THE ADHD Field Guide FOR ADULTS

THE ADHD Field Guide FOR ADULTS

Cate Osborn & Erik Gude

WITH RENNIE DYBALL

monoray

Originally published in the United States in 2025 by
Gallery Books,
an Imprint of Simon & Schuster, LLC
1230 Avenue of the Americas
New York, NY 10020

First published in Great Britain in 2026 by Monoray,
an imprint of Octopus Publishing Group Ltd
Carmelite House
50 Victoria Embankment
London EC4Y 0DZ
www.octopusbooks.co.uk

An Hachette UK Company
www.hachette.co.uk

The authorized representative in the EEA is Hachette Ireland,
8 Castlecourt Centre, Dublin 15, D15 XTP3, Ireland (email: info@hbgi.ie)

Text copyright © Cate Osborn and Erik Gude 2026
Illustrations by Lucy Engelman

All rights reserved. No part of this work may be reproduced or utilized
in any form or by any means, electronic or mechanical, including
photocopying, recording or by any information storage and retrieval
system, without the prior written permission of the publisher.

ISBN: 978-1-80096-241-5
eISBN: 978-1-80096-240-8

A CIP catalogue record for this book is available from the British Library.

Typeset in 8.36/14.70 pt Lexend by Six Red Marbles UK, Thetford, Norfolk.

Printed and bound in Great Britain.

10 9 8 7 6 5 4 3 2 1

This FSC® label means that materials used for the
product have been responsibly sourced.

This book is not a substitute for the advice of your healthcare provider.
It is intended as a general information resource. The publisher and
the author cannot guarantee the complete accuracy, efficacy, or
appropriateness of any recommendation contained in this book.
The publisher is not responsible for, and should not be deemed to
endorse or recommend any treatment or cure, in any respect.

To those who've been told they're too much, not enough, or just needed to try harder.

You are never alone.

Contents

Authors' Note: How to Read This Book 8

Foreword by KC Davis 10

Introduction: You Are Not a Fuckup 12

PART 1: An ADHD Primer

1. The Technical Stuff 23
1B. A Bonus History of ADHD 49
2. ADHD and . . . Comorbidities 56
3. How ADHD Affects Your Body and Brain 78
4. Coping with ADHD: Stress, Boredom, and Other Experiences 104
5. ADHD and Identity 123

PART 2: Getting the Help You Need

6. Asking for Help 151
7. Making It Official: ADHD and Diagnosis 161

PART 3: Systems and Organization

- **8** Time and Task Management 181
- **9** Get Down with the Systems 200
- **9B** Setting an Alarm to Pee and Other Personal Hygiene Systems 228
- **10** So, You Need to Eat and Sleep, Huh? 238
- **11** Why Folding Socks Is Overrated, aka the Household and Organization Chapter 266

PART 4: Work and Money

- **12** Work, Work, Work 289
- **13** Money: It's a Gas 306

PART 5: Relationships, Sex, and Loved Ones

- **14** All About Relationships 325
- **15** Let's Talk About Sex 343
- **16** The Chapter for Loved Ones 364

Afterword: Signing Off ... for Now 378

Appendix: ADHD Evaluations 380

Acknowledgments 382

Notes 384

Index 393

Authors' Note

How to Read This Book

This book might look a little different from others on the shelf, and that's because it was carefully constructed to make it accessible. Many people with ADHD struggle with reading difficulties, including Erik, and benefit from nontraditional texts.

With this in mind, we've broken down dozens of topics about living with ADHD into a Q&A format based on the questions we get most from our audience. You'll also hear from other members of our community, plus guest experts on key topics. The answers are bite-size, so you won't be overwhelmed by pages upon pages of straight text, **and the key points are in bold**. We structured our book this way so that as many people as possible can benefit from it.

IF COLOR-CODING OR ANNOTATING
a text for yourself makes you more
likely to retain the information, you have our
full, enthusiastic permission to mark up
this book however you please!

☐ **I'm going to use this color for**
_____

☐ **I'm going to use this color for**
_____

☐ **I'm going to use this color for**
_____

Whether you read cover to cover or flip
to a random page, you'll be greeted with at
least a nugget of helpful information.
There is no wrong way to read this book!

FOREWORD

I first came across Cate on TikTok, where we were both sharing bits of our journey with ADHD and offering tips to others who were navigating the ups and downs of being an adult with this diagnosis. I knew then she had a gift for connecting and communicating. Every video held my attention and taught me something new about my brain. This book is an extension of that.

When Cate and Erik first shared their manuscript with me, I was immediately struck by how accessible this work is. It's a rare thing for someone with ADHD to feel that they can stay focused through a whole book (barring books that happen to coincide with our current hyperfixation, of course), but I was able to read this one with ease. As someone who has given a lot of thought to how to write books for people with ADHD, I can honestly say they've nailed it.

> **When Cate and Erik first shared their manuscript with me, I was immediately struck by how accessible this work is.**

Of course, being accessible is only beneficial if the book's content is helpful. I can say with enthusiasm that this one is. What I wouldn't have given to have this book when I was diagnosed with ADHD in my mid-thirties, trying to figure out how to manage my money and clean my house and deal with rejection sensitivity. There's no fluff here—just straight-to-the-point information on how to understand your brain and how to work with it in all areas of life. I imagine it will be sitting on the shelves of ADHDers and therapists alike for decades to come.

What makes *The ADHD Field Guide for Adults* so powerful is that it normalizes the ADHD brain. Many of us with ADHD have spent our lives feeling broken, always aware we aren't quite staying on top of life in the way the world says we should. We view our struggles through the lens of moral failure—we are lazy, irresponsible, chaotic, messy—even resources that aim to help us get our life together often reinforce this message by offering solutions that don't work for our brains. Perhaps you, too, have felt like a square mind living in a round world.

This book shines because both the message and the delivery are effective. And, what's more, not only have Cate and Erik written a book that gives solid information and practical tips in a format that you can actually consume but they have a way of making you feel like you are not alone anymore. Because you aren't. You're one of us.

—KC Davis

INTRODUCTION
You Are Not a Fuckup

~~~~~~~~~~~~

It is September 2018, and I am sobbing uncontrollably on my couch. In less than two weeks, I'm supposed to play Miranda in *The Tempest* and Maria in *Twelfth Night*, and despite my nightly efforts to sit down and focus on studying my lines, I am wildly unprepared.

I sit and read, and I reread, and I try to learn the lines forward and quite literally backward. Nothing sticks. I try writing them down. I try listening to recordings. I try making up songs and anagrams and I try every single trick and skill I've ever developed to memorize, but nothing stays in my head for longer than a few minutes, if I can even sit down and focus for that long.

I am terrified. This has never happened before. I have two master's degrees in Shakespeare. This has always been easy for me, and this is the thing I love to do. Why can't I sit down and focus? Why can't I memorize my lines like usual? I am sure that I must have early-onset dementia—something is definitely wrong. But how do I say, "I'm having trouble remembering Shakespeare lines" at the doctor and be taken seriously?

> **Over and over, day after day, I wake up and promise myself that today is the day that everything changes.**

I can feel the *wrongness* lurking around corners, in stacks of dishes gone undone, in piles of laundry and clutter that crowd my hallways, in the unsent emails and unanswered texts, in the plans I keep making and breaking, in the way that I seem to be outside myself, watching my world fall apart. I am drowning, and the water is invisible to everyone but me.

I keep willing myself to get up off the couch.

Just send the email just send the text just put the dishes away this time don't forget to take out the trash why can't you ever keep anything clean just do the laundry or can you at least brush your teeth or take a shower you really are a piece of shit why can't you do anything right why are you such a fuckup . . .

I start having panic attacks. I start finding reasons to miss rehearsal—if I don't go, they won't know that I'm a fuckup, and they won't know that I'm suddenly too stupid to memorize a bit of Shakespeare. I can just quit; I can just hide. I can never do anything I like, ever again, because fuckups don't deserve nice things.

I am ashamed and embarrassed. I'm a terrible wife, a crappy partner. I am an embarrassment to my family, and I'm lazy and worthless, and I simply need to buckle down and try harder. And so I do. Over and over, day after day, I wake up and promise myself that today is the day that everything changes. Today is the day we sit down, focus, and learn the lines. And then, at the end of the day, I am exhausted from simply existing, but the laundry piles remain, the dishes are still undone, and my depression, shame, and anxiety grow and grow until finally I confess to a friend, through sobs, that I'm worried I'm going crazy.

He pauses thoughtfully and says, "I don't know if you're going crazy, but I do think you have ADHD."

The part I often leave out of the story was that he made the phone call to make the first appointment with my doctor, because at the time, even that was something I couldn't find the motivation to do.

That phone call became the catalyst for great change. Four months later, the day before my thirtieth birthday, I sat in a psychologist's office and told her my story, convinced the whole thing was ridiculous. I told her about how I'd been incredibly successful academically, how I'd earned multiple degrees, how I'd been told several times in my life that I couldn't possibly have ADHD. People with ADHD don't get good grades, I'd been told. "People with ADHD aren't smart like you, aren't good students like you, aren't pretty and outgoing and talented like you." I believed them.

She smiles at me and says, "Yeah, I believed them, too."

In that moment, I am seen. And for the first time in thirty years, I begin to understand myself. A year later, I begin devoting my life to helping others do the same.

AT THE START OF 2020, I was the entertainment director of the Georgia Renaissance Festival, while Erik was working as an artisan pizza chef at a high-end restaurant in California. We were unaware of each other's existence, both of us climbing our own ladders. Then in March, Covid-19 shut down the entertainment and restaurant industries, and our careers ended in an instant. Stuck at home with nowhere to go and no fast-paced careers to distract us, our ADHD had us all to itself.

We both started to make videos about how ADHD affected our lives, sharing our struggles and triumphs. Our videos started to resonate through the ADHD community, and eventually both of us went viral. Then one of us got tagged in the other's video. On August 8, I sent a message to Erik that read, "The laws of ADHD TikTok demand that we do a collab." The first time we got onto the phone, we talked for three hours.

Eventually, we started a podcast together, *Catie and Erik's Infinite Quest: An ADHD Adventure*. It turned out that there were a lot of people in the world who wanted to hear two people—with vastly different experiences of ADHD—talk honestly and openly about how

ADHD has affected their lives. We ultimately became full-time content creators and advocates for the ADHD community, making a career of educating and supporting other adults with the disorder.

But this book isn't our story. Although you'll learn about us along the way, our book is a guide and a resource to help other adults with ADHD navigate their way through the world, too. We decided to write this book mostly in a Q&A format because the questions you'll see in these pages are the ones we get most frequently from our audience. We hope that you'll find some answers that prove helpful in navigating life with a neurodivergent brain.

ADHD used to be something that people believed existed only in context and that affected only children. It wasn't viewed as a debilitating, chronic condition; an insidious disorder that infiltrates all aspects of a person's existence.

But guess what?

DRUMROLL, PLEASE . . .

That's exactly what it is.

ADHD (formerly ADD), or **A**ttention **D**eficit **H**yperactivity **D**isorder, is a neurodevelopmental disorder that affects the brain's executive functions. These are a set of mental processes that help us regulate our behavior, plan and organize tasks, pay attention, and control impulses. They act as the conductor of your brain's orchestra, ensuring that all the brain's intricate processes are working together effectively.

In people with ADHD, the brain's executive functions don't work as effectively as they should; the conductor isn't paying attention. This leads to, among other things, difficulties with attention, organization, and self-control. Individuals with ADHD may struggle to focus on tasks that are not stimulating or interesting to them, or they may have trouble completing long-term projects because they struggle with planning and time management.

People with ADHD may also exhibit physical hyperactivity and impulsivity, which can make

> We hope that you'll find some answers that prove helpful in navigating life with a neurodivergent brain.

it difficult for them to sit still or wait their turn. These behaviors are thought to be related to difficulties with inhibiting motor responses and regulating emotions, which are also controlled by the brain's executive functions.

Scientifically, we now know that the construction of an ADHD brain is fundamentally different. When it comes to your ADHD-related struggles, the issue is not as simple as

- you haven't been trying hard enough,
- you just "need to apply yourself," or . . .
- you're "lazy" or you "just don't care."

In short, your executive functions don't work the way they're supposed to, *and that is not your fault*. This can be really, really hard to internalize, especially for those who were diagnosed later in life, but it's incredibly important to keep in mind as you read this book.

Regarding your diagnosis with shame or guilt or embarrassment (or a tasty cocktail of all three) will stop you in your tracks when it comes to making progress. We're speaking from experience here.

> **Scientifically, we now know that the construction of an ADHD brain is fundamentally different.**

It is okay to need to look up resources on how to get your laundry done, how to organize, or how to maintain friendships.

It is healthy to develop systems (anything that makes tasks easier) and structures that work FOR YOU, regardless of what conventional society might think. It is FINE to need assistance and to work around your limitations, because you are not a fuckup. You are neurodivergent, and therefore your brain works differently. Plus—more good news—there are tools, structures, systems, and support available to help you.

But there is a *but*.

Having ADHD does *not* mean that you can't develop coping strategies and systems that minimize the impact on your life. You most definitely can.

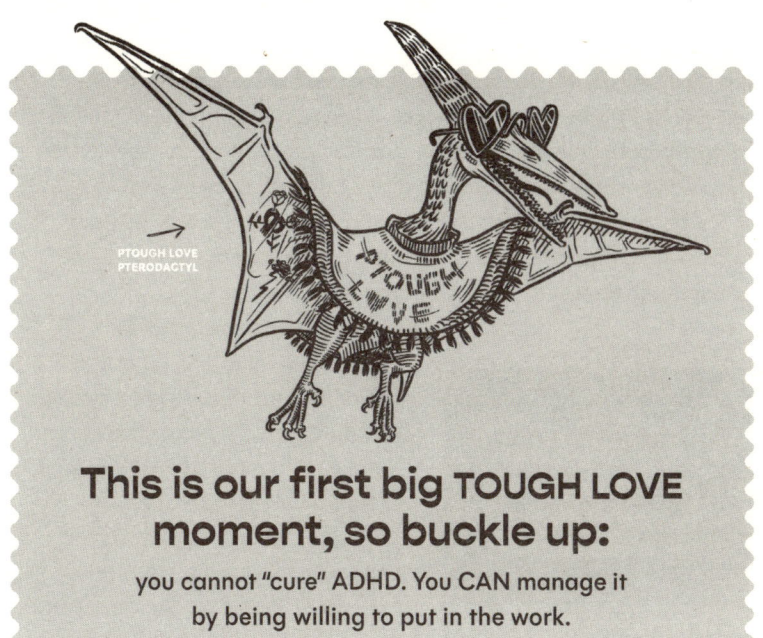

PTOUGH LOVE PTERODACTYL

This is our first big TOUGH LOVE moment, so buckle up: you cannot "cure" ADHD. You CAN manage it by being willing to put in the work.

WELCOME to the Club

You are not alone. While ADHD is generally considered to be a chronic, lifelong condition, recent efforts to decrease stigma among doctors and the public have led to an increase of late-diagnosed adults—*anyone who's learned they had ADHD after high school or beyond*. If that's you, then you are the intended audience for this book! As well as the people who love you.

According to a 2019 study, the prevalence of adult ADHD diagnoses has doubled since 2009. ADHD diagnoses are growing four times faster among adults than for children in the United States, and many scientists believe the disorder is *still* thought to be highly underdiagnosed in adults.

But why are we seeing so many more diagnoses now than we did ten, twenty, or thirty years ago? When ADHD was first recognized as a disorder in the 1960s and '70s,* it was largely seen as a behavior problem that could be controlled through discipline and punishment. Many people believed that children with ADHD were simply lazy or unmotivated and that their parents were to blame for not being strict enough with them.

> **In the '60s and '70s, many people believed that children with ADHD were simply lazy or unmotivated.**

As more research was conducted on ADHD, it became clear that the disorder was caused by differences in brain chemistry and structure rather than a lack of effort or willpower. But even as this understanding of ADHD evolved, stigma surrounding the disorder persisted. Many people with ADHD have been subjected to negative stereotypes and discrimination, with some people viewing them as unreliable, irresponsible, or even dangerous.

One of the most significant factors is that the diagnostic criteria for ADHD were historically based on research conducted primarily on young boys. As a result, the symptoms of ADHD in girls and women (not to mention trans and nonbinary people) were not as well understood, and they were often misdiagnosed with other conditions such as anxiety or depression.

Not only is it possible for girls and women with ADHD to present with symptoms that are different from those seen in boys and men, but social and cultural factors may play a role in the underdiagnosis of ADHD in women, gender-nonconforming people, and other minority groups whose experience of the condition has not been well researched. *It wasn't until 2022* that the *Diagnostic and Statistical Manual of Mental Disorders (DSM)* first included a section on gender and racial differences, noting that lived experience and socialization can have a major impact on how neurodivergence is both detected and diagnosed.

---

* Cate, the resident historian here!

There is also a strong hereditary component to ADHD, so when a child is diagnosed, the symptoms may seem familiar to a parent, leading that adult to seek out an evaluation for themselves. College is another common time to be diagnosed, as it's the first time people with ADHD are out on their own. Marriages, divorces, and other major life events are also well-known catalysts for seeking treatment. In short, all sorts of adults are being diagnosed with ADHD, and many more already know they have it.

So now we're playing the world's worst game of catch-up, in which all the previously undiagnosed adults (or adults who are starting to understand the scope of the disorder) are now learning that the struggles they live with are actually due to ADHD.

Since there's no ADHD fairy that comes down on your eighteenth birthday and takes your ADHD away (that we know of), those of us who grew up in the 1980s and '90s are now adults who still must live with the condition, the difference being that now we have the agency to ask questions. We want to understand ourselves and why we are struggling, and we seek help to make life easier.

Fortunately, research on ADHD is catching up. Where it used to center on the needs of children with ADHD, it is now, finally, starting to address more adult concerns. For example: How does ADHD impact sex and intimacy? Now we can confidently say that ADHD can profoundly affect your experience with intimacy. There's research behind it, and there are things you can do about it.

> **Our book is an ADHD guide that addresses all the subjects you haven't read about before.**

This is just one area of adulthood where we dive into the implications of life with ADHD. It's not all sunshine and rainbows, but we've learned through our work how important it is to have these tough conversations.

Our book is an ADHD guide that addresses all the subjects you haven't read about before. It is a comprehensive manual on life as an adult with this chronic condition, as told by two people who are living it and educating about it. We'll employ the help of medical professionals here and there as needed, but this survival guide is mainly about offering real-life suggestions on every page from our own lived experiences—as well as permission to ignore whatever doesn't suit you.

We believe adults with ADHD need a tool to help them get through the day and, perhaps more importantly, a reminder that everything is going to be okay. *You* are going to be okay.

LIFE HACKS: Take 'Em or Leave 'Em

Many self-help books are predicated on the ableist notion that if you just try hard enough and pull yourself up by the bootstraps, your issues will magically disappear, and you'll finally reach ultimate self-fulfillment.

If that works for you, awesome.

Some of us need a little more than that.

There is no one "right way" to ADHD. There is, frankly, no WRONG way to ADHD, short of hurting others—don't do that. We are not here to tell you that your systems are invalid because they aren't how *we* do things. Because what works for you might not work for one of us, and that is okay.

You don't have to employ any ADHD "hacks" if you don't want to.

It's really that simple.

We didn't write a book to tell you how to live your life. However, between our own lived experience and the feedback we receive from millions of people with ADHD, we've got some solid advice for you to take if you want it and leave if you don't.

Want to be able to find your pants more easily? Great! A pants hook (trademark pending) can be a genius solution for this issue. Is your floor covered in socks and you are absolutely fine with it? Hell yeah, friend, you do you. We're here to offer suggestions.

At the very least, we hope that this book will provide you with some useful tools to manage parts of your ADHD that you choose, some insight into how your brain works (or doesn't work), and some strategies for building systems that might work for you in the long run. Most importantly, we hope that you remember, once and for all . . .

YOU ARE NOT A FUCKUP, YOU SILLY GOOSE

That's you. That's you being a silly goose.

INTRODUCTION: You Are Not a Fuckup

PART

1

An ADHD PRIMER

1

THE
Technical Stuff

The date is February 17, 2010.

I'm fifteen years old. I'm sitting next to my mom on a too-soft couch, waiting for a psychologist, Dr. Emerson, to return with the results of my seemingly endless ADHD evaluation process. My shoes are wet from the Michigan slush, and the microfiber fabric of the couch pulls and twists under my jeans every time I move. Despite this discomfort, I'm having trouble staying awake because of the room's warm lighting and the hum of the building's heating system droning in the background.

Dr. Emerson enters the room and, after some pleasant conversation, hands us a thick packet printed on firm, authoritative stationery. It feels heavy in my hands.

PSYCHOEDUCATIONAL REPORT
PATIENT NAME: Erik Gude

Dr. Emerson takes us through sixteen pages of confusing jargon, esoteric charts, and technical acronyms that, all together, apparently prove one thing: I definitely have ADHD.

On the very bottom of the sixteenth page, the last page, is a section titled "Recommendations," which reads:

Erik may benefit from a trial of medication to help with the ADHD and depression symptoms.

It will be another four years until I learn that my ADHD doesn't affect me only in an academic environment. It will be seven years until I learn that my ADHD makes me more prone to addiction. And it will take ten years before I hear the term *executive dysfunction*.

It is our hope, dear reader, that the following section will serve to enlighten you about the various facets of ADHD in a format that will hopefully save you a decade or two of wondering why your brain works the way it does.

—**Erik**

What Is ADHD?

 Attention deficit hyperactivity disorder (ADHD) is a neurodevelopmental disorder that affects both children and adults. It is characterized by persistent patterns of inattention, hyperactivity, and impulsivity that can impact various aspects of an individual's life—including academic performance, work, relationships, and daily functioning.

 So, what does that ACTUALLY MEAN?

It means your brain works differently than the brains of neurotypical people, and you will very likely need systems and support in your life to make ADHD more livable.

But it does **NOT** mean you are a fuckup.

 **Neurodevelopmental**

Neurodevelopmental refers to the processes that shape the development of the brain and nervous system from early embryonic stages through childhood and adolescence. This includes the growth and organization of neural cells, the formation of neural connections, and the establishment of neural networks that support various cognitive and behavioral functions.

TL;DR: Neurodevelopmental: the way your brain develops neurological pathways that influence how you function.

Is ADHD a DISABILITY?

 Yes. ADHD is considered a neurodevelopmental disability, depending on the severity. However, it is not considered a *learning* disability (at least not in the United States in 2025). This can make it very hard to get disability benefits for ADHD. ADHD often comes *with* learning disabilities—dyslexia, dyscalculia, dysgraphia—so you can get work accommodations in that regard.

Dyslexia

"A condition of neurodevelopmental origin that mainly affects the ease with which a person reads, writes, and spells, typically recognized as a specific learning disorder in children."[1]

Dyscalculia

"Dyscalculia is a learning disorder that affects a person's ability to do math. Much like dyslexia disrupts areas of the brain related to reading, dyscalculia affects brain areas that handle math- and number-related skills and understanding. Symptoms of this condition usually appear in childhood, but adults may have dyscalculia without knowing it."[2]

—CLEVELAND CLINIC

> **DEFINITION BREAK 4/18**
>
> ## Dysgraphia
>
> "Dysgraphia is a neurological disorder characterized by writing disabilities. Specifically, the disorder causes a person's writing to be distorted or incorrect. In children, the disorder generally emerges when they are first introduced to writing. They make inappropriately sized and spaced letters, or write wrong or misspelled words, despite thorough instruction. For example, writing 'boy' for 'child.'"[3]
> —National Institute of Neurological Disorders and Stroke

 In other words, *neurodevelopmental* refers to the way in which the brain and nervous system mature over time, which can have important implications for a wide range of developmental outcomes, including cognitive, emotional, and social functioning.

It's also important to note that **ADHD is a spectrum disorder,** and disability is not a monolith. Then we have the conversation of **comorbidities (other conditions that exist in a person alongside their ADHD; lots more on this in chapter 2).** Because a large percentage of people with ADHD also have depression and anxiety, substance use disorders, sleep disorders, eating disorders, and more.[4]

I always say, "If you know one person with ADHD . . . you know one person with ADHD."* **One person with ADHD might be great at things like organization or task management and be absolutely garbage at the relationship side of things. It may not look like a disability on that person, but that doesn't mean it's not disabling.**

---

* We actually found out while editing this book that Stephen Shore says the same thing about Autistic people!

You have the right to think of your ADHD however you want—you don't have to think of it as a disability. You can think of it as a superpower. You are entitled to your own understanding of your own brain and your own mind and your own ADHD.

ABOUT THE TERM
DISORDER

Many neurodivergent advocates believe that applying the word *disorder* to things like ADHD and/or Autism pathologizes a natural variation in the vast array of human experiences. By doing so, we stigmatize traits that are simply different from the average person's; we are inclined to agree.

It's difficult, in particular, when the actual *medical name* of the condition *attention deficit hyperactivity disorder* contains two different ways of emphasizing and amplifying that we're deficient and disordered, simply by existing as we are. And that sucks.

Celebrating neurodivergence doesn't mean ignoring the challenges that these traits might cause, but rather understanding that every person's experience with ADHD (or any other difference) is unique and should be tailored to their individual needs.

In this book, we have tried to avoid using the term *disorder* as much as possible, but in some cases, particularly when addressing where ADHD lives in psychological and medical contexts, it's difficult to avoid.

CHAPTER 1:
The Technical Stuff

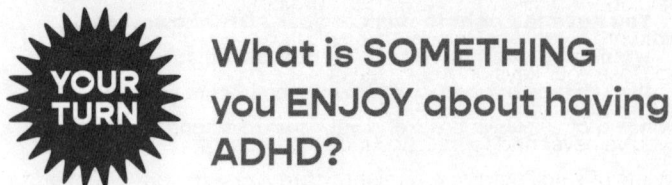

YOUR TURN: What is SOMETHING you ENJOY about having ADHD?

> I love my ability to retain knowledge, and the empathy I have for others as not all maladies are visible.

—Andrea from Calgary

> I enjoy the hectic noise in my brain. Now that I know how to self-regulate better, I find times when the "bees in my brain" help me be more creative and spontaneous and allow me to think in ways that neurotypical people wouldn't think to. It keeps me moving, and while it's harder to manage at times, sometimes work gets best accomplished when I take the reins and go for the ride.

—Mattie Rose from Atlanta

Can a person develop ADHD LATER IN LIFE, as an ADULT?

 If you're reading this, we assume that you're an adult, perhaps even an adult who had no idea that you had ADHD until recently. Welcome to the club. First and foremost, you're not a fraud.

It is not uncommon for a person not to really notice the difficulties presented by their ADHD until after they reach adulthood and are expected to manage their own lives.

For the most part, researchers agree that ADHD can often go unnoticed and unrecognized, especially in scenarios where you have a lot of support, structure, and access to resources.

The ADHD Field Guide for Adults

PART 1:
An ADHD Primer

Think about it this way: if you had a luxurious apartment with a butler who provided everything you needed, you would find out how often you lose your keys only once the butler left and stopped finding them for you.

If you've never had to make your own schedule that demands juggling lots of small details, you might not realize that your attention to detail sucks until you're making that schedule.

You might not notice that you constantly lose track of time until you're staring down a deadline wondering where all the time went.

This is why lots of people are diagnosed with ADHD in college. College is the first time that many people navigate the "real world," without the structure and support of parents and teachers, and they find that the sudden shift into direct personal responsibility comes with a crash and burn, resulting in an ADHD evaluation.

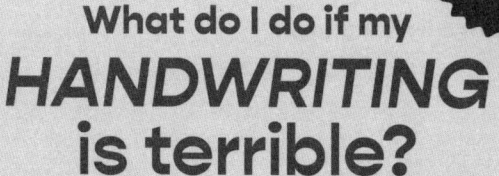

What do I do if my HANDWRITING is terrible?

sidenote

First of all, I get it. I know that feeling of getting a really important form to fill out, and they give you **a pen**, and you think: *Okay, no screwups. I better nail this first try.* Or the pressure of writing down something in front of your boss. A large percentage of people (some studies say up to 59 percent)[5] with ADHD also have **dysgraphia**.

Personally, I indent a lot and make space between paragraphs to make the page at least look more organized. I use different colors as much as I can. Try to find your own preferred utensil.

For me, writing with a smooth, gliding pen is a nightmare. I love the twisty-top pencils. It took me a long time to figure out, but they are very comfortable for me to write with. **Find *your* utensil and then get as many as you can so you always have one nearby when you need to write something down. It helps control the variables.**

Let's Learn Some
SCIENCE TERMS!!!

"Adult ADHD is considered to be a part of the **externalizing spectrum** with which it shares both **homotypic comorbidity** and **heterotypic continuity** across the lifespan."[6]

HERE'S WHAT ALL THAT MEANS . . .

● The **externalizing spectrum** refers to a group of disorders that are expressed outwardly and often involve disregarding social norms by way of hyperactivity, impulsivity, aggression, etc. ADHD, oppositional defiance disorder (ODD), antisocial personality disorder, and even substance use disorder all fall into this category.

● ADHD having **homotypic comorbidity** means that it often occurs alongside other disorders within the externalizing spectrum.

● ADHD having **heterotypic continuity** means it's for life, but its presentation, the way it **externalizes**, is likely to change throughout a person's life. My ADHD looks different at thirty than it did when I was fifteen and than it did when I was nine. And it will look different when I'm fifty. Yours probably will, too.

ADHD can also make itself known after major life changes: a marriage, a move, the death of a loved one, a new job, the onset of menopause, and for many in the LGBTQIA+ community, transitioning or coming out. Much more on all that later.

Since ADHD is a neurodevelopmental disorder, that means you're born with it, and your brain is structured differently. Something happens during brain development that results in this disorder.

You're not going to *develop* ADHD. You don't *catch* ADHD. What winds up happening in a lot of cases is that through childhood and your teenage years, you have a lot of support and structure, so you don't really notice it.

Or maybe you're a little bit messy, like me. And then major life changes are often what make the ADHD symptoms and struggles much more profound. For some, it's going off to college, living with a new partner, or having kids. It can happen for others in menopause.

So, no. **You didn't magically wake up one day with ADHD, but your systems and your structures burned down because you started living your life differently**, and that's probably why you're reading this book.

What is the DIFFERENCE between ADD and ADHD?

 There isn't one. ADD is an antiquated term.

 Cate the historian chiming in here, with a tiny bit of background. ADHD has always been around. This isn't about the rise of the Internet or Adderall or whatever. **People have been experiencing these issues for centuries. And when it first got a name in the *DSM*, that name went through a few changes before we ended up with ADHD.**

The Diagnostic and Statistical Manual of Mental Disorders (or DSM) is the reference book used by mental health professionals to aid in diagnosis and treatment of various mental health concerns. It's also important to remember that it's a LIVING document—the American Psychiatric Association often publishes updates or clarifications when new research comes to light, like in 2013 when they made it "officially" possible to be co-diagnosed with ADHD and Autism. Before that, psychiatrists had to choose one. The newest version, the DSM-5-TR, came out in 2022.

A lot of doctors and psychiatrists still call it ADD. And that is an indicator that they were trained at a certain time. If they *persist* in refusing to call it ADHD, that may be a red flag.

> Sometimes that "H", the hyperactivity portion, isn't physical. Sometimes it's just mental hyperactivity.

The term was changed in the *DSM*, but ultimately **experts figured out that ADD and ADHD were actually different presentations of the same underlying disorder.** Sometimes that "H", the hyperactivity portion, isn't physical. Sometimes it's just mental hyperactivity. There are different *presentations* of ADHD, but not different *types*, despite what you may read on the Internet.

There is some pervasive junk science on the Internet about the different "types" of ADHD. So you'll probably see this, and you may come across people who say they have a certain type of ADHD, but the scientific community identifies different presentations. There are no subtypes.

How did you FIND OUT about your ADHD?

> My brother was diagnosed as a kid. I had to wait until thirty-one for them to care about looking at women.

—**Sarah from Utah**

Can GIRLS have ADHD?

YES.

ADHD and ADD used to be inadvertently genderized, where girls were often diagnosed with ADD because hyperactivity looks different on different people based on things like socialization and expected behaviors. So there was a big divide between diagnoses—boys were primarily being diagnosed with ADHD, while girls were primarily being diagnosed with ADD. As we've done more research, the *DSM* changed, because we've learned that it comes back to that presentation conversation—presentations change. It's why we stopped saying "types" and we started saying "presentations."

When we talk about "gendered" differences of ADHD, we also have to keep in mind societal factors—for many women, ADHD symptoms aren't necessarily a visible, external thing. The hyperactivity, the distractibility, the managing . . . all that is happening internally, with racing thoughts, trouble sleeping, struggling with clutter, impulsive spending, and for some, using substances to self-medicate. Many women find themselves spending all their time and energy with this internal struggle while externally looking just fine.

On top of that, normal hormonal fluctuations throughout the month can also severely impact ADHD, as can pregnancy and menopause.

This is the late diagnosis story of many. According to Patricia Quinn, MD, the average age of diagnosis for women with ADHD who weren't diagnosed as children is thirty-six to thirty-eight years old.[7] If a doctor tells you women can't have ADHD, that doctor is wrong, plain and simple. That narrative was around for a long time, but it's been refuted.

EXECUTIVE DYSFUNCTION

What is executive dysfunction?

DEFINITION BREAK 5/18

Executive dysfunction is one of the defining characteristics of ADHD, in which the part of your brain that controls thoughts, emotions, and behavior (your executive functions) is disrupted. People with ADHD experience this dysfunction with a higher frequency and magnitude than neurotypical people. Everyone struggles with impulse control from time to time. Those with ADHD struggle with it intensely, nearly all the time.

What are the executive functions?

It's surprisingly hard to find a definitive list, but for simplicity's sake, we'll use the one on the ADDvantages Learning Center website.[8] This list is similar to the list that many doctors also use. The executive functions are impulse control, emotional control, flexible thinking, working memory, self-monitoring, planning and prioritizing, task initiation, and organization. **People with ADHD are generally deficient when it comes to executive functioning.**

Also, if you have comorbidities—like if you're ADHD and Autistic, or have ADHD and depression, or ADHD and anxiety—these executive functions are going to behave in different ways.

1. Impulse Control: This term may make you think of a little kid in the back of the classroom, unable to control themselves. **With adult impulse control, it looks more like overeating, overspending, gambling issues, alcoholism, or risky sexual behavior.** People with ADHD also have more traffic accidents as a whole because their brains don't automatically focus in driving situations.[9]

Or it could seem like a really good idea one night to spend thousands of dollars you don't have on something, and the next morning you wake up and hate yourself for spending that money. Checking your phone constantly can be related to impulse control as well.

Impulse control has a lot of implications in relationships, like speaking before you think or acting on impulse when you're working through conflict rather than taking the time to reflect.

2. Emotional Control: ADHD is not an emotional disorder. However, we do have trouble regulating our emotions. People with ADHD struggle with regulating dopamine and serotonin, which are responsible for things like regulating your emotions and your focus/concentration. So a person with ADHD might seem like they get angrier or more joyful than most people. The wall between what we're feeling and what we're outwardly presenting can be less consistent than others'.

Having ADHD is like driving a manual car. Your car (brain) can still do all the things that automatic cars do, but you've got to learn how to drive a stick. We have to make a concerted effort to manually regulate our emotions, because we tend not to do it as automatically as other people.

**3. Flexible Thinking:** Flexible thinking is, generally, your brain's ability to quickly shift gears and adapt to new information, situations, or strategies, and it's WEIRD to me how little this gets talked about in context with ADHD. There is literally a functionality in your brain that is responsible for adapting to change. Deficits in this functionality can result in a lack of flexibility, creating rigid thinking patterns and even just difficulty seeing things from someone else's point of view. This can have a HUGE impact on how we navigate through our day, especially planning, organizing, and emotional control.

4. Working Memory: If you think of your brain like a computer, your working memory is like your desktop.

Your computer is storing an immense amount of information—it's got documents and pictures and all sorts of stuff in there, but anything you're working on at any given time is on your desktop.

People with ADHD can have a very hard time managing what's on our brain's "desktop." Files are opening and closing at random, getting pushed to the background, until eventually we forget what's even open. Working memory is completely different from long-term memory, or your storage capacity. As an example, working memory can look like forgetting somebody's name right after they said it, or forgetting your coffee cup on top of your car.

For me, working memory is very different depending on where I'm at in my depression and anxiety levels. It's much harder for me to function, get off the couch, do the dishes, take a shower, or brush my teeth if I'm in the throes of depression.

That depression is often compounded by anxiety—while I am struggling to do basic care tasks, I'm also watching those care tasks: The dishes go from a single dishwasher load to four or five days' worth of dirty dishes. The tasks start to feel bigger and scarier and more overwhelming the longer they sit, so I become less and less likely to start. The anxiety and depression cycle continues while I keep putting off tasks and then beating myself up when it happens. It's fun in my brain.

---

5. Self-Monitoring:

Self-monitoring is being consciously aware of your actions and the effect they have not only on you, but on your environment and others **AND** the ability to regulate/control your behaviors, emotions, and responses. For ADHDers, this includes not only managing impulsiveness (interrupting, making comments, etc.), but also regulating your emotions and focusing attention. This is the executive function that informs reflecting on behavior and noticing if it requires adjustment.

Self-monitoring can be difficult for neurodivergent brains. It's what gives us insight into things like social cues and appropriate behavior, but if our attention or interest is focused elsewhere, we might miss those vital social cues and wind up with awkward or uncomfortable social interactions.

6. Planning and Prioritizing: Starting a task is different from planning and prioritizing for that task. They're actually different processes. With planning and prioritizing, imagine you're building an IKEA shelf. Do you make sure you have all your tools in place first, or do you just get into the middle of it and realize you don't have the right tool, and now the shelf is going to sit there unfinished for the rest of your days?

You need to ask yourself, *What do I need in order to start?* and *How will I finish this?* as part of the planning process. As for prioritization, what is more important? Building the shelf or getting to your grandmother's birthday party on time? Or doing the dishes? Or eating a snack? For people with ADHD, it can be extremely difficult to look at a to-do list and say to yourself, *Okay. I need to make sure that I'm on time to my grandmother's birthday party, so I shouldn't get a tattoo right now.* That's a real story from my real life.

 7. Task Initiation: Simply put, this is your ability to start a task. This involves a transitional space (the time between one activity ending and another one beginning), which can be very hard for people with ADHD.

 8. Organization: When we talk about organization, we're not just talking about your ability to keep your DVD collection organized,* we're talking about the broad IDEA of organization and how it applies to your life. Bringing order to the chaos that surrounds us all.

As well as keeping our physical spaces tidy, organization also relates to prioritizing tasks, setting (and sticking to) deadlines, avoiding procrastination, setting goals, creating schedules and plans, categorizing information, and summarizing information—ALL those things deal with organization in your executive functioning.

---

* Do people still have DVD collections?

How do people with ADHD PERCEIVE TIME differently?

People with ADHD perceive time differently than neurotypical folks, but "time blindness" isn't real. Before you get mad, let me explain: *Time blindness* is a colloquial term that the neurodivergent community has sort of adopted to refer to the **very real** time perception deficits in people with ADHD. There is ample science to prove that ***time perception deficits*** are measurable when you have ADHD.

There have been a bunch of different studies on how people with ADHD perceive time. It breaks down like this:

People with ADHD have a really hard time knowing how much time has passed. We have a really hard time estimating how long something is going to take. We have a really hard time estimating how long it will be until something happens in the future. For example, if something is happening in a week, that's forever! Until it's tomorrow, and then you're fucked.

Often that time perception deficit is written off as "You're just being lazy, you're just not keeping track of time, you're not being responsible, you're being rude, or you're being disrespectful to your boss and your fellow employees." But people don't always realize that there's actually a measurable difference in our brains.[10]

Planning for the future can be super hard for people with ADHD. Saving money, too, though it's less about the actual action of saving money. What it comes down to is that time perception deficit: "Well, of course I'll have enough money by the end of the month to pay my rent." And then you don't.

Many of the struggles, and even the relationship issues that happen with people with ADHD, boil down to time deficits. "Oh, I didn't realize it's been six months since I called my mom. I didn't realize that I haven't texted my partner back in four hours, even though I said I was gonna call him at noon."

The ADHD Field Guide for Adults

PART 1:
An ADHD Primer

The way I see it, there are three different types of time deficits that come with ADHD, any of which can mess with your day-to-day life in different ways. It's useful to recognize which one of these is the problem at the moment:

1. **Boredom Time:** when you're bored, any amount of time feels like forever. If one thing is true about people with ADHD, it's that we *hate* being bored—it's painful to us.

2. **Default Time:** these are your "Oh, I lost track of time" moments. Just your day-to-day forgetfulness, like "Oh no, I have to leave in fifteen minutes . . . Oh my gosh, it's been fifteen minutes!"

3. **Hyperfocus Time:** no amount of time seems long enough, and any amount of time seems too short.

Hyperfocus and *hyperfixation* are similar, but we don't use those terms interchangeably. We use **hyperfocus** to refer to individual instances of intense focus, during which people with ADHD are liable to lose track of time (this is also known as "flow state" and is not exclusive to people with ADHD).

We use **hyperfixation** to refer to a period of enthusiastic interest in a specific subject or activity, usually resulting in multiple instances of hyperfocus. For example, if you've been **hyperfocusing** while making puppets a lot lately, puppet-making is your current **hyperfixation**.

So it's useful to figure out which type of time deficit you're dealing with. Are you struggling with things not moving fast enough? That's #1. If you tell someone, "I'll be there in a minute, I just have to finish tidying this up," and then you keep tidying and it's been ten minutes, that's #2. If I'm in the shop building models or if Cate is in a deep research dive, we may lose track of time being immensely focused on something. That's #3.

Once you get better at recognizing these different types of deficits as they happen, you'll start to be able to anticipate them and plan systems and strategies accordingly.

A few examples:

> 66 I know I'm going to be bored to death helping my grandmother set up her Gmail spam filter, so it's going to feel like it's taking forever, making me liable to get unduly frustrated with her. I'll make sure to bring a paper clip so I can fidget with it to pass the time more easily.

> 66 My friend I'm meeting for dinner just asked me for an ETA. I think I'll be there in ten minutes, but I'm going to say fifteen minutes because I'm often a bit off about that sort of thing.

> 66 I have to go work on something in the shed, but I also have to pick my kids up from school in two hours. I know I tend to hyperfocus on projects in the shed and lose track of time, so I'll set a timer on my phone for an hour and a half.

The boredom example ties in a lot with frustration tolerance. Remember, as much as you deserve to have people be patient with you, considering the way that your brain works, you also must be patient with other people, considering the way that *their* brains work.

QUICK TIP FOR
Time Blindness

Keep easy-to-read clocks readily visible around your home and workplace. That way you can check the time with just a quick glance rather than having to remember to check the time on your phone—the ultimate distraction.

Very small durations of time during which we're bored can feel like a really big deal and make us irrationally mad at whatever is causing this boredom. That's one of those moments when you have to realize, *This is a ME thing.* This person is talking at a reasonable rate, or this line is moving at a reasonable rate, and this is my own frustration coming up.

Some other examples of how time perception deficits can really ruin your day . . .

- "I'll just set this stuff here for a minute." (Two weeks later, that stuff is still there.)
- "These bookshelves will take me only a couple of hours to put together." (Three months later, they are still unassembled in the hallway.)
- "Switching these cabinet doors shouldn't take too long. I've definitely got time to do that before the party starts . . ."

Awareness that you might have real, measurable issues with time is an important first step in planning how and when to implement helpful systems in your life.

 ## Will I GROW OUT of ADHD?

 No. Hopefully you'll get better at dealing with it, though, and it'll affect your life less negatively over time. Also remember that ADHD has *heterotypic continuity*, meaning it can change how it presents itself over time, but it doesn't go away.

 There is this narrative that people grow out of their ADHD. **What is actually happening is that the ADHD presentations change over time.**

Externally, it may look a lot like you're growing out of your ADHD. What you're actually doing is developing coping mechanisms, systems, and structures that allow you to manage your life.

You also become more aware of the social and professional costs of unchecked ADHD behavior. There's relatively little cost to running around the room as a kid—you might get yelled at or embarrass your parents. Whatever. As you get older, your awareness of the cost begins to grow. As an adult, there's a big cost and very little benefit to running around the room during a meeting.

A **PSYCHIATRIST** says I have ADHD, but I don't **IDENTIFY** with what people say about it. What's up with that?

There is no one correct way to have ADHD. I think people have a fundamental urge to be seen and understood . . . to describe their own experience and just to have people get what it's like to be them.

So when you're looking into the experience of others and the online content that gets made about ADHD, it can often feel like there are some people who have ADHD who do it right or do it well. That's not the case. Nobody knows what the hell they're doing. We're all just doing our best to try to live a nice life. **Your experience of ADHD is just as valid as every other thing that you've seen about ADHD, and might feel very different from how other people describe theirs.**

❓ What are the LIFE EVENTS that often contribute to making SYMPTOMS more NOTICEABLE?

Transitioning in academic environments is a big one—high school to college, especially. Other big transitions include losing a job, prolonged illness, moving, moving in with a partner, getting married, breaking up with a partner, or the death of a family member.

You also might notice ADHD symptoms or be prompted to seek a diagnosis when the things you're expected to manage change drastically. Something like a job change can bring difficulties with organization and time management right to the surface.

❓ Is ADHD GENETIC?

Yes. **If your parents have ADHD, there's a much higher likelihood that you will have ADHD.** We don't know specifically what causes ADHD yet, but we do know that there is a strong genetic component.

We can MAP THE ENTIRE FREAKING HUMAN GENOME NOW, so science is chugging away, and I'm really excited for all the new data we're going to get over the next few decades.

MORE Myths and Misinformation

> **Is it true that if I just eat better, my ADHD will be cured?**

Nah. But eating like crap might make you feel like crap, and feeling like crap isn't really known for easing the symptoms of neurodevelopmental disorders.

Eating terribly can also muddy the waters as you try to sort out exactly how your ADHD is affecting your life. Is your brain fuzzy because of your ADHD? Or because you've only eaten cupcakes and half a roll of Werther's Originals today? (It's okay, we've all been there.) Making sure you're well nourished will help isolate ADHD as a variable.

There have also been a number of studies and reviews about whether fish oil (omega-3 fatty acids) alleviates ADHD symptoms,[11] and the results range from "no" to "meh." Still, if you find it helps you, go for it.

> **Is it true that if I stop eating red dye no. 5, my ADHD will be cured?**

We have no reason to believe that your ADHD will go away if you stop consuming red dye no. 5. However, a fair number of studies have been done concerning synthetic food dyes and child development,[12] leading California's Office of Environmental Health Hazards Assessment to conclude that "[t]he scientific literature indicates that synthetic food dyes can impact neurobehavior in some children" and that the FDA's current Acceptable Daily Intake (ADI) "may not provide adequate protection from neurobehavioral impacts in children."

Then a bunch of Internet grifters used these studies to get views and sell supplements by claiming that red dye no. 5 is the sole cause of ADHD as part of some vague conspiracy.

So if you want to steer clear—or have your children steer clear—of synthetic food coloring, go for it, but it certainly won't make your ADHD go away or prevent your kids from having it.

Is it TRUE that if I just TRY HARDER my ADHD will be fixed?

 Abso-fucking-lutely not. As we've mentioned and will continue to hammer home, **the ADHD brain works differently than a neurotypical brain. No amount of "try" can change this.**

That reality can be hard to accept, but there are many ways to manage your ADHD that may help. A whole book's worth of strategies, in fact.

And remember: you don't need fixing, because . . .

YOU ARE NOT A FUCKUP.

While we're here . . .

 I was told by an ENIGMATIC OLD MAN that there is a mystical herb that grows only in Tibet on the tallest peak during the longest day, and that this herb would CURE MY ADHD. Will it?

 NO. He's probably trying to sell you something. Herbs are not mystical.

 Have you eaten EVERY HERB, Cate?

 No, Erik. I have not eaten every herb.

 Then how do you know some of them aren't super mystical?!

 . . .

 Where's your sense of wonder, Cate?

CHAPTER 1:
The Technical Stuff

Chapter 1 in short:

- **Attention deficit hyperactivity disorder (ADHD)**, formerly known as ADD, is a disorder that makes your brain not very good at deciding what you should be doing at any given time. This is because your brain's **executive functions** don't work properly.
- Your **executive functions** are the processes your brain uses to decide what you should be doing. They are IMPULSE CONTROL, EMOTIONAL CONTROL, WORKING MEMORY, FLEXIBLE THINKING, SELF-MONITORING, TASK INITIATION, ORGANIZATION, and PLANNING AND PRIORITIZING.
- **Anyone** can have ADHD.
- You are **more likely** to have ADHD **if members of your family do**.
- ADHD is a **neurodevelopmental disorder**, which means you have it from birth and cannot "catch it" later in life.
- **ADHD presents itself differently to different people**. If you don't identify with another person's experience with ADHD, that's okay!
- ADHD has **heterotypic continuity**, meaning **it doesn't go away**, but factors like major life events and changes in circumstance can change how symptoms present themselves throughout your life.
- In particular, the **female hormonal cycle affects ADHD** not only on the day-to-day but through a person's life and can make treating ADHD challenging.
- There is **no known "cure"** for ADHD.
- **There is a lot of BS out there** about ADHD these days. Be careful where you get your information from!

A Bonus History of ADHD

WARNING: The next several pages are basically a long, weird digression where I dig into historical excerpts of old manuscripts. If this is not for you, PLEASE SKIP THIS SECTION! Move along. You won't hurt my feelings. And if you're a history nerd like me, well, you're welcome ... —Cate

One of the things that I find more fascinating than anything else in the world is context. We, as humans, fit into a context—our cultural background, our religious beliefs, where we went to school, what we do for work—and context is often necessary to understand why and how things are today.

The history of ADHD is something that we don't talk a lot about when discussing the disorder, but it provides an *immense* amount of context to understanding the attitudes and ideas that currently shape our understanding of ADHD.

Hippocrates (460–375 BC), almost universally considered the father of modern medicine, provided the earliest report of a condition that appears to be comparable with what is currently identified as ADHD. He described patients who had "quickened responses to sensory experience, but also less tenaciousness because the soul moves on quickly to the next impression."[1]

An ADHD TIMELINE

Early Observations

Melchior Adam Weikard* (1775): Published the first edition of *Der Philosophische Arzt*, which received harsh criticism and backlash, particularly from the German Catholic Church, which objected to his theories that the usual solutions to mental illness—namely prayer and exorcism—were less effective than an informed medical approach to treatment.

Most notably for our purposes, this book contained a chapter titled "Attention Deficit" ("Mangel der Aufmerksamkeit") or "Attentio Volubilis." He describes this "attention deficit" phenomenon:

> Those, who have a lack of attention, are generally characterized as unwary, careless, flighty and bacchanal. [There's more, but he goes on to say:] ... A young chaplain for example is supposed to meditate about the savior's sufferings. Every humming fly, every shadow, every sound, the memory of old stories will draw him off his task to other imaginations. Even his imagination, if and when it is copious, entertains him with a thousand minor subjects. He laughs so cordially when he is contemplating a nun who saw a soldier getting caught on the fence of the garden and his trousers getting snagged while he is to meditate on when Christ was taken prisoner. That is what I call lack of attention.

→

---

* The childhood of a doctor in the 1700s might seem like a small digression, even in a book about ADHD, but context begets context, and so it is important for you to know that Weikard was disabled, having what is described in memoirs as a "spinal deformity" and nearsightedness. This lived experience would inform his opinion that mental and physical ailments were not the result of God's punishment, demons, or witchcraft, but rather all had causes rooted in specific and measurable causes. Even more specifically, he concluded that social and economic factors could affect a person's cognitive function. This was an incredibly progressive take for the time, and this belief would spur his interest in medical science—particularly in the fields of what we'd now call psychiatry and psychology.

> ... An inattentive person won't remark anything but will be shallow everywhere. He studies his matters only superficially; his judgements are erroneous and he misconceives the worth of things because he does not spend enough time and patience to search a matter individually or by the piece with the adequate accuracy. Such people only hear half of everything; they memorize or inform only half of it or do it in a messy manner. According to a proverb they generally know a little bit of all and nothing of the whole.

Sir Alexander Crichton (1798): Described a condition similar to ADHD, focusing on inattention and distractibility.

> In this disease of attention, if it can with propriety be called so, every impression seems to agitate the person, and gives him or her an unnatural degree of mental restlessness. People walking up and down the room, a slight noise in the same, the moving a table, the shutting a door suddenly, a slight excess of heat or of cold, too much light, or too little light, all destroy constant attention in such patients, inasmuch as it is easily excited by every impression. The barking of dogs, an ill-tuned organ, or the scolding of women, are sufficient to distract patients of this description to such a degree, as almost approaches to the nature of delirium. It gives them vertigo, and headach [sic], and often excites such a degree of anger as borders on insanity. When people are affected in this manner, which they very frequently are, they have a particular name for the state of their nerves, which is expressive enough of their feelings. They say they have the *fidgets*.

Heinrich Hoffmann (1844): Illustrated stories like "Fidgety Phil" and "Johnny Look-in-the-air," which depicted behaviors akin to ADHD.

> "Let me see if Philip can
> Be a little gentleman;
> Let me see if he is able
> To sit still for once at table":
> Thus Papa bade Phil behave;
> And Mamma looked very grave.
> But fidgety Phil,
> He won't sit still;
> He wriggles,
> And giggles,
> And then, I declare,
> Swings backwards and forwards,
> And tilts up his chair,
> Just like any rocking horse—
> "Philip! I am getting cross!"

Sir George Frederic Still (1902): Discussed "defect of moral control" in children, a concept overlapping with ADHD, especially in impulsivity and attention issues.

> 1) passionateness; (2) spitefulness—cruelty; (3) jealousy; (4) lawlessness; (5) dishonesty; (6) wanton mischievousness—destructiveness; (7) shamelessness—immodesty; (8) sexual immorality; and (9) viciousness. The keynote of these qualities is self-gratification, the immediate gratification of self without regard either to the good of others or to the larger and more remote good of self.

THE EVOLUTION OF ADHD

DSM edition	Year	Terminology for ADHD/ADD	Key Characteristics
DSM-I	1952	Not specifically mentioned	ADHD/ADD was not explicitly recognized or defined in this edition.
DSM-II	1968	Hyperkinetic Reaction of Childhood	Characterized by overactivity, restlessness, distractibility, and short attention span, especially in young children.
DSM-III	1980	Attention Deficit Disorder (ADD) with or without Hyperactivity	Introduced the term ADD, distinguishing between types with and without hyperactivity. Emphasized attention deficits.
DSM-III-R	1987	Attention Deficit Hyperactivity Disorder (ADHD)	Combined symptoms into a single list, removing the distinction between ADD with and without hyperactivity.
DSM-IV	1994	Attention Deficit Hyperactivity Disorder (ADHD)	Identified three subtypes: predominantly inattentive type, predominantly hyperactive-impulsive type, and combined type.
DSM-IV-TR	2000	Attention Deficit Hyperactivity Disorder (ADHD)	Maintained the definition of ADHD from *DSM-IV*, with updates to the descriptive text that served to highlight the variability of symptoms over time.
DSM-5	2013	Attention Deficit Hyperactivity Disorder (ADHD)	Preserved the three subtypes from *DSM-IV* but renamed them as "presentations," and included examples of symptoms in adults, acknowledging the disorder's persistence into adulthood. This change was part of the broader updates and revisions in the *DSM-5*, which aimed to more accurately reflect the fluidity and variability of symptoms over time. This was also the *first* time that ADHD and Autism could be diagnosed concurrently.
DSM-5-TR	2022	Attention Deficit Hyperactivity Disorder	Makes a much longer note of gender variances in ADHD, including that women with ADHD have higher rates of comorbid disorders, including oppositional defiant disorder, autism spectrum disorder, and personality and substance use disorders. A section about the prevalence of sleep disorders and sleep difficulties in people with ADHD was also added.

Kramer and Pollnow (1932): Identified a "hyperkinetic disease of infancy," closely resembling modern ADHD.

They described children with "a chaotic character, lack of concentration, insufficient goal orientation, increased distractibility, walking around aimlessly, touching of chairs, boards, etc.—of everything that comes their way." At school, children "affected by hyperkinetic disease often cause extreme educational difficulties,"[2] particularly in motor restlessness and inattention.

Charles Bradley (1937): Inadvertently discovered the positive effects of stimulant medication on children's behavior and accidentally paved the way for medication treatment.[*]

So why does all this matter?

Because the "why" of ADHD, the foundational understanding, is still shaped by these ideals and viewpoints.

We have to look at the history of writing on mental illness and the attitudes of those old times to start understanding how and why we talk about neurodivergence the way we do today.

It's frustrating, right?

Medical ideas from a time when things like "being born under the wrong star" and "an imbalance of humors" were believed affect *your* ability to get treatment *today*. Stigmas about "moral defects" are still present in conversation about ADHD.

Furthermore, there is quantifiable, sourceable, historical evidence that ADHD has always been around. It's not a "new thing," it's not a "trend," it's not a "fad," and we can look as far back as the BC years to prove it.

ADHD has been part of the human experience for as long as there have been people. So you, dear reader, or someone you love, are part of a long, storied history. You, by the very nature of your existence—with your own set of experiences, your own background, your own strengths and weaknesses and dreams and goals—are part of that story. You're part of the context by which we understand ADHD.

And I think that is pretty cool.[3]

---

[*] Listen, I can't in good conscience write this section without at least mentioning that the reason this happened was because this guy was doing terribly painful experiments on kids in a mental institution; he's not a hero.

ADHD and...

Comorbidities

Imagine you're moving and you've got a big, heavy box of books. The moving truck is parked out back, so you've got a bit of a distance to walk. You manage, but you're kind of sweaty and it takes some energy to get there.

Now imagine someone hands you two boxes at the same time. A little tougher, but you do it, and you're very proud of yourself.

Now imagine you're holding those two boxes and someone starts stacking a third, a fourth, a fifth . . . At some point, getting to the truck is going to be REALLY difficult. Maybe even impossible.

That is what living with comorbidities can feel like. For a HUGE number of people living with ADHD, it's not *just* ADHD. It's a stack of ADHD, depression, anxiety, PMDD (premenstrual dysphoric disorder), substance use disorders, eating disorders, issues with sleep, or maybe even Autism.

All those boxes "stack." All those boxes interact with one another, their component parts sometimes supporting other parts, other times causing a profoundly negative reaction.

This is why we feel it's so important to just yell this over and over:

For the MAJORITY of people with ADHD:
IT'S NOT *JUST* ADHD.

For a huge percentage of the ADHD population, those comorbidities are going to impact the success of the systems and solutions they use. We cannot talk about, say, executive functions (see page 36) without acknowledging that executive functioning is vastly different with depression, anxiety, or sleep issues—or all three. We cannot talk about strategies to feed yourself without acknowledging that many people with ADHD have issues with binge eating and food restriction. The list is long.

These Venn diagram scenarios are different for everyone, but no matter the type of overlap, ADHD rarely exists in a vacuum, so why do we keep talking about it like it does? We're going to break it all down for you instead.

In this chapter, we will discuss some of the most common comorbidities that come with ADHD. Before we do that, we should probably take a definition break . . .

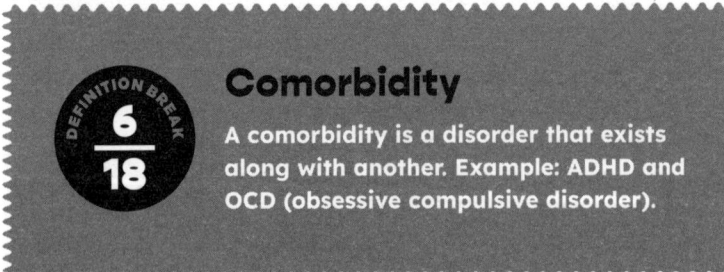

DEFINITION BREAK 6/18

Comorbidity

A comorbidity is a disorder that exists along with another. Example: ADHD and OCD (obsessive compulsive disorder).

What COMORBIDITIES are ASSOCIATED with ADHD?

Some of the most common comorbidities with ADHD include **depression, anxiety, eating disorders, sleep disorders, and substance abuse.**[1] Having any comorbidity is going to affect how you're moving through the world. I think there is a lot of misunderstanding because comorbidity sounds like multiple things mixed together in the same pot. But it's not like soup.

It's like salad.

Yes, that's way better. It's like salad.

Are there other COMMON COMORBIDITIES of ADHD?

Sexual dysfunction, erectile dysfunction, balance issues, vision issues, learning disabilities, and dyslexia are all relatively common comorbidities of ADHD.

Recently there has been a push by some educators to say "sexual disappointments" or "difficulties" rather than "dysfunction," and I think that's an important idea to highlight.

Dysfunction implies that there is something broken or "wrong" (usually medically), whereas difficulties or disappointments highlight that some of the issues we as ADHDers face are exactly that—disappointing and/or difficult. **It's not because our orgasm button is broken or that having sex is physically impossible, it's that we need a very specific set of circumstances to be right for us to manage the factors—like focus, physical connection, relaxation, and communication—it takes to get in the right headspace to make something sexy happen.**

Studies are starting to come out suggesting people with ADHD "report more sexual desire, more masturbation frequency, less sexual satisfaction, and more sexual dysfunctions than the general population."[2] So we generally have **a higher sex drive but less of an ability to satisfy it.** In males, this often manifests as what we would describe as "erectile dysfunction," so let's talk about that, too.

In Western pop culture, not being able to get or maintain an erection is almost ALWAYS portrayed as a shameful and embarrassing thing—a sign of a weak, ineffective person. While the *real* men, the ones who matter, can throw someone up against the wall and go at it anytime, anywhere.

That's just the movies.

Because of the manufactured shame surrounding erectile dysfunction in popular media, I can hardly think of any public figures

The ADHD Field Guide for Adults

PART 1:
An ADHD Primer

who've spoken openly about erectile dysfunction besides a handful of elderly men paid to appear in advertisements by pharmaceutical companies. And that's unfortunate. So I think it's important that I share my experience.

No matter your age, there is nothing wrong with experiencing erectile dysfunction. I have since I was fourteen years old, and still do today. I promise if you start talking about it openly with your friends, you'll realize ED is something that is experienced by nearly everyone with a penis. If you talk to your sexual partner(s) about it, which I highly recommend you do, I guarantee they will be more compassionate and understanding than you'd think.

There are helpful products available (none of which I'm willing to plug in this book). A quick Google search should put you on the right track; just make sure whatever products you try are safe for you and your physiology—be particularly careful if you have high blood pressure. Much, MUCH more on sex and intimacy in chapter 15, beginning on page 343.

How do DEPRESSION and ADHD work together?

The actual number varies depending on what studies you look at, but on average, 20 to 40 percent of people with ADHD also have depression.[3] There're a lot of package deals going on.

One of the struggles in diagnosing any sort of mental health condition is that a lot of things look like a lot of other things. Depression and anxiety can look like ADHD, but you can also have them comorbidly. Sometimes treating depression can genuinely help support your ADHD.

So, from a scientific perspective, we know that clinical depression is pretty commonly comorbid with ADHD,[4] but we don't have the slightest clue why, medically speaking.

Anecdotally speaking, it's not hard to see how ADHD can lead to depression once you start looking. Consider the following scenarios:

D'artagnan is about halfway through a hobby project when it suddenly stops bringing him any joy. It feels like the tenth time this month he's gotten enthusiastic about a project, only to get bored of it and have to agonize over cleaning up the mess he's made. He thinks to himself, *I never care about anything for long enough to finish it, so I should save myself the hassle and just never start.*

In the following days, D'artagnan thinks of several projects he'd like to start, but each time he thinks, *Eh, why would I? I'm just going to spend a bunch of time and money making a mess, just to abandon it and have to mournfully clean it up.* He starts feeling useless, like the only thing he can offer himself or others is disappointment. D'artagnan crawls into bed.

This "ADHD/Depression Cycle" seems to be pretty common in those with ADHD. I find it helps to remember that **the point of hobbies and projects is to enrich our lives, and even if you never finish any of them, your life is still enriched by the joy you feel while working on them. So if you abandon a project, you did not *fail*.** You succeeded in allowing a hobby to enrich your life, even if only briefly. Keep your eye on the ball.

Beuford's friend Marta is having a really hard time and invites him out to coffee. While at the café, Marta tells Beuford about what's going on with her: work stuff, family stuff, things she would only ever tell a good friend. Beuford is honored that she trusts him so much but is having an immensely hard time paying attention to what she's saying with all the hustle and bustle going on around him. It seems like the harder he

> **When stopping a project,** try storing all the materials and workpieces in a single box. I recommend buying and tucking away a stack of cardboard shipping boxes in assorted sizes somewhere. That way, they don't take up any space when you're not using them, and you'll always have a box that is an appropriate size for the project you're putting away. It's also important to LABEL THE BOX. That way, if you ever feel like working on it again, you know exactly which box your project is stored in and can pick up where you left off. Even if you never touch it again, it will feel more like you "paused" the project rather than abandoned it.

tries to pay attention to Marta, the less he actually does, to the point where all he can hear are his own thoughts screaming, Pay attention! This is important!

"Anyways, thanks for listening," Marta says, wrapping up. "You're a good friend."

Beuford wasn't listening. He didn't catch a single word of what his friend said. Beuford feels like a bad friend, and thinks it'd be best if he just stopped letting people get close to him and saved them the disappointment. Beuford doesn't talk to Marta for a long time.

This has happened to me more times than I can count, and it feels really shitty. Ask yourself: If the roles were reversed, and you were confiding in a friend who was having a hard time paying attention, would you be mad at them for struggling? Would you think that person was a bad friend? Or would you have compassion and patience for them, and hope that they ask for what they need so you could help support them? Do you think they would feel the same?

Assume that others have the same compassion for you as you do for them.

Scenario 3

Steve is on vacation with his wife and two daughters, standing in line at the place his youngest daughter, Marie, has been begging to visit: the British Lawnmower Museum. She is vibrating in excitement watching the front of the line grow nearer and nearer. When the family finally reaches the ticket-taker, Marie practically levitates with enthusiasm.

Steve's wife looks expectantly at him. He stares blankly back at her. "I gave you the tickets," she reminds him. Steve has absolutely no memory of receiving the tickets, but she's never wrong about this sort of thing. Steve frantically pats his pockets and tears through his backpack looking for the tickets, but it becomes clear he doesn't have them.

Steve watches Marie hang her head in dismay as she turns away from the entrance, dragging her feet on the long walk through the parking lot back to the car. She doesn't say anything on the drive back to the hotel. Steve thinks to himself, *I'm such a terrible father*.

In my opinion, forgetfulness is one of the most insidiously destructive symptoms of ADHD, especially when it inconveniences other people, and it can lead to strong feelings of guilt, shame, and depression.

No amount of mental illness is an excuse to harm other people, even through negligence. Figuring out how to keep track of important stuff is one way of minimizing your harm to others. That said, getting super pissed off at yourself isn't useful when it comes to amending the behavior you're trying to change.

> **No amount of mental illness is an excuse to harm other people.**

The ADHD Field Guide for Adults

PART 1:
An ADHD Primer

THIS APPLIES TO MUCH OF LIFE WITH ADHD!

> **There are many ways** ADHD stuff can lead to depression stuff, and they all have one crucial thing in common: They all start with *shame*.

Now, shame is inevitable. You are going to feel shame in your life, and there's no sense in feeling shame about feeling shame. Developing a healthy relationship with shame is arguably one of the hardest and noblest endeavors we can undertake as adults.*

As for distinguishing guilt and shame, we feel *guilt* over things we *did*. We feel *shame* over what we *are* (or what we believe we are). Guilt can be useful, because we can change what we do, and guilt lets us know when we should. Shame is useless, because we can't change who we are. Guilt is actionable; shame is not. Don't use shame as an excuse to neglect the lessons of guilt.†

When we feel shame, it is because we think we are something worth being ashamed of. So in those moments, ask yourself, "What do I think I *am* that is making me feel ashamed?" For example:

"I am ashamed that I am unreliable."

Now reword that as a statement of guilt:

"I have been guilty of behaving unreliably."

Notice how the shame statement pertains to the past, present, and future, as if dooming you to a life of being unreliable, whereas the guilt statement refers only to the past, leaving the future open for change.

Once you have framed behavior in terms of guilt rather than framing yourself in shame, you can begin to modify your behavior.

---

* I've said the word *shame* too many times, and now it just sounds like weird mouth sounds. Fun fact: that's called "semantic satiation."
† Okay, now *guilt* just sounds like a nonsense word, too. Is that really how it's spelled? It looks so weird.

It's never pleasant to be mad at yourself, so it could be seen as a useful deterrent for bad behavior, but too often we stop at the anger.

When we dwell on feelings of self-loathing, it can grow into a type of self-obsession, in which all feelings, including our compassion for others, are displaced by our bloated disdain for ourselves. It's tough to consider others when all you can think about is how much you hate yourself.

Remember, believing that you *are* bad serves only as an excuse not to address the situation. Sometimes you *do* things you think are bad, but you have the power to change that.

Here are some systems that might have helped Steve.

When somebody gives you something to hold on to, announce it out loud: *"You're giving me the tickets!"* The other person can then respond (if they're cool): *"I'm giving you the tickets!"* You can then elaborate from there if you'd like: *"I'm putting them in my wallet!" "You're putting them in your wallet!"* Anything you can do to manually mark something you're liable to forget.

If it fits in your wallet, it goes in your wallet. Having a default place to put important items (doesn't have to be a wallet—it can be a zipper pocket in the bag you always carry, or whatever) is always a good move.

Refuse the call! *"I really shouldn't be the one holding the tickets, do you mind holding on to them?"* You can't lose something you don't have!

How do ANXIETY and ADHD WORK together?

About 25 percent of people with ADHD also have an anxiety disorder.

What's tricky about the combination of ADHD and anxiety is that in some cases, it can actually help mitigate some of the symptoms of ADHD. Many studies talk about this comorbidity pairing literally *changing* the clinical presentation of ADHD.

For people living with both, it can be much, much harder to detect.

Think of it as kind of like a seesaw. On one side, you have ADHD. You might be impulsive, disorganized, and struggling with executive function. On the other side is a little anxiety gremlin whispering things like "If you don't get this done, everyone will be mad at you!" Or "If you do that impulsive thing, you're going to get in trouble and it's going to go on your PERMANENT RECORD!"

When you've got a little gremlin making you worry about every choice and every decision you make, it often results in less externally visible impulsivity or hyperactivity. That's because you're spending all your time living in your head, worrying about that thing you did, or meant to do, or need to do, or still haven't done.

This combination is often how many young women end up struggling with ADHD silently.

However, since this combo tends to work like a seesaw, these effects can go both ways. ADHD can make anxiety symptoms worse, and anxiety can make ADHD symptoms worse.[5]

That might look like:

- Difficulty concentrating/paying attention
- Racing/intrusive thoughts
- Procrastination/overwhelm/avoidance
- Struggles with decision-making: *ARE you making the right decision? What if you aren't?!*
- Perfectionism/people-pleasing: *If I do everything perfectly, no one will know how hard I'm struggling.*
- Physical symptoms like tight muscles, headaches, jaw aches

One of the most important things I've ever done was getting my ADHD under control, because when I did, I realized that easily 80-90 percent of my struggles weren't actually about ADHD. It was the anxiety I was feeling ABOUT my ADHD symptoms, thanks to years of navigating without support.

I am hypervigilant and a people-pleaser (both things I'm working on in therapy), and I also struggle with intrusive and catastrophizing thoughts. I struggle with making the "right" decision because I tend to overthink everything to death, and a lot of my impulsive behavior is followed immediately by extreme anxiety about whether it was a good or bad decision.

I have never, once, ever, lived in "the now." I'm worried about what happens afterward, this week, this month, next year. *Am I having fun wrong? Am I not enjoying this beautiful sunset HARD ENOUGH?*

For me, my ADHD medication is not NEARLY as valuable as my antianxiety medication. The difference between my taking it and not taking it is staggering. I can spend HOURS worrying about Erik being mad at me because of some weird way he moved his shoulders when I asked him a question, and then I take my anxiety medication and my brain goes, *Actually, that's dumb as hell and we both know this is silly.*

ANXIETY + ADHD
Scenarios You May Recognize!

▶ When Anxiety Makes ADHD Symptoms Harder to Notice

Maleficent is a straight-A student with diagnosed general anxiety disorder and undiagnosed ADHD. Every day, she wakes up obsessing about all the stuff she needs to get done and runs through her to-do list constantly in her head throughout the day to make sure she's not forgetting something.

She exerts a gargantuan amount of energy keeping her backpack and study area meticulously organized, to the point of near compulsion.

A teacher once scolded her in front of the class for having a messy backpack, and she would do just about anything to have that not happen again. People frequently compliment her on her organization, and for some reason, it never feels like a good thing or a nice thing. It feels like more pressure being put on her, because if she has a messy day, she'll be letting all those people down.

She is popular at school and very outgoing; she participates in a lot of different activities. During club meetings, she is terrified people will think she's not paying attention, so she diligently manages her facial expressions and the things she says so she always comes off as the picture of attentiveness. This is often at the expense of actually paying attention.

At the end of the day, she can't shake the nagging feeling there was something she forgot to do or didn't get done, so she starts planning tomorrow's tasks and goals and lists to feel more in control. She worries that if she doesn't go to bed early, she'll be too tired to get everything done the next day, so she forces herself into bed at 10 p.m.

→

She can't fall asleep for another several hours, getting out of bed several times to make sure her backpack has all the necessary material for the next day. It always does.

▶ When ADHD Makes Anxiety Symptoms Worse

Captain Farkman has ADHD and general anxiety disorder. He and his partner, Bobbie, have just arrived at a dinner party at his boss's house. He's up for a big promotion, and he knows if he nails this dinner party, he's sure to get it. Walking up to the front door of the tacky estate, Farkman notices that he's not feeling very anxious, but his ADHD meds are starting to wear off.

Ten minutes after arriving, he finds himself standing with Bobbie listening to Allister Stigman, the head of marketing, tell a long-winded story about his dog. Farkman takes great pains to seem engaged, nodding occasionally, smiling when Allister smiles, and making an appropriate amount of eye contact. Allister is just wrapping up the story when Farkman realizes he was tuned out almost the entire time. He has no idea what the story was actually about.

"Anyways, that's Duke for ya!" Allister finishes, making expectant eye contact.

Farkman panics and says something he thinks is general enough to get him out of this situation. "You should bring Duke by the office some time, I'd love to meet him!"

Allister Stigman's face turns puzzled, then pained. "I'm going to refresh my drink," he says before walking away.

Captain Farkman's heart sinks into his stomach.

Bobbie yanks him aside and leans in close. "What the hell was that? He just finished telling us how much he misses his dead dog, and you make fun of him?!" Bobbie whisper-yells at Farkman.

"I-I'm . . . ," he stutters.

Farkman rushes to the bathroom, his heart now beating out of his chest. Splashing cold water onto his face, he notices his hands shaking, breath shortening, and mind racing. *I can't go back out there. He's probably told everyone how inconsiderate and dense I am! I can't, I can't!*

Farkman knows he's having a panic attack and texts Bobbie to make up an excuse for them to leave.

▶ When Anxiety Makes ADHD Symptoms Worse

Vernon has a big quarterly report due at the end of the week. They've known about it for a long time now, but every day when they start working on it, they are overwhelmed with fear and anxiety that what they come up with won't be good enough, so they put it off.

Now they have one more night to get it done, and they're in the midst of an actual panic attack because the scope of work is so big and they have so little time left. Their brain sounds like a cacophonous choir of derisive half thoughts, each voice vying for supremacy.

... ifyouhad**startedsooner**youcouldhave ...
whydoyou**always**dothi ... youhave**nothing**tooffer ...
you're**never**goingto**amounttoanyth** ...
it's**gettinglate**areyousureyou**have**the**time?** ...

They try desperately to regain control of their brain, but each time they look back at their computer screen, the voices get faster, louder, and angrier. For hours, Vernon is able to type only a couple words at a time before losing their train of thought. They feel like a failure. They're worried someone will find out that they left it to the last minute; they're worried about the project being successful.

Vernon finally finishes the report as the sun slowly starts to rise.

This thing is a piece of shit, they think, looking over the discursive mess of words in front of them. *When I present this at work, everyone is going to know I left it to the last minute and I'm going to get fired.* Vernon begrudgingly copies the file onto a flash drive. *I bet they're going to laugh at me.*

Later that day, an exhausted Vernon is standing in front of the projector screen in a packed conference room, about to present their report to the office. They take a few deep breaths before double-clicking the lone file on the flash drive.

Vernon hears a few chuckles and notices a confused expression on their boss's face. They turn around to look at the screen, their blood running cold as they find themselves standing in front of the huge projected image of Richard III.

Vernon was so caught up in their anxious thoughts that they had copied their son's book report onto the flash drive by mistake.

Vernon quit two months later.
... This has just become autobiographical at this point.

Are ADHD and AUTISM the same thing?

 No. That's important to say right away. Autism and ADHD are NOT the same thing; they are two different, separate diagnoses that can occur in a person at the same time.

HOWEVER

I'm about to sound like one of those SAT math problems, so hang tight. Right now, the current research gives us numbers that look like this:[6]

- 20–50 percent of children with ADHD also meet the criteria for Autism.
- 30–80 percent of Autistic children meet the criteria for ADHD.

That's a HUGE amount of overlap.

> It's time for another **SCIENCE MOMENT with CATE!** Feel free to dig in or skip this part and move along. Choose your own adventure . . .

Where ADHD and Autism* start and end, especially for people with the AuDHD "combo platter," is currently something of a contentious topic. Much of this stems from the damage that the *DSM* caused by not allowing joint diagnosis until 2013.

---

* You might be wondering why we capitalize *Autism* and use the term *Autistic* rather than *person with Autism*. Many in the Autistic community prefer "identity-first" language. The idea is that being Autistic is an integral part of their identity, much like cultural or gender identities. Saying "Autistic person" emphasizes that the condition is not something separate from the person, but a key part of who they are. This contrasts with person-first language, which some feel implies that the condition is a problem or illness separate from their identity. Preferences for language can vary among individuals, but in writing this book, we've chosen to listen to the community on this one at the time of writing.

The ADHD Field Guide for Adults   PART 1: An ADHD Primer

> Many Autistic people struggle with sensory issues; so do people with ADHD.

Doctors were not allowed to give a dual diagnosis of ADHD and Autism—they had to basically pick the one that seemed the most obvious. This inadvertently created very disparate research, which, in turn, inadvertently created the idea for some that certain traits are exclusively "an Autism thing" or "an ADHD thing." Combine that with the utter lack of nuance on the Internet, and you wind up with some truly vitriolic arguments about the validity of various neurodivergent experiences. And that helps nobody.

The reality is that many Autistic people struggle with sensory issues; so do people with ADHD. Some of those Autistic people may not know they have ADHD, and some of those ADHD folks may not know they're Autistic. One of the criteria for ADHD is "not seeming to listen when spoken to directly," and that's also DEFINITELY the case for a lot of Autistic kids. Again, the WHY might be very different.

That "why" is really important only when we look at it from a diagnostic standpoint—for an Autistic person, sensory issues may lead to meltdown because of the overwhelm they cause. For an ADHD brain, that scratchy tag might ruin your focus or ability to think about anything else before it's resolved. Both of those are "sensory issues" that show up differently for different people. At the end of the day, the issue is that both people struggle to function with scratchy tags. Research shows that up to 70 percent of people with ADHD have some kind of sensitivity to light,[7] but that, too, is often labeled as exclusively an "Autism thing."

The "Is it Autism or ADHD" conversation has resulted in a lot of *us vs. them* mentality: "ONLY Autistic people stim" (not true, even the most average, neurotypical people in the world stim; it's part of human behavior). "ONLY ADHD people struggle with focus/attention, ONLY Autistic people have sensory issues." This is all fundamentally untrue, and claiming things for a "side" only results in further misunderstanding and division in the neurodivergent community.

This overlap between ADHD and Autism also makes treating ADHD much, much more difficult for some people. One half of me craves structure and order and gets really, really upset when plans change and things are different than I expected. The other half of me craves spontaneity and whimsy, and those two things are VERY difficult to navigate together. I spend a lot of time genuinely not knowing what I want or what I need to do because I am constantly being pulled in two different directions. Similarly, I love being with friends and going out and doing things, but loud and crowded restaurants are overwhelming and social situations exhaust me.

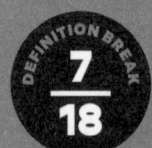

What is a stim?

A stim, or "stimming," refers to repetitive motions or activities that are used to help self-soothe and/or process emotions and release energy. Examples include tapping your pencil or bouncing your knee when you're bored . . . twirling around until you're dizzy to feel excitement . . . twirling your hair around your finger or chewing your lip to help you concentrate.

Some stims can be classified as "body-focused repetitive behaviors," or BFRBs. These stims include things like skin picking, nail biting, nose picking, hair pulling, and chewing the inside of your cheek. The problem is that, like many other stims, these activities can be incredibly self-soothing but also physically damaging, leaving you with bloody fingers or a spot in your mouth that won't heal. About 10–20 percent of people with ADHD struggle with BFRBs, and sometimes it can be prevalent enough to classify as clinical trichotillomania (pulling out hair, including eyebrows) or dermatillomania (skin picking).

What About OCD?

About 30 percent of people with OCD also have ADHD. Besides the conventional obsessive-compulsive behaviors that most people recognize as OCD,[8] a number of disorders also fall under the umbrella of OCD, including, but not limited to:

**hoarding disorder • tics • tourette's disorder
• body-focused repetitive behaviors
(skin picking, nail biting, hair pulling, etc.)**

If you have ADHD, you have a slightly higher likelihood of experiencing ALL these conditions.

In particular, OCD, body-focused repetitive behaviors (BFRBs), and hoarding disorders can be challenging to navigate with ADHD because of the executive functioning deficits that are made even more difficult when dealing with these issues.

A Brief Note on Hoarding[9]

About 20-30 percent of ADHDers struggle with hoarding disorder. It's important to note that not every person who struggles with clutter or disorganization is a "hoarder." Hoarding is a specific, separate diagnosis. A person struggling with ADHD and depression might have a pile of moldy coffee mugs in their office and be deeply embarrassed about it, want to do something about it, but struggle with the shame and guilt of asking for help.

A person with a hoarding disorder might adamantly refuse to get rid of the moldy coffee cups, or experience fear and panic at the thought of having to move them or change the way they are, even if they're offered help. These are two very, very different scenarios that can look very similar if you're not asking the right questions.*

---

* According to *Hoarding Disorder: A Comprehensive Clinical Guide* by Dr. Carolyn I. Rodriguez and Dr. Randy O. Frost, there are three major "manifestations" of hoarding: *excessive acquisition* (buying/getting too much stuff), *disorganization*, and *compulsive saving*. What's even MORE interesting is that they break down compulsive saving into three separate categories: sentimental, instrumental (useful), and intrinsic (they just ... like the thing).

What about EATING DISORDERS?

Binge eating and bulimia tend to occur at a higher rate in the population of people with ADHD.[10]

Interestingly, while some people with ADHD do struggle with anorexia, most research indicates that anorexia is less common (about 18 percent vs. 35–40 percent for binge eating disorder and bulimia).[11]

There are several things going on with this comorbidity. One, you have executive dysfunction, so maybe you forget to eat all day long, and then by 9 p.m. you're starving so you eat an entire pizza.

You also may have a lack of impulse control, so you start eating a bag of chips and you end up finishing it because you just can't stop. You also may have "time blindness," like when you're watching a show and focusing on something other than eating, and then the same thing happens—you eat the entire pint of ice cream along with the entire bag of chips.

Similar to addiction, there's a dopamine issue here. **Sugar releases dopamine and serotonin, which make you feel good. And for people who struggle with regulating their emotions, turning to food (like turning toward substances or alcohol) can be a way of coping with that.** I'm sad, I eat a cookie; I'm happy, I eat a cookie, but for a lot of people with ADHD, it's not just one cookie, it's the entire box of cookies, in a chaos loop.

Personal note: I have been bulimic for over half my life, and I suffered for a lot longer than I needed to. I think that if somebody had told me when I was a teenager that I'd be much more predisposed to binge eating and bulimia, my life would look a lot different. I would have sought help.

In closing . . .

Despite the fact that many ADHD books discuss the topic singularly, the truth is that if you have ADHD, it is far more likely that you are dealing with other stuff on top of it, and that stuff you're dealing with can start to stack. It can be REALLY easy to say "Just keep a planner" to manage your ADHD. But it's a lot harder to encompass the lived experience of ADHD—and what sort of support you need—when you factor in comorbidities.

For a long time, I thought about my ADHD as though it existed in a vacuum, but the more I learned about the disorder (and myself), the more I realized that I was actually dealing with so much more. Personally, I am facing a bunch of common comorbidities—depression, anxiety, bulimia/binge eating, sensory processing issues, as well as a host of problems related to my executive functioning deficits.

It would be useless for me to look only at my ADHD as a singular issue, because that would be ignoring how my depression and anxiety affect my ability to manage my ADHD. My hormonal cycle affects my mood, my mood affects my executive functioning, my executive functioning affects how I navigate through the day . . . Everything is interconnected.

—Cate

FROM THE
INTERNATIONAL CONSENSUS STATEMENT ON ADHD

> ADHD often co-occurs with other psychiatric disorders, especially depression, bipolar disorder, autism spectrum disorders, anxiety disorders, oppositional defiant disorder, conduct disorder, eating disorders, and substance use disorders.

How ADHD Affects Your Body and Brain

Right now, as I write this, I am looking at two forearm crutches and a wheelchair sitting quietly in my hallway, waiting for another Very Bad Day to be of service. (I am very proud of one of the crutches, because it has a dragon on it, the kind you'd see on the side of a shag-carpeted van in the seventies.) In this moment, there is constant, shooting pain that stems from my lower back and runs down my thighs, and I can feel my nerves being compressed. Sometimes, when I shift in my chair too quickly or sit up in bed without preparing properly, it feels like I am being stabbed. Having spent all day at the keyboard working on this very masterpiece, my wrists and my fingers feel like they're filled with red-hot concrete.

In learning how to navigate life as a disabled person, I've had to learn not only how to handle the complexities of a worsening disability and chronic pain but also how to do all that while ALSO managing my ADHD.

As I have aged, as my body has changed, as I have learned to thread the needle of managing pain while not doing too little but also not doing too much, I have had to accept difficult truths and learn to navigate a life that is adapted to what I can do today.

When I am having a Very Bad Day, my systems can collapse if I'm not proactive. My usual habit of resetting the kitchen every night can fall by the wayside, so dishes are more likely to stack up. So, on Very Bad Days, I use disposable dishes. My frustration tolerance grows much smaller, so I remind myself to take a deep breath before I lash out at the people around me. My days look different depending on where I am on the pain scale. We don't talk about it much, but aging is a disabling event, whether it be hearing loss or memory issues or the cartilage in your knee breaking down—our bodies naturally deteriorate with age, and with that deterioration comes the challenge of being able to develop new systems that work for you. At the ripe old age of thirty-six, I can no longer lift a laundry basket off the floor without pain, so I use a rolling cart.

If I'm being honest, one of the most frustrating parts of ADHD is the changeability of it: the need to constantly adapt, and the way that our bodies and our brains need to work together to function. But when one thing changes—a broken arm, a deteriorating knee, an unfixable spine injury—the careful balance we've built can shift imperceptibly, or drastically, but we suddenly find ourselves looking back up the mountain and feeling like we're starting all over again.

The important thing to keep in mind is that you're not a fuckup if your systems need to change on a daily, weekly, monthly, or life-event-ish basis. There is no shame in admitting that you need help or more support, nor is there any weakness in figuring out the work-around that allows you to facilitate your day-to-day without injuring yourself further or spending a bunch of time exhausted because you're in pain.

—Cate

❓ I have **TROUBLE REGULATING** my body **TEMPERATURE**. Is that an **ADHD** thing?

 It's not a symptom of ADHD per se, but ADHD medication can affect your body temperature, and sensory processing can make temperature changes more difficult to navigate. ADHD medication can make some people run really hot and can make them more sensitive to heat. Other types of medication can do things with your circulation where you feel cold, or your hands and your feet are cold.

Anxiety and depression medication can have an effect here, too. Being sensitive to heat or cold is also a sensory thing, and tied into your interoception (in short, the processing of signals from your body—more on interoception on page 231).

 My ADHD meds cause excessive sweating, so I rely on products like Carpe, Certain Dri, and Drysol (not sponsored at the time of writing) to keep me from sweating through my clothes.

 Sensory issues can also compound. I hate being hot, but I would rather be hot in my car than have the air conditioner on full blast, because I cannot stand the sound of it, so then I'd have to get out my headphones. It becomes a whole thing.

Does ADHD make me CLUMSY?

Kinda, yeah.

When your brain tells your body to do something (stand up, reach for your phone, raise your hand, etc.), your body's nervous system activates specific circuits (known as "inhibitory cortical circuits") designed to *prevent* you from doing it. It's called "cortical inhibition." It's basically your body sending your brain a little pop-up that says, "Are you SURE?"

Studies suggest that the nervous systems of people with ADHD are not super great at this.[1] Inhibitory cortical circuits have even been measured to be weaker in ADHD children than children without ADHD.[2]

Basically, your brain doesn't always get the "Are you sure?" pop-up, so our physical bodies tend to move a bit more . . . brazenly.

 If you've got ADHD, you also may have dyspraxia. This can show up as being clumsy, falling down, and having more accidents. It can also be part of some learning difficulties, like with handwriting, because handwriting is a muscle control thing.

 **Dyspraxia**

Dyslexia is to reading what dyspraxia is to movement. It basically means your brain is challenged at coordination—controlling what your body does physically.

I CAN'T PICTURE THINGS in my mind. Is that an ADHD thing?

 There's a great deal of overlap between ADHD and aphantasia. So, what's the big deal if you can't picture an apple in your mind? What happens differently in your life because of that?

Well, as someone who just moved two pieces of furniture out of my house today, I can tell you it shows up in a lot of interesting ways! I struggle with a sense of direction. I can't picture how roads interact or relate to each other. So if I don't have a GPS or a map, I'm screwed.

DEFINITION BREAK 9/18

What is aphantasia?
The inability to picture things in your mind.

Similarly, I can't picture how things would look in my house, or what would fit. Same with packing or conceptualizing what will fit into the car. Plus, there's face blindness, which is different from aphantasia, but lives in the same realm. I really struggle with remembering people, and it's because I can't picture what you look like. Even buying clothes is difficult because I can't picture how they're going to look on me.

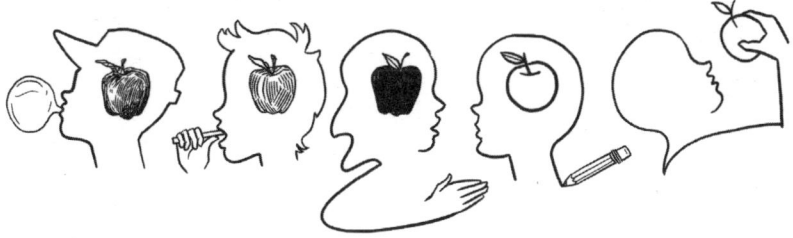

Are SENSORY ISSUES related to ADHD or are they just an Autism thing?

 Sensory processing disorder (SPD) can be associated with both ADHD (attention deficit hyperactivity disorder) and autism spectrum disorders (ASD), although it is more commonly discussed in the context of Autism. However, as we've talked about, a huge number of people out there are AuDHD (Autistic and ADHD).

I really believe that a better way of talking about sensory issues is removing the idea of them being an exclusively *neurodivergent* thing from the conversation. Every human being alive has different sensory needs. Maybe you don't like the feeling of velvet. I don't like the texture of ranch dressing. But it's the intensity and the frequency that we focus on with ADHD symptoms to differentiate between just "preferences" and "processing disorder" (and the disorder paradigm is a whole other conversation anyway).

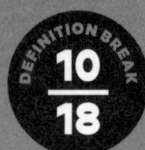

Misophonia

A disorder in which certain sounds trigger emotional or physiological responses that some might perceive as unreasonable given the circumstance.[3] Aka when the sound of someone eating potato chips sends you into a blind rage.

The ADHD brain is always looking for stimulus, whether it's positive or negative. So that element of distractibility can also become a hyperfocus. My husband Chris's jaw clicks when he eats chicken wings in a way that makes me want to commit a murder. The problem is that the minute I notice it, it's all that I can think about. To be abundantly clear: misophonia is not a symptom or a criterion of ADHD, it's just another thing that can correlate to the difficulties we already face.

I HAVE SENSORY ISSUES:
IS IT ADHD OR AUTISM?

▶ **Sensory processing issues** are frequently seen in Autistic people. These sensory processing issues can manifest as hypersensitivity (overresponsiveness) or HYPOsensitivity (underresponsiveness) to sensory input. For example, some Autistic people might find certain textures or sounds overwhelming (microfiber is Satan's toilet paper) or might not react to—or even enjoy—sensory inputs that others would find intense, like being very cold or very dizzy. (Shout-out to the twirly girlies who spun around all the time when they were little as a stim.)

In ADHD: While sensory processing issues are not a symptom of ADHD in the *DSM*, children and adults with ADHD may display hypersensitivity to various sensory experiences, which can contribute to distractibility and restlessness. (Imagine you're trying to take a test and you realize that your shirt has a scratchy tag.) Similarly, ADHDers can be distracted or hyperfocused and overlook stimuli. (Have you ever found a bruise and wondered where it came from or realized all of a sudden that you haven't eaten anything all day?)

It's important to note that sensory processing disorder as a stand-alone diagnosis is a hot-button topic in the medical community. It is not currently recognized as a distinct medical diagnosis in the major diagnostic manuals like the *DSM-5* or *ICD-10*, but the symptoms are widely acknowledged by both medical professionals and the neurodivergent community as a whole.

However, as we've said, ADHD is not a monolith, so the nature and impact of these sensory issues can differ from person to person. What really bugs the crap out of one person might be pleasant to another.

We are not researchers, we are not doctors, and we cannot tell you if your sensory issues are part of the ADHD experience or the Autism experience (or both, or something else). But if you're reading this section, it's probably because there's some sort of sensory issue that you are experiencing, and we're here to support you.

 There's also a higher rate of misophonia for people with ADHD. (See the Misophonia Definition Break, opposite page.)

❓ Can I smoke **WEED** if I have **ADHD**?

Well, we aren't your parents.
Still, this is one of those moments when we need to discuss the VAST discrepancy between "official scientific research" and "anecdotal/self-reporting."[4] Most scientific studies on cannabis either remain neutral[5] or outright discourage cannabis use for people with ADHD due to issues like exacerbated anxiety, executive dysfunction difficulties, and, to a smaller extent, the rate of substance use disorders in the ADHD population. In fact, 34–46 percent of people seeking assistance for cannabis use disorder have ADHD.[6]

We can tell you that lots and lots of people with ADHD self-report using cannabis (effectively) to mitigate the symptoms of their ADHD or, in many cases, use it as a tool to self-regulate things like anxiety or sleep. Many people with ADHD also report that using certain cannabis or THC products can help with executive function and improve focus.

It's also important to note that talking about "recreational" use is tricky because "recreational" means different things to different people.

> **We can't tell you what to do, but we do want to encourage you to be informed.**

There is also an entirely different conversation about the inherent privilege of being able to have these conversations while many people remain incarcerated for minor drug-related offenses.

HOWEVER. This is not us blanket-stamping cannabis as a one-size-fits-all solution to your ADHD woes. In reality, as the legal cannabis industry has grown in the United States, a wide variety of products of varying intensities and strains have been developed. Each individual is going to react to those things differently. This is why it's important to make your own informed decision.

The ADHD Field Guide for Adults

PART 1:
An ADHD Primer

You might want to talk to your doctor or your mental health team to discuss potential drug interactions and/or negative side effects. (PS—if you get judged or shut down, it may be worth your while to ask why. Many older medical professionals have a strong bias against cannabis due to the antidrug campaigns of the 1980s and '90s.)

We can't tell you what to do, but we do want to encourage you to be informed, do your own research, and, if you do choose to partake, please partake responsibly.

How does CBD interact with ADHD?

First off: WTF is CBD?

CBD is short for *cannabidiol*, which is a type of chemical compound called a "cannabinoid" found in the cannabis plant. It does not have the same psychoactive effects as THC. (That's science for "It won't get you high.")

There is some evidence to support the use of CBD to treat ADHD, but not much. CBD as it relates to ADHD is a relatively new area of study, meaning no statistically significant long-term studies have been completed yet, so the jury is still out.[7] That being said, many people claim CBD is a useful tool for treating their sleep difficulties and/or chronic pain. If it's legal where you live, you are welcome to try CBD products for yourself (we still aren't your parents).

If you do, you should know that **ingesting CBD can alter the concentration of other drugs in your system**. CBD can compete or otherwise interfere with how your liver normally breaks down medication, resulting in either higher or lower amounts of the drug in your system than intended. For some drugs, these small discrepancies can be harmless, but for others, they can be dangerous.

A number of medications can be affected by CBD, so if you're taking any kind of regular medication, you should always speak with your doctor and research potential conflicts.

My ADHD feels like it got WORSE as I got OLDER. What's up with that?

 Getting older often means managing more stuff, and ADHD doesn't like managing more stuff. So you might feel like your ADHD is getting worse, but really, it's just that you have way more to deal with than when you were thirteen. There were no insurance payments to worry about when you were a teenager.

 There are also many physical and mental changes that occur as we age. (See pages 90-98 for a discussion about the interplay between ADHD and hormones.).

For some people, memory loss and/or a loss of physical and executive function can also impact ADHD. If you already struggled with memory issues as a young person, that can make navigating ADHD more difficult as you age. If you have new physical limitations as you get older, those can also make a difference in how you get through the day. When your health and lifestyle changes over the course of your life, the systems you have in place to help you manage your ADHD will need to change and adapt, too.

This also goes for new, temporary, or complex disabilities. If you break your arm or your leg, a lot of your day-to-day tasks and how you physically move through the day are going to change. You'll have a shift in energy and ability to get stuff done. We also know that being in pain reduces your ability to focus and concentrate.[8]

Some temporary disabilities, like a broken arm, will heal and you can go back to your old systems. If you are permanently disabled, you may have to rework a lot of your life to accommodate.

If you are complexly and/or chronically disabled, your symptoms may change from day to day, month to month, or year to year. Disability can absolutely exacerbate symptoms of ADHD because it takes away the structure and flow you were used to.

 **Can you tell us about some "small hurts," things people have said or done around you that made you feel invalidated or bad about your ADHD?**

> I HATE when my family says, "Oh, we're all a little ADHD." Oh, are we??? Did we all almost flunk out of college and have mental breakdowns from the lack of structure and paralyzing executive dysfunction?? Did we all exhibit signs of massive depression and impulsiveness that were chalked up to bipolar rather than my actual dx of ADHD??? No? Then hush.

—Cait from New Jersey

 ### Does having ADHD mean I'll get ALZHEIMER'S?

 No. We have no evidence to support the idea that ADHD can cause Alzheimer's. However, some research suggests that certain genetic markers of ADHD (remember how ADHD is likely a polygenetic disorder, and is the result of many tiny genetic mutations) may also be used to predict mental decline in older patients (fifty-plus).[9] If your brain is already bad at remembering stuff, staying organized, and generally keeping things together, it's probably not going to get *better* as it ages.

Can HORMONES (periods, pregnancy, and menopause) AFFECT ADHD?

YES. **Hormones are inherently related to ADHD. In particular, for people who get periods, we absolutely get the shit end of the stick when it comes to managing ADHD.** This is also a topic that is extremely personal to me—the whole reason I got diagnosed with ADHD was because of a massive, overnight shift in my hormones.

> **PRO TIP:** This has nothing to do with ADHD but it might save your life (or your junk): make yourself aware of the symptoms and signs of ovarian or testicular torsion. That's how I found out I have ADHD—I had my ovary removed in emergency surgery, and the resulting hormonal shift set off a sequence of events that would change my life forever. (Very dramatically phrased, but it's TRUE.)

Whenever people ask me how I found out I have ADHD, I tell them that we have to start with an ultrasound technician who was late for a birthday party. I'd been waiting in the ER for about six hours at that point. I hadn't been feeling well that morning—cramps, I thought—but by midafternoon I was concerned enough with the throbbing pain in my pelvis to go to urgent care. The cramps had intensified to a point where I was curled in a ball and shivering. I'm told I passed out on the floor of the urgent care with a temperature of ninety-four degrees. When I woke up in the ER, I realized it was probably serious.

The ultrasound tech was pissed. She was supposed to take her kid to a birthday party, and I'd been tacked on to the end of her very busy day. She bustled back and forth with annoyed efficiency, and, while kind, she told me matter-of-factly, "I'm sorry you aren't feeling well, but I'm definitely going to be late because of—"

And then there was a long silence. She squeezed my shoulder and said, "I need to step out for a moment." Less than ten minutes later, I was surrounded by a team of surgeons explaining that the ultrasound had revealed an ovarian torsion that had cut off circulation to my left ovary for around eight hours. My ovary had died, and my body was going into septic shock.

One emergency surgery and a couple of weeks of recovery later, I was in a follow-up appointment with a doctor who told me that everything looked fine. "But," he said, "your hormones will probably take some time to even out. No big deal."

Three months after that, I was curled up on the couch in the throes of an anxiety attack, weeping and googling "symptoms of early onset dementia." At the time, I'd put my master's degrees to use by picking up some acting work with a classical theater company in town. They'd cast me as a lead in two linguistically complex plays by one of Shakespeare's contemporaries, and for the first time in my life, I couldn't remember my lines.

I'd sit down to learn them. I'd read the first line and . . . forget what I'd just read. I'd read another single line, over and over again, unable to get it to stick in my brain long enough to commit it to memory. Suddenly, I remembered that I'd left the laundry in the washer for two days, so I went to rewash it when I noticed that the sink was full of dishes. So I started doing those, realized I was hungry, made some food, and turned around to an even bigger mess and a very thick script of unlearned lines.

The people around me noticed, too. My husband, Chris, was used to quizzing me on my lines, and even he set the script down at one point and said, "This isn't like you," as I struggled through Act 1, Scene 1. I felt shame and guilt and panic, knowing full well that there were four more acts for me to learn and the show opened in two weeks.

I was convinced I was losing my mind. My ability to synthesize verse and poetry was something I was deeply proud of. I'd earned two master's degrees in Shakespeare while feeling, honestly, moderately bored the whole time because it was easy for me. The rhythm and the meter flowed like a heartbeat and felt right inside my body and inside my mouth, but now I couldn't even sit down for long enough to read those beautiful words and commit them to memory.

I was scared of what I was becoming. I'd always been messy, I'd always been a person who left things maybe a LITTLE bit to the last minute, I'd always been rather impulsive about the strange decisions I'd make in following my passions (that year, I'd also become a professional magician and I'd used the money I made to buy a hurdy-gurdy), but I intrinsically knew that those passions made me who I was and I ran toward them—now I couldn't even find the motivation to get off the couch.

When I confessed what I was going through to a friend (as I share in the introduction on page 13), he gently suggested that I might have ADHD.

My immediate response was "That's impossible, I was fantastic in school, I have multiple master's degrees, and I was a straight-A student." But then, as I read and researched, the puzzle pieces started coming together.

My lifelong struggle with disorganization. The teacher in third grade who'd repeatedly dumped my desk in front of the rest of the class for being messy. The struggles I'd had fitting in with my peers. My beloved hobbies and interests, inconstant as the moon.

"Catie is a joy to have in class, but she consistently speaks out of turn without raising her hand." The moldy coffee cups, the messy car, the ruined friendships because I'd forget to text back. "Catie would have such an easier time if she would really apply herself." The racing thoughts, the constant anxiety about forgetting something, the way I'd overextended myself in the hopes of being liked. The way I put all my self-worth into proving that while I might not be able to keep my locker or my room clean, I was smart and talented and capable. "Catie is intelligent and capable but often misses assignments because she loses them."

Suddenly the trail of red flags came starkly and glaringly into focus. So did several moments from my childhood and teenage

The ADHD Field Guide for Adults

PART 1:
An ADHD Primer

years. The time I'd seen a Newsweek article about ADHD in girls (fun sidenote—years later I would find out that Erik's dad illustrated that article) and brought it up at home, only to be told I was being dramatic. I got such good grades; how could I have ADHD? The "do you know ADHD" flyers in the college mental health center where I sat waiting after being sent for an evaluation—after a summer of bingeing and purging, I'd arrived back to school a size 0 rather than my usual and comfortable size 12.

I was filled with feelings of hurt, betrayal, shame, guilt, and the overarching question: "Has everything I've struggled with been ADHD the whole time?"

The answer came hilariously quickly, as the day before my thirtieth birthday I found myself sitting in the office of a psychiatrist who also happened to be a late-diagnosed burned-out gifted kid with ADHD and depression. I told her everything that was going on, and she took me through the various screeners that would determine on paper whether I had enough ADHD. Then she winked at me and said, "I feel like I'm meeting myself."

I was stuck on one thing—how had I gotten this far? Why had my brain chosen this moment to suddenly go from "struggles but survives" to "incapable of sitting still and focusing on anything at all"? I clung to my master's degrees like they were proof of my sanity and ability, insisting over and over to myself that I must be exaggerating. I must be acting overly dramatic. If I really buckled down and tried, I'd have been able to manage and maintain the life I'd built. My doctor asked me what had changed recently, and I said very honestly that the only thing of note was that I'd lost an ovary about three months ago.

"Oh yeah," she said. "Sudden changes to hormones can absolutely exacerbate ADHD."

The relationship between hormones and ADHD cannot be overstated, but it's something that is often overlooked because we're just now starting to really understand the full impact that they can have on ADHD.

—Cate

> When I was pregnant with my son and my daughter was four, my sister came over to see me. She immediately called my mom and told her she had to fly in to help me. I hadn't done a thing to get ready for my son and was about to give birth. No clothes, crib, nothing. My mom flew in and got me organized. I didn't know yet at the time that I had ADHD, but in hindsight it makes total sense. My entire life just felt chaotic and disorganized all the time. It was SO embarrassing. **—L.R.**

SCIENCE MOMENT with CATE!

To really understand the depth and seriousness of hormones + ADHD, we need to take a quick look at the menstrual cycle. Don't worry, this will be more interesting than your middle school health class. Learning this visually really helped me understand why I struggle so much during my period.

The four phases of the menstrual cycle are menstruation, the follicular phase, ovulation, and the luteal phase (note: not all cycles are twenty-eight days). The luteal phase is the one that will screw up your life.

Hormonal changes during the menstrual cycle, particularly changes in estrogen and progesterone levels, can affect neurotransmitter activity in the brain.

That luteal phase, especially days 21–28(ish), are the days when your estrogen tanks. So does your progesterone. Some people with ADHD may notice that their symptoms—such as mood swings, irritability, or impulsivity—intensify during this time. Many period-havers with ADHD also report feeling like their medication is less functional on these days.

HORMONES & MENSTRUAL CYCLE

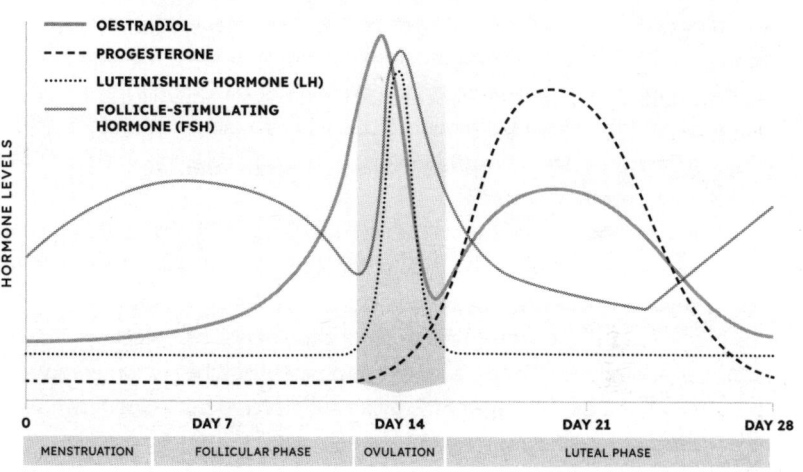

For some people, this effect is incredibly pronounced. **There was a FASCINATING study done where people with periods were screened for ADHD during different parts of their menstrual cycle, and depending on where they were, it made a difference on whether ADHD was clinically diagnosable.[10] That is, in scientific terms, a BIG FUCKING DEAL.** It's also one of the reasons why it's really important to inform yourself and prepare for the diagnostic process if you choose to go through it. "Do you struggle with focus?" is a very different question if you're looking at it today, now, this week, or overall from month to month.

Not only that, but people with ADHD also have higher rates of PMDD, or premenstrual dysphoric disorder (45.5 percent of ADHDers and 92 percent of Autists with periods experience PMDD versus the 5–8 percent prevalence rate in the general population), and other hormone-related mood disorders. We get periods, but they're turned up to ELEVEN.[11] People with polycystic ovary syndrome (PCOS) also have higher rates of ADHD symptoms.[12]

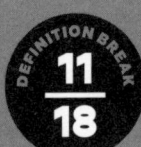

PMDD

PMDD causes extreme mood shifts that can disrupt work and relationships. Symptoms include depressed mood, sadness, irritability, increased anxiety, mood swings, decreased interest in normal activities, concentration problems, fatigue, changes in appetite, changes in sleep patterns, feeling overwhelmed, headaches, joint or muscle aches, weight gain, and bloating.[13]

Now, obviously, every person's cycle is different and doesn't operate on a strict twenty-four-hour Gregorian calendar, but this can be super useful in terms of planning around your ADHD and/or PMDD symptoms.

Hormones also change with pregnancy. So if you're pregnant or you're going through menopause, you may feel like your ADHD is getting worse. Many people say their symptoms improve while they're pregnant, but then their hormones reregulate and they may make you feel, well, like you're going insane.

So, to put that in context:

As a reminder, people with ADHD struggle with regulating dopamine and serotonin, which are responsible for things like regulating your emotions and your focus/concentration. These hormones fluctuate a LOT during the month—more so if you have PMDD.

Hormones start naturally diminishing in menopause, so your ADHD can feel a lot worse. ("Am I losing my mind? Is this early-onset dementia?") **Actually, it may be your hormones regulating, and that has an impact on your neurodivergence. In fact, in recent years, many women in their fifties and sixties have gotten diagnosed with ADHD, with menopause as the catalyst for previously livable symptoms becoming much more prominent and life-altering.**

What about HORMONE REPLACEMENT THERAPY during perimenopause and menopause?

There have been conversations about ADHD and menopause dating back to the ancient year of 2001, but **science has only very recently started to catch up with the revolutionary idea that women with ADHD continue to have ADHD for their entire lives**. And the natural hormonal changes we go through might, y'know, affect it a li'l bit, maybe kinda sorta.

In a study done in 2023, **61 percent of women said that their ADHD most impacted their life between the ages of forty and fifty-nine**.[14] Couple that with the woeful lack of understanding of what ADHD looks like in women . . . imagine how many undiagnosed women have been struggling through menopause because we were never represented in the first place. All that struggling? It didn't have to be part of it. It never did.

If you are in perimenopause or menopause, it may be worth bringing up ADHD with your doctor and discussing if your symptoms are making your life more difficult. During "the change," your estrogen levels fluctuate and decline, which can worsen your ADHD symptoms, mess with your executive functioning, and worsen emotional dysregulation.

There has been some interesting research lately into HRT (hormone replacement therapy) and how it may not only provide benefits in reducing hot flashes/sleep disturbances/mood changes but also improve ADHD functioning. Before you get excited, results are *super* mixed and vary widely from person to person. In some cases, HRT can make symptoms worse instead of better, and it can be more or less effective based on when you start treatment in your menopause. *I cannot stress enough that this is one you'll want to confer with your doctor about.*

> **Undiagnosed women have been struggling through menopause because we were never represented in the first place.**

PEOPLE WITH ADHD MAY ALSO
Struggle With...

▸ Substance Use Disorder (Addiction)

About half of all people with ADHD will experience problems with addiction in their lifetime, both behavioral addiction and substance use disorder.[15] The science isn't crystal clear just yet, but *ADHD appears to be a disorder that's fundamentally related to our brain's relationship to dopamine.* Our brains are basically dopamine-starved, all the time. And do you know what's really good at releasing dopamine at the drop of a hat? Drugs. It's almost as if ADHD is a disorder that was tailor-made to make someone more prone to addiction.

Contrary to what you may think, however, most studies indicate that being on ADHD medication actually decreases your likelihood of dealing with addiction. There is a militant portion of the population who like to treat ADHD medication like a gateway drug, as though you're going to be all hopped up on Adderall and become an addict. But the studies show that when kids are diagnosed and properly medicated, their likelihood of turning toward substances *decreases* because they're not self-medicating.[16]

▸ Gambling

If you were to invent an activity for the sole purpose of getting people with ADHD addicted to it, it would likely look a lot like gambling. Many places where gambling occurs, like casinos or hotel lounges, are specifically designed to bombard you with stimuli, diminish your decision-making skills, encourage impulsivity, and even make you lose track of time. Be careful when going to such places. Plan beforehand the maximum amount of money you are willing to spend, check the time often, and make sure at least one person knows you're there and what time you intend to leave.[17]

TRIGGER WARNING... →

Self-Harm[18]

Self-harm is really interesting when coupled with ADHD, because it's often talked about in the context of "I am using self-harm because I hate myself so much," or "I'm suicidal and I'm testing the waters." But with ADHD, self-harm can be something to alleviate boredom. That's a really uncomfortable concept, but it seems surprisingly common, and it's not something that gets talked about a lot. There's a bit of a stigma.

NOTE FROM CATE: Speaking very honestly to my own experience with self-harm, I did it because I wanted someone to notice and ask if I was okay. I didn't know how to process what was going on with me, especially in college when I didn't know that I was neurodivergent. I didn't have a diagnosis, I didn't understand why I struggled to accomplish basic tasks and fit in with my peers, and I started using self-harm as a way of saying, "Maybe someone will reach out?" The phrase "doing it for attention" has a negative connotation. In my case, I was seeking help externally because I didn't know how to help myself, nor did I understand what was going on with me internally.

Ironically, later on I learned that some studies suggest that my behavior patterns were exactly in line with ADHD in women—that self-harm can be a useful sign of undiagnosed ADHD and can often be a major indicator of the disorder.[19]

Years later, the first summer I got a job working for a Shakespeare company, I celebrated the occasion by having the dozens of thin white scars covered with a tattoo that runs up and down both forearms. It reads: "My scars can witness, dumb although they are, that my report is just and full of truth." It's a quote from *Titus Andronicus*, my favorite Shakespeare play. My scars are silent, easy to look over. They stand as witness and remain a constant reminder for me of that pain and hurt I felt as I struggled to know myself and understand my brain.

NOTE FROM ERIK: When I first started cutting myself, sometime in seventh grade, it was because I was so incredibly bored all the damn time. It had nothing to do with depression, or punishing myself, or anything the adults in my life worried (or insisted) it was about. It was about my contempt for boredom, and the impulsive things I was willing to do to avoid it.

When I saw some of the "emo" kids (mind you, this was 2006) using various school supplies to cut themselves, I was immediately curious. That day I went to the bathroom, pried the metal straightedge out of a wooden ruler, and scratched it against my left arm hard, producing a white line that would slowly seep red.

It was . . . fine. I felt no great relief, or sadness, or whatever you were "supposed" to feel. I just remember not being bored anymore. So I continued this little ritual, getting less and less discreet about it over time, the thrill of maybe getting caught being one of the most exciting parts.

And I would get caught, many times, by other kids, teachers, and my parents. But I would always keep on cutting. It felt like I was playing a big game with everybody, where every few months they would catch me and watch me more closely, requiring me to be more and more clever about acquiring sharp objects and where on my body I'd cut. It was fun, and it didn't have anything to do with depression. Yet.

When my depression eventually did start pestering me to self-harm, I was a practiced cutter. I was already attending mandatory meetings with visibly concerned guidance counselors. I was already mistrusted around sharp objects. The transition from self-harming out of contempt for boredom . . . to self-harming out of contempt for myself . . . felt perfectly natural. I had unknowingly been practicing what would become a decades-long behavioral addiction, and it all started with acting on an impulse, without contemplating the possible repercussions. Poor impulse control is often what allows us to take the first step down a dark path.

I think as we get older we discover more and more ways to not be bored—it's up to us to embrace the healthy ones and be vigilant in sussing out and avoiding the unhealthy ones.

You are going to form a lot of habits in your life for the purposes of alleviating boredom. Most of them will be harmless, and some of them can kill you. Be mindful of what you do when you're bored.

TRIGGER WARNING . . .

Suicide[20]

Rates of suicidal ideation are higher for people with ADHD. People with ADHD, as a whole, are impulsive. Think about it like this: Are you regulating your emotions? No. Do you have underlying issues like depression and anxiety? Quite possibly. Do you struggle with task prioritization and management? Probably. ("I'm so behind, I'm under this mountain of stuff, it would be easier to take my own life than it would be to navigate through this.") Once you start breaking it down by executive functions, it's easy to see how somebody who is struggling and has a lack of resources would go, *This is the solution.* Trying to remember that *this will end* is important, difficult as it may be. **Because you never want to make a permanent decision based on a temporary state of mind.**

There is help available: blog.opencounseling.com/suicide-hotlines/

Money troubles and sleep issues are also common among people with ADHD. More on those on pages 306–323 and 239–251, respectively.

Will BIRTH CONTROL affect ADHD?

YES. Kind of.

Different types of birth control work in different ways. The kinds that can impact ADHD more than others work by using hormones,* particularly estrogen and progestin. Some pills contain both; some only contain progestin. Anytime you are adding or subtracting hormones, it can affect the severity of your ADHD symptoms. (As an ADHD sidenote, it's important to know that progestin-only pills need to be taken within the same three-hour window every day for them to be effective.)

Before we get to final thoughts, how are you?

Really, though. Actually. Are you breathing? Is your jaw clenched? Hearing some of this for the first time can be a lot, and it can be very overwhelming. It's okay to be worried or stressed right now.

Closing thoughts on ADHD and your body and brain, from Cate:

It can be difficult and feel overwhelming to look at a pile of other potential struggles alongside your ADHD. "I have to figure out all THIS before I can start helping myself?" Or "I'm at risk for ALL this?"

That is where I can offer you some assurance. **The reason we need to talk about comorbidities and increased risks is not to overwhelm you, doom you to a lifetime of misery, or add to the pile of stuff to**

---

* This is also why many trans and nonbinary people often find their ADHD is different after beginning hormone therapy. Unfortunately, there have been [checks notes] zero studies done specifically on the interactions between gender-affirming hormones and ADHD.[21]

deal with. Rather, it's so you can organize and strategize around the challenges that you face every day. **Naming things takes away their power, and knowing your risk factors increases your ability to be proactive.**

Once I really homed in on my antidepressant dosage and got into therapy, I realized how much the other issues were affecting me, so I was able to work on those. ADHD became part of my journey, but I wasn't focused on *just* solutions for ADHD. My systems and support needs are based on the whole of me, and, if you're catching on to the Main Theme here, the more you know and understand yourself, the more you can start building and creating and asking for the support and systems and structures you need to succeed.

It may be useful to explore systems, tools, and techniques outside the usual ADHD conversation. For example, you don't have to have OCD to benefit from techniques to quell racing thoughts. You aren't taking anything away from anyone (nor are you "faking it") if anxiety relief practices help you navigate your day. **Treat yourself as one whole, complex person, not simply a person with ADHD.**

Closing thoughts from Erik:

It's necessary for you, dear ADHD reader, to know about your increased likelihood for all these different disorders and behaviors so that you can internalize the idea that **struggling with them is not your fault, it's just a statistical probability**.

To be clear, your behavior is always your fault. You are always accountable for the things that you do. However, your struggles with managing your behavior are not your fault, and getting mad at yourself for those struggles is counterproductive.

But even in those moments when you really screw up, remember that the feeling of guilt can be healthy, letting you know what behavior to avoid and pushing you to make better choices (see page 65). Managing your behavior with ADHD is a noble if difficult endeavor, and there's no sense in getting down on yourself for having a hard time doing it.

Coping with ADHD:

Stress, Boredom, and Other Experiences

I am twelve, lying awake in the thick humid soup of a Midwestern summer, unable to sleep. I have the familiar tummy ache that means I have Messed Up Very Badly. I stare at my Nickelodeon Time Blaster alarm clock as it grows later and later, and finally give up.

I head out to the living room, where my parents are watching *The West Wing*. I try to play it cool for a few minutes, but suddenly the guilt and the shame and embarrassment wash over me and I am crying as I confess that I am supposed to turn in a three-page essay on my chosen confirmation saint[*] tomorrow. I haven't even started. This was one of the assignments my teacher had warned us would be "on our own." We were important grown-up Catholics now, so it was our job to create the structure we needed to write the report.

"I don't have a confirmation saint! I can't choose! There are too many!" My teacher talks about the decision to choose a saint as a massive, life-altering deal, and I want to be sure I'm making the right decision. But flipping through book after book of saints is boring and tedious, and it's much more exciting to wander a bit farther down the library aisle to the coffee table books full of Renaissance paintings and make up stories in my head about them.

---

[*] Confirmation is kind of hard to explain, but in the Catholic faith, it means that you're "sealed with the gifts of the Holy Spirit." Sort of the final-boss level of Catholicism after baptism and first communion. During this process, kids take classes, take a "confirmation test," do community service, and choose a confirmation saint they'd like to emulate. The name of the saint is unofficially added to your Christian name, so thanks to that half-assed book report I did with my dad at 5 a.m., technically my second middle name is Joan.

I am sure God is going to punish me for not taking my confirmation saint seriously. I see my dad try not to laugh at my almost teenage dramatics, and my mom sighs. Once again, I've left something Very Important to the last minute. There are literally so many saints in the Catholic Church that they don't have an official number—it's somewhere around ten thousand. I am overwhelmed with choice paralysis, although I will not learn that term for another twenty years.

"I don't understand why you leave everything to the last minute! You've known about this for months! If you just kept an assignment notebook . . ." My mom launches into the familiar tirade, a bingo card of red flags.

It then occurs to me to lie, to protect myself. "It's not my fault! My teacher forgot to give me the assignment!" Not true, and they both know it. They'd been told at the last four parent-teacher conferences that while I was an excellent student, I was incapable of keeping my desk and backpack organized. As per usual, I'd lost the assignment sheet, and then I'd forgotten to ask for a new one.

"Can you turn it in late?" my dad asks. I cry harder. Doesn't he understand that everyone will know I'm a bad student? The shame of not having a paper to pass to the front of class is too much to bear. If I fail this assignment, I'm going to get a bad grade; if I get a bad grade, then I won't get into a good college; if I don't get into a good college, then I'll never be able to be a writer.

That night, my dad sits up with me until 5 a.m. on our dial-up Internet to help me write a passable essay on Joan of Arc because she has the longest entry in the 1972 *Encyclopedia Britannica* set my grandparents gave us when they moved. I turn it in and get the usual A and compliments about what a coherent and talented writer I am for my age. I am soothed by the praise and make a promise to myself to never, ever leave anything to the last minute again.

Two months later, I wake up in a panic at 3 a.m. when I remember my rainforest diorama is supposed to be due later that morning.

Eighteen years later, I will learn that I have ADHD. And that none of this is my fault.

How does STRESS affect ADHD and my ability to FOCUS?

Stress can positively and negatively affect ADHD, but stress also becomes a learned behavior when it comes to managing ADHD. A lot of people need the *Oh crap, my paper is due tomorrow* to get over the speed bump of starting it.

The problem is that your brain learns that if you leave something to the last minute, that stress is going to get you over the hump so you can complete the project. **That is useful to a point, but it can then develop into an unhealthy coping mechanism—your brain starts manufacturing reasons for you to be artificially stressed.**

A great example of this is the phenomenon of being an amazing house cleaner when you know someone is coming over. It's become kind of a joke in the ADHD community, but it works for a reason: the stress of knowing someone you like and care about (and who you fear might judge you a little bit) is visiting can be the impetus your brain needs to finally break down that pile of boxes or clean the bathroom.

Issues arise when you start either self-sabotaging (*I "work best" when I leave things to the last minute, so I won't start this super-important work presentation until the night before it's due!*) or adding on complications that may or may not actually be true (*If I don't sweep the floor, my husband is going to want a divorce!*). Those complications are—hopefully—not true, but if you say something to yourself long enough, you can start believing it, which then makes sweeping an anxiety-driving task instead of just a neutral chore you need to do sometimes.

I find it useful to think of stress as either "time-based" or "quantity-based." I tend to thrive under time-based stress, like having a project due tomorrow, but crumble under quantity-based stress, like having a bunch of different projects due in a month. **Being aware of what type of stress your brain likes and what it doesn't can help you leverage them appropriately.**

The ADHD brain does better under stress, as long as that stress stays under a certain threshold.[1] Then you also get into frustration tolerance. Say you have exactly the right amount of stress you need to finish a paper and then your computer crashes. Now you've blown through your frustration tolerance. It's a fine line.

I have TROUBLE holding on to a THOUGHT for very long, like something I was about to do or something I meant to say in a CONVERSATION. What can I do about this?

If I think of something and don't want to interrupt a conversation or lose that thought, **I like to put a finger on my nose.**

This is called **externalization**.

Externalization

The act of giving yourself an external sign in connection with your train of thought.

It's a physical, external cue to yourself that you have something to remember. **People do this all the time—crossing their fingers, putting a string on their finger or a rubber band on their wrist, or just taking notes. Put the reminder on the outside for the thought inside.** Get it?

One of the really common experiences of ADHD is that our brains are working a lot faster than our mouths (or our fingers, if we're typing). And so, by the time that you've said the thought that is coming out of your brain, you've had ten more thoughts. That's often where losing your train of thought can happen.

If I'm having an argument or a heavy discussion, **I will sometimes take notes** on my phone or with a pen and paper. This allows me to make sure I hit all my important points.

My other big piece of advice is just to **slow down, pause, find the thread, and go from there**.

There can be this weird shame and embarrassment attached to having to pause in conversation or to employ tools like externalization or note-taking. The idea that this is weird or that you shouldn't have to is a waste of time. It's just how your brain works. I once heard someone say, "If computers with infinite processing speed are allowed to have a little circle loading bar, so can I," and I think that's a great way to think about it. There isn't any shame in needing to load or organize your thoughts before you start talking again.

Some strategies that might help:

→ **For remembering that you were going to do/say something:**

- Touch two fingers together.
- Hold something in your hand.
- Put one finger in your pocket.
- Move something in the environment.

→ **For remembering what it was you were going to do/say:**

- Scribble it on whatever is in front of you (if available).
- Retrace the conversation to hopefully arrive at it again.
- Retrace your thoughts to hopefully arrive at it again.
- Ask if you mentioned anything about something you wanted to say.

- Picture one of the people you're talking to or something in your environment as being something that has to do with the thought. (Like your mom dressed as Napoleon because you have a super-hot Napoleon take, or a paper towel roll monster chasing you into the garage because every time you go into the garage to get paper towels, you immediately get distracted by something else in there and forget to get paper towels. Anyone? Just me?)

I trust you get the idea and can brainstorm from here, but, spoiler alert: none of these strategies will have a 100 percent success rate.

At the end of the day, you have to come to terms with the fact that you simply are not going to remember all the thoughts you want to remember, and you're not going to be able to say all the cool, smart things you want to say. So, **however much effort you put into practicing techniques to not forget those fleeting thoughts, you should put an equal or greater amount of effort into *forgiving yourself* when you do**.

Forgetting your train of thought sucks, but it doesn't suck as much as being furious at yourself. Sometimes you can't help forgetting something, but you can always practice taking a deep breath and being kind to yourself when you do.

I feel TEMPTED TO LIE a lot. Why is that?

The short answer is impulse control.[2] It's not that people with ADHD are liars, it's that oftentimes, depending on how your executive function works, you can be more predisposed to speaking before you think, and sometimes the things you say aren't exactly true.

In all honesty (ha), I lied ALL THE TIME as a kid. About dumb, silly stuff that didn't matter. What I had for lunch. Who my favorite band was. What movie I watched that weekend. I used to feel a profound amount of guilt about it afterward, too, because I'd get asked a question and blurt out *The Little Mermaid* before I even stopped to think about WHY I felt the need to obscure the fact that I'd actually watched *Beauty and the Beast*.

 This is probably less frequent but still worth addressing. It can also be a manufactured stressor where there simply isn't enough going on for you. Maybe you can barely manage sitting through class and paying attention on a Tuesday, so you lie and tell your teacher that your dog just died or something. It's not true, but it adds some interest to a typical Tuesday. I certainly did that when I was a kid. *Screw it, let's make up a harmless lie just for fun.*

 Sometimes it also comes from the trauma associated with growing up neurodivergent. Sometimes we use lying as a coping mechanism to navigate social situations or to manage our challenges discreetly.

It can be really, really embarrassing to tell your mom that you forgot her birthday for the fifth year in a row, so making up a story about how the florist delivered her birthday flowers to the wrong address can help soften the blow.

It's not GOOD to lie, but I defy you to show me a single person with ADHD who hasn't sent a less-than-truthful "I'm sorry for the delay in my response, your email got buried in my spam folder" at least once in their life. We all do it occasionally. Telling a white lie to adjust for the ways executive dysfunction manifests can be a way of mitigating harm.

NOW, THIS IS VERY IMPORTANT:

We are not advocating for lying, nor are we excusing it. We are also not saying that if you have ADHD, it is your God-given right to lie to people. What we are doing is acknowledging that yes, sometimes, people with ADHD lie, and you're not a monster or a terrible person for doing it sometimes. Being aware of it, knowing when and how you start to lie, can be a really useful tool to unlearn the habit.

What is RSD (rejection sensitive dysphoria)?

DEFINITION BREAK 13/18

RSD is condition that interferes with a person's ability to regulate their emotional response to rejection and failure.

 Can you explain REJECTION SENSITIVITY?

Rejection sensitivity (sometimes called rejection sensitive dysphoria)[3] is generally defined as a person's tendency to anxiously expect, readily perceive, and intensely react to rejection or criticism. It manifests as extreme emotional sensitivity and (very, very real) emotional pain triggered by the perception by the person with ADHD that they have

- been rejected,
- been teased,
- been criticized,
- disappointed important people in their lives, or
- failed to attain their own standards or goals.[4]

 What are some common symptoms of RSD?

- Difficulties maintaining relationships
- Withdrawing from social situations
- Isolating yourself

- Negative self-talk
- Low self-esteem
- High levels of anxiety
- Rumination and perseveration
- Sudden emotional outbursts following real or perceived criticism or rejection

While rejection sensitivity isn't a specific diagnosis (nor is it specific to ADHD), it IS an observable phenomenon in up to 95 percent of people with ADHD. *About a third of people who experience rejection sensitivity name it as the most impairing aspect of their ADHD—and that's a big deal.*

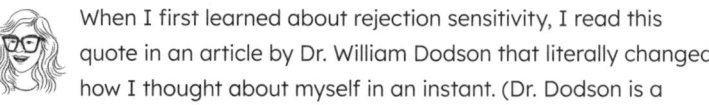When I first learned about rejection sensitivity, I read this quote in an article by Dr. William Dodson that literally changed how I thought about myself in an instant. (Dr. Dodson is a board-certified adult psychiatrist who has specialized in adults with ADHD for the last twenty-five years. In particular, his work on rejection sensitivity has made him a leader in the field of ADHD research.)

I cannot fathom a better way of writing this, so here is Dr. Dodson's quote in its entirety. I beg you to read this:

> To some degree or another, most people with RSD become people pleasers. They quickly scan every person they meet and have a remarkable ability to figure out exactly what that person would admire or praise. They then present that very pleasing false self to the world. They are so intent on avoiding the possibility of displeasure from others and keeping everyone happy that they often lose track of their own goals and desires. By the time they get to their forties, they have built up a huge well of resentment about having given up their own lives to attend to the perceived needs of everyone else and getting nothing in return.

> The other most common way of protecting oneself from the extreme pain of RSD is to give up trying anything new unless one is assured of quick and complete success. The notion of trying and failing or being turned down is just too painful to risk. They don't go on dates. They don't apply for jobs. They don't speak in meetings or make their ideas and needs known to anyone.

I'd never even HEARD of rejection sensitivity before that moment. Imagine how many undiagnosed people with ADHD haven't either.

Flaming-hot take that might get me canceled: **RSD is a *learned* behavior and can therefore be *unlearned*.** Laura Mears-Reynolds, host of the *ADHD AF* podcast, calls RSD "Really Shit Daydreams," and I think that's an *excellent* way to contextualize what RSD really is—lies your brain tells you, and we have to learn to recognize them as such.

I experienced brutal RSD from the age of eleven to about twenty-two. I spent the majority of my waking hours obsessing over what I *imagined* others were thinking about me and vainly devising ways to make sure they viewed me *exactly* the way I wanted. I'd especially never let anyone see me fail.

Then my life absolutely fell apart. Like, "I don't know where my next meal is coming from or where I'm going to sleep tonight" fell apart. It's a long story for a different book. With my life in ruins and my friends and family disappointed in me, I was faced with the monumental task of building a new life.

Then I thought one of the most powerful things a person can think: *Fuck it.*

Fuck living my life based on what I imagine others want from me. Fuck wasting energy wondering if people are thinking bad things about me. Fuck wondering if I'm good enough. *Fuck it.* It was time to ask myself who this "Erik" guy really was, to find out what he really wanted his life to look like.

I resolved to fight back against the RSD voices in my head. I decided, *every day*, to prioritize my own opinion of myself over the

> "You wouldn't worry so much about what others think of you if you realized how seldom they did."
> —Eleanor Roosevelt

assumed opinions of others, and to insulate my sense of self-worth from those liable to harm it. I practiced this for years, and I still do.

So now there are a very select few people whose opinions I care about. I spend zero time worrying that the waiter doesn't like me, or that the people behind me in line at the grocery store are mad at me for typing my PIN wrong. Maybe they are, maybe they aren't. I genuinely don't care.

You can work your way out of RSD, but you have to decide, every day, that you are going to combat those negative voices and respond to them with an assured sense of self-compassion.

You've got this.

 For those not living with RSD, it can sound ridiculous. "Your entire day was ruined because I sent a text with a period instead of an exclamation point?" And that's an important thing to understand, especially if you love someone with ADHD. Rejection sensitivity isn't just "feeling bad." It's a gut-punch, heart-wrenching, anxiety-inducing feeling.

It can be debilitating, and it can show up in a lot of different ways. It can make navigating social situations more difficult: Have you ever said something slightly awkward at a party and then thought about it for weeks afterward? RSD can dramatically impact how we navigate and build safe and healthy relationships. How can you give enthusiastic consent if you're terrified of saying no?

MORE COGNITIVE DISTORTIONS,
AKA FORMS OF NEGATIVE THINKING WITH ADHD

> **Cognitive distortion:** a pattern of negative thinking that can cause people to perceive reality in a way that isn't necessarily accurate and usually results in negative emotions and/or anxiety, depression, and low self-esteem.

These can all FEEL real—if you lose your job, it can absolutely seem 100 percent true that you're a failure and a fuckup, but it's important to remember that just because something seems true, it doesn't mean it is. And even if it is kind of true, it doesn't mean it will be true forever, or that you're incapable of learning, changing, and doing better.

Lots of neurodivergent people struggle with cognitive distortions due to extremely literal thinking, but also because of the experience of living in a world that isn't built for our brains. It can be easy to develop negative thinking habits that create a negative bias toward . . . pretty much everything. That then can lead to negative emotions being reinforced, which creates a vicious cycle that can be REALLY difficult to step away from.

Specifically naming and discussing these thought patterns can be super helpful for neurodivergent people because, to be quite honest with you, I am guilty of a LOT of these. I never stopped to consider that perhaps my thought processes weren't actually based in **what was true and accurate**, but rather **my brain perceives everything as shitty all the time**.

Here are some common cognitive distortions:

- **All-or-Nothing Thinking (aka Black-and-White Thinking):** Viewing situations in only two categories instead of on a continuum. For example, if you're not perfect, you see yourself as a total failure. It's not worth running a marathon if you're not going to win; it's not worth learning the violin if you can't be first chair. This can also look like thinking: *I am happy now! I've always been happy, and I will always be happy for the rest of my life!* Then, something negative happens and that changes to *I'm sad, I've always been sad, I will be sad for the rest of my life.*

- **Overgeneralization:** Making broad interpretations from a single or few events, like thinking you'll never succeed in anything after failing at a particular task.

- **Mental Filtering:** Focusing exclusively on the negative aspects of a situation and filtering out all the positive ones.

- **Disqualifying the Positive:** Dismissing positive experiences or attributes by insisting they "don't count" for some reason. *Oh, you won an award? Cool, you lucked into it! Your success isn't because you worked your ass off, it's because you were in the right place at the right time.*

- **Jumping to Conclusions:** Making negative interpretations without actual evidence.

- **Mind Reading:** Assuming you know what others are thinking, usually negatively.

- **Fortune-Telling:** Predicting future events, usually negatively, as if they were certain.

- **Magnification (Catastrophizing) or Minimization:** Blowing things out of proportion (magnification) or inappropriately shrinking something (minimization). *Yeah, I called my boss an asshole to his face, but it wasn't that big of a deal, because he was yelling and he deserved it.*

- **Emotional Reasoning:** Believing that because you feel a certain way, it must be true. For example, feeling like a failure means you are a failure, because only failures feel like failures, obviously.

- **"Should" Statements:** Using *should, ought to,* or *must* can lead to guilt or frustration. For example, thinking *I should be able to keep my house clean* or *It should be easy for me to stay organized* is just setting yourself up to feel awful.

- **Labeling and Mislabeling:** Attaching a negative label to yourself or others based on a single instance or event. *I got an F on this math test; I'm terrible at math. Why did I even bother?* This is an extreme form of overgeneralization.

- **Personalization:** Blaming yourself for events outside your control or assuming responsibility for things you're not responsible for. Contrary to what a LOT of neurodivergent people have internalized, you're not solely responsible for everyone's happiness.

 **If you could tell someone who doesn't understand ADHD one thing about your lived experience, you'd want them to know...**

> I'd want them to picture what it would feel like to be superglued to a chair while all of your interests, obligations, and worries are yelling and dancing all around you. And then someone turns on the most annoying song possible and chides you for not getting up and doing the dishes.

—Sarah from Portland

> What you may see as lack of effort or drive is in fact the opposite. I'm doing everything I can to make myself as functional as possible with the tools I have.

—Ashtan (@cricketandlace)

> Imagine your brain is a computer. Every thought and action is a different window, and every time you click on something it opens another tab. But you can't close any of the tabs until you've read through the whole thing. And sometimes you have to pass a test to close it first. And you have more and more tabs and windows opening with every thought until suddenly everything just freezes up. You can't do anything but wait or turn everything off and start over. So, if I'm not doing things I need to do, I'm not being lazy. I'm just stuck. I'm frozen or I'm trying to close out the new tabs that have opened or I'm taking a test and I can't move on. I'm not lazy. I just need help.

—@curiousalice09

> It's so unpredictable. Some days I can function almost perfectly. Other days I can barely get dressed. But the worst part: I can't predict what day it's going to be. There's no logic. Sure, there are things that influence the severity of my symptoms, like sleep, diet, and exercise. But even if I've had a good night's sleep, eaten well, drank enough water, taken my meds, and gone for a run, my brain might still be fully uncooperative. And sometimes I have a really productive day on three hours of sleep. There's no logic, no fix, nothing I or anyone else can do to make sure I can do what needs to be done. At the end of the day, it's a roll of the die.

—Marjolein from the Netherlands

> Hyperactivity physically hurts. It's not like, "I have all this energy, I can now do everything." It's more like my body is so restless and it feels so icky I want to crawl out of my skin, but I'm using all my energy trying not to crawl on the walls so I can't physically do anything, just sit here like a bouncing ball. Also, impulsivity is not cute. It's usually stupid, not well-thought-out decisions.

—Mathilde from Norway

> The ADHD tax is real. You will "waste" money on food that you forget to eat . . . on appointments that you forget to cancel . . . on fees because you forgot to move that money or pay that bill. It feels shameful and embarrassing when you've used all your energy to shower and pick out clothes for the day, and then when you finally get to work, find yourself in task paralysis because you have no more focus energy. The anxiety to remember all the things that are important as an adult is overwhelming. I have had to be realistic with what I can do with my energy and my time. I want to do all the things, but at the end of the day, after making all those decisions (which feels hard and exhausting), I just really want to go to bed.

—Amanda Vest

❓ I tend to CATASTROPHIZE. Is that an ADHD thing? Can you HELP me there?

If you grew up with undiagnosed ADHD or have anxiety, you might be a catastrophizer. And frankly, catastrophizing is a very slippery slope. **Catastrophizing is a cognitive distortion that causes individuals to jump to the worst possible conclusion, often with very little evidence or no evidence at all.**

It's very easy to fall into a pattern of thinking like *Oh no, my boss sent me a text with a period instead of an exclamation point . . . I'm definitely getting fired and then I'm not going to be able to pay my rent and I'll be homeless and I'll never recover from that setback.*

Hot and spicy take—some catastrophizing is learned, because parents tend to catastrophize around their kids, especially neurodivergent kids: *Oh no, my ADHD son is struggling in school, he's never gonna get into college, he's never gonna get a good job.*

No matter where your catastrophizing comes from, you can learn to break that cycle and that thought pattern through repetition. *My boss sent me a text with a period instead of an exclamation point . . . maybe she's in a bad mood today. Maybe she had a fight with her partner. Maybe her thumb slipped. MAYBE HER PUNCTUATION HAS NOTHING TO DO WITH MY JOB SECURITY.*

Some people with ADHD jump quickly to "pattern matching." It is a learned trauma: *A message with no exclamation point means that they're mad at me and then we're gonna get into a fight and that means that we're probably not gonna be friends anymore and then I'm not gonna have anybody to talk to at lunch, so then I'm gonna be sad and lonely forever.* **Noticing your own pattern matching and when you catastrophize can be helpful on the ride.**

This is the worst Disney ride ever—the ADHD Experience!

Remember that your brain's job is to solve problems to keep you alive and safe. Your stomach digests stuff, your kidneys filter your blood, your eyes see stuff, and your brain solves problems. And if there aren't problems to solve, then your brain is gonna try to come up with one. Your brain is a state-of-the-art, nail-seeking hammer, but the "nails" are problems.

It's not helpful to vilify your own brain, although this is tempting. Even when it does bad things, it's just trying to do its job the best it can, like when your dog destroys your vacuum trying to protect you from it.

The ADHD brain also craves new stuff to think about, so when it's looking for problems to chew on, it's gonna flip over every stone in search of a big, juicy, catastrophic train of thought.

That's your brain trying to suck as much newness out of a given situation as possible, thinking of all the horrible ways something could go. ADHDers can't stand to be bored, and the more your brain can worry about something, the less likely it is to be bored. Enter: catastrophizing! Fleeing frantically away from boredom.

Catastrophizing has a lot in common with all-or-nothing thinking: *OMG, I'm so anxious, and I'm going to feel anxious until the end of time.*

Try reframing that as *I feel anxious RIGHT NOW, but I'm not going to feel like this forever.* That can be really helpful for things like difficult discussions or managing your own feelings about the catastrophe that's sure to follow a terse email from your boss.

In closing...

Your ADHD is going to be with you for the rest of your life, so it's good to develop an understanding of the immediate problems it presents you with on a day-to-day basis, and have real, practical tools for addressing them. The good news is that with some introspection and practice, it doesn't have to feel like such a heavy burden from day to day. It gets easier.

→ **Here are some questions to get you thinking about your own ADHD coping skills.**

- What types of stress does your brain like? What types does it despise? Identifying the good kinds of stress is the first step... use them to your advantage when you need to focus.

- How hard is it for you to handle real or perceived rejection? How does rejection sensitivity rank on your list of ADHD symptoms—in the middle? The hardest part?

- Do you have a habit of catastrophizing—imagining the very worst outcomes? If so, the next time your brain paints a terrible picture, try breaking that cycle by imagining more positive scenarios. Example...

    - Your friend canceled plans at the last minute.

    - Catastrophizing: *They hate me! I must have really screwed up! The friendship is already over!*

    - Breaking the cycle: *Maybe something came up at work. Maybe their dog got sick. Maybe it's one of a hundred things that have nothing to do with me.* This takes a lot of repetition to be effective. See if you can make it a habit.

Remember: discovering and developing ADHD coping skills that work for you can feel tedious at times, but if you stick with it and keep the faith that the tools you need are out there, we promise you will get to a point where your use of them is so commonplace in your life, you'll hardly realize you're using them at all.

5

ADHD and Identity

A fun fact about me is that I spent a lot of my youth planning to become a nun. *Sister Act* full habit, the whole shebang. This arose from a series of factors, namely that my parents were staunchly religious Catholics who'd enrolled me in Catholic school.

I actually wanted to be a teacher, but most of my teachers were nuns. Therefore, in my experience of the world, to be a teacher, I would have to be a nun. Later, once I'd stepped away from organized religion (turns out I was way too bisexual and liked birth control too much to thrive in Catholicism) and begun to work as a sex educator, I realized that many, many, MANY of my attitudes around mental health, sex, and intimacy were still foundationally shaped by what I can mildly call the indoctrination I experienced in my youth.

"Cate, what does this have to do with ADHD?" Nothing . . . but also kind of everything. My identity as a kid who went to Catholic school still impacts me today. I was told not only that it was bad to be messy and disorganized, but also that being messy and disorganized was a sin. In "disrespecting" my parents/surroundings, I was sinning. God was mad at me.

We talked earlier about how kids with ADHD receive more negative messaging. Now consider repeatedly telling an eight-year-old that because of the struggles they have (even though they don't know why they have them), they're a sinner and they're more than likely going to burn in hell. Then you'll see how that can start to impact how one might think about themselves.

When it comes to conversations about identity and ADHD, it can be hard to even get past the first step. How do you literally identify that you have ADHD? "I have ADHD." "I am an ADHDer." "I am a person with ADHD." "I live with ADHD." "I struggle with ADHD." "I'm ADHD." There is no real consensus in the ADHD community.

Then we zoom out a little farther and see that our ADHD is just one component of who we are. Growing up knowing you have ADHD with support at home and in school is a very different experience than discovering you have ADHD at age thirty.

All this—our cultures, our religions, our backgrounds, the beliefs we hold in our communities, and our families—shapes the way we navigate the world, from how we build systems to how we think about ourselves in context with ADHD. Keep reading for the questions we get most often about ADHD and identity.

—Cate

Am I a BAD PERSON for not liking having ADHD?

 No. People are just trying to live their lives in a way that makes them not miserable. **A lot of highly vocal people claim that they like having ADHD. We're not saying they're lying, but** claiming this publicly is one of the ways some people cope with having this debilitating mental disorder. **To each their own.** As long as you aren't hurting other people, you are entitled to your own way of coping with ADHD.

 I just got DIAGNOSED with ADHD and I'm finding out that what I thought was my PERSONALITY is just a bundle of ADHD symptoms, and now I'm having an EXISTENTIAL CRISIS! What should I do?

First, dear reader, everything about you is related to ADHD because you have ADHD. But that doesn't mean that everything about you is because of your ADHD. Just like everything that you do is related to planet Earth because everything you do happens on planet Earth. But that doesn't mean everything happens *because* you're on planet Earth.

As with the rest of this book, we want you to take what you can use and leave the rest. If thinking about parts of yourself in the context of ADHD makes you a happier, healthier person, then great. However, if your entire understanding of yourself is shattering because suddenly everything that you've ever done is just "because of" your ADHD, that's probably not helpful.

Remember: you are an entirely unique person, with likes, dislikes, mannerisms, tendencies, and quirks born of an infinitely complicated dance between your experiences, neurochemistry, physiology, location, temperament, and a million other ever-present things. It's frankly not possible that your entire personality is because of any one thing, including your ADHD. All humans, including you, are simply much more interesting than that. We promise.

What was finding out that you had ADHD like? What emotions came up for you?

> I was diagnosed at forty, and it retroactively made so many report cards, employee evaluations, and tantrums and punishments from my parents make sense. There was palpable relief and also anger that it hadn't been recognized earlier.

—Jeremy from Atlanta

> I knew in my gut that I functioned differently than other people, I just didn't have the words or language for it. Once I knew what I was dealing with, it was a huge burden lifted from my shoulders.

—Kate from Homer

> It was a relief and sad at the same time. I wasn't broken but man, how much easier would things have been if I had known. My brain wasn't broken. I was just made different. Relationships would've been different since I could've maybe understood why the emotions were so hard to relate to at times.

—Kelli from Kentucky

WHEN and to whom should I DISCLOSE that I have ADHD?

 Unless you are seeking formal accommodations or you're trying to work certain top-level-clearance government jobs, you are not required to disclose your diagnosis to anybody. This goes for Autism. This goes for depression. This goes for anxiety. **You are not legally or morally obligated to disclose your diagnosis to anybody you don't want to.**

There can also be this stigma of "If I get an ADHD or Autism diagnosis, it's going to hurt my career." **Unless you want to be an astronaut or a CIA agent, you're probably gonna be fine.** That's the argument that I get the most frustrated about—because people use these very rare jobs to say, "It hurts everybody's career." But for the most part, employers really don't care. Or, more specifically, they care only if your disclosure will hurt the bottom line, because we live in a failing capitalist hellscape in which our labor has been commodified. But I digress . . .

 I've always been generally hesitant to divulge my ADHD to my coworkers.

Context is important. In a perfect world, everyone could name their strengths and weaknesses and receive the support they need unquestioningly, but unfortunately, we live in a world where a disappointing number of people feel the need to throw out a "Well, why does ERIK get special treatment?" at the mention of even basic accommodations. It's not fair, and it's certainly not okay, but this is a book about getting you through the day, and getting through the day requires a fair amount of realistic perspective to make it useful.

It may be super easy for you to disclose, or you may incur judgment or difficulty. In some circumstances, it might not even be SAFE for you to disclose. Your place of work might have an incredible HR department that is well-versed in ADA law, or your HR department might just be the owner's son who would rather be literally anywhere else.

We would never encourage people to keep ADHD a secret in their personal lives, as though having it is shameful, or because you should worry about the negative opinions of others. However, people are gonna view you in a negative light because of it. There's still a lot of stigma about ADHD.

It's really nuanced. I get questions like "I'm starting to date this person. When do I disclose?" There's this main-character-energy idea that it has to be this serious, tearful conversation where you uncover the deep, dark secret of your ADHD. If you wanna do that, that's fine, but for a lot of people it's more like: I have brown hair. I have ADHD. And it doesn't have to be a whole thing. In some cases, it's so profoundly obvious that disclosing is more of an official confirmation than a surprising revelation.

Is ADHD a SUPERPOWER?

ADHD is not a superpower, because superpowers aren't real. That said, **you have the right to think about your neurodivergence however you want**! If you want to think of your brain as superior and that being neurodivergent is your superpower, absolutely go for it.

You do *not* have the right to tell other people how to think about *their* neurodivergence. ADHD is a disability, straight up. So just be aware that if you're saying it's a superpower, people who struggle with this disorder every day may tell you to fuck all the way off. You don't want to make people feel like they're doing ADHD wrong. If your life is better thinking about your neurodivergence this way, fantastic. But consider how telling others that their lived experience is wrong might be damaging or hurtful.

When I was in my early twenties, I landed a job in a fancy kitchen. A *really* fancy kitchen. Picture the movies—it was like that. Frankly, I was not at all qualified, but I knew a guy.

So while trying to keep my head above water in this restaurant, I would periodically check in with my guy to see if I could glean any information on how I was doing. It almost always went something like this:

"Hey, guy! Chef say anything about me?"

"All good things! Says you're a little out of your depth but working through it!"

This went on for a while, with me prodding for information on any backroom conversations surrounding "the new sweaty kid" and receiving some mixture of platitudes and "Nah, you're good, man."

Then one day, while feeling the breeze on the line (that's Cool Chef-speak for chatting while it's slow), I let it slip that I had ADHD and took Adderall.

Suddenly, although I swore my performance hadn't changed, reports from my guy started to contain things like "scattered" and "all over the place." I had reframed myself to my coworkers.

I became chronically nervous, convinced that every little lapse in memory or organization would be noted and logged, with an eventual grand day of judgment (I was like twenty-one; I thought I was the main character). I spent every day absolutely terrified. Eventually, I would quit that job, but only after I found myself trying to break my fingers so I wouldn't have to go to work and face the kitchen again.

Now, I want to be clear about something: At no point do I think I was treated unfairly. I was given the same chances and opportunities as everyone else, and everything that was said about me could be considered reasonable.

The big change for me was *knowing they knew*.

So although I was not discriminated against, revealing my ADHD started a chain of events that ended with me leaving that job. I kept it closer to the vest after that.

When considering divulging your ADHD at work, it's good to do a little cost-benefit analysis. Do the potential benefits of accommodations outweigh the potential social, mental, and emotional costs of revealing your neurodivergency?

 I have a different perspective:

Before I started doing the work I do now, I was the entertainment director of a Renaissance festival. (I know, right? It was a VERY cool job.) It was also a very *complicated* job. The festival ran on an extremely small, full-time staff, so I had to manage a lot of different stuff. Payroll, contracts, hiring actors, finding acts for the stages, getting the festival ready for the season, painting, costumes, rehearsals—it was a LOT, and it was every single day.

As a result of the huge variation of tasks and how I like to work on multiple things at a time, my office got really, really messy. My office was part costume shop, part admin office, part props storage, and part . . . whatever else the space needed to be.

My boss was an incredibly nice guy, but he was, shall we say, unaccustomed to working in that type of environment. He came to me several times and asked me to clean up my office.

(It's important to note that I have a LOT of trauma around mess/organization. As a kid, my room was NEVER clean enough for my mom. So as an adult, I carry a lot of shame around how my spaces are perceived by those in authority.)

During my employee review, I got great feedback about how I was doing, but a LOT of criticism about the mess, about how I tended to forget stuff, and how generally, my (undisclosed) ADHD was impacting the office.

At that point, I did exactly what Erik did: I reframed myself to my coworkers. I shared with my boss that I have ADHD, that my task management might look chaotic and disorganized, but I had systems that worked for me. I also asked for better support on things like deadlines—my boss had a habit of saying, "Can this get done?" and I'd say, "Sure!" but with no deadline, those tasks would get back-burnered until they disappeared.

For me, disclosing my neurodivergence helped, especially during the busy months when there was always way too much to do. My boss was more understanding when things fell through the cracks and tended to be forgiving when I'd screw something up badly, which, thankfully, happened only a couple of times.

The moral of the story is that for many of the questions you may have, there's more than one way to handle a situation, and quite a few interpersonal dynamics you have to think through. As Erik said previously, in a perfect world, everyone would receive the support they need, but unfortunately we live in a world where a disappointing number of people feel the need to throw out a "why does Erik get special treatment" at the mention of even basic accommodations. It's not fair or okay, but this is a book about getting you through the day, which requires a large amount of realistic perspective to make it useful.

The INTERNET keeps saying ADHD is a GOOD thing, but I find it really HARD. Am I doing ADHD WRONG?

No. ADHD *is* really hard, which is why a lot of people have to make it work in their brain by saying that it's a good thing. Everybody's just trying to live their lives and trying to like themselves at the end of the day.

Hot take: Who is telling you that ADHD is a good thing? Is it somebody with your similar background? Is it somebody from a wildly different economic bracket? Are they trying to sell you something? To convince you that you need their specialized "coaching" for a fee?

Is there a RIGHT WAY to have ADHD?

NO. There's no rightness and wrongness here. It's more about intending to enjoy your life while having ADHD. Not being defeated by it, because, ultimately, defeat can be an excuse for not doing anything. You may want to try thinking about living in partnership with your ADHD. Because it can make life more difficult, but there can still be a whole lot of joy in your life with ADHD.

> There can still be a whole lot of joy in your life with ADHD.

Does My ADHD Make Me . . .

> **Smarter?**
No, there's no correlation between intelligence and having ADHD.

> **Forgetful?**
Yes.

> **More creative?**
Anecdotally, yes. Scientifically, no.[1]

> **Think faster?**
Anecdotally, kind of, but there's no science to prove it. Many people with ADHD do claim to think faster. Faster does not always mean better.

> **A better artist?**
Who knows?

The ADHD brain is like a big pile of wadded-up paper—everything from random things you learned in seventh grade to your boss's wife's name, which is not always ideal. However, when it comes to creative pursuits, it can be useful because creativity is arguably just mixing concepts deliberately for whatever reason—taking seemingly unrelated concepts and smashing them together. Your brain may be more inclined to smash things together 'cause they're already right next to each other.

Is there ANYTHING GOOD about having ADHD?

 You may find that you pick up new concepts really quickly because your brain is hungry for new stuff all the time. You may also fail a lot, because you pick up new hobbies and try new things all the time. This builds a healthier relationship with failure—you get used to it.

Disclaimer: if you don't identify with the paragraph above, you're not doing ADHD wrong.

Universally, the "good" parts of ADHD tend to be things like problem-solving, creativity, and thinking outside the box. But not every person with ADHD has those qualities, so it's a slippery slope. Try not to pathologize your entire life experience.

 ## Why are BIPOC left out of the ADHD CONVERSATION so often?

 Listen, you may have noticed that we are two white people, and this is absolutely not our lane. We believe in listening to and amplifying the voices who represent the lived intersectional *experience* of being both BIPOC and ADHD. As such, we've interviewed guest experts to weigh in on this subject.

We've also compiled a list of resources that highlight the work and perspectives of BIPOC experts and advocates and provide support for members of those communities most affected by the inequity of care and access to diagnosis, treatment, and support.

BIPOC and ADHD Resources

American Society of Hispanic Psychiatry
https://www.americansocietyhispanicpsychiatry.com

Melanin & Mental Health
https://melaninandmentalhealth.com

African American/Black Diaspora +ADHD Peer Support Group
https://add.org/african-american-adhd-peer-support-group/

Dr. Kimberly Douglass
https://www.instagram.com/drkimberlydouglass/

Black Mental Health Alliance
https://blackmentalhealth.com/connect-with-a-therapist/

The IEP Strategist/IEP Advocate
https://www.theiepstrategist.com

ADDitude Magazine
https://www.additudemag.com/clinicians-of-color-advocacy-diversity-adhd/

Unicorn Squad: For Black People of Marginalized Genders with ADHD
https://www.facebook.com/groups/234973573573055

What is your lived experience being trans or BIPOC and having ADHD?

> Being transmasculine and biracial exacerbates a lot of what is stressful about having a neurodivergent brain—navigating a world that isn't built for me, feeling fundamentally misunderstood, and encountering pressure to mask or pass for things that I'm not. That being said, these intersecting experiences of marginalization have also been a huge gift. Because there was no chance of me living up to normative standards of "achievement," I've been able to design a career and a community on my own terms. It can be exhausting having a mind that is constantly moving and making connections, but it's allowed me to be innovative in ways that I otherwise never would've been. Having such a fluid experience of identity has only deepened my creativity, as I'm able to see things from so many different angles.

—Avery Garrett, MSW

> My experience with ADHD is heavily influenced by being both bisexual and biracial in that I can instantly clock the intersectionality of it all. Specifically, there are MANY aspects of ADHD that I see how White ADHDers get to use it as a crutch to pretend that they can't be expected to engage in how politics works, or be expected to still maintain order in their lives in a way that Black people are NEVER given grace with. I have to work twice as hard to get half as much recognition as a Black woman as it is. And then I was dealt the "dopamine regulation, what's that?" card on top of it all.
>
> The performance I am required to put on for society to be seen as worthy is amplified in so many ways. Being fat and Black, I have to be diligent about my hygiene and grooming to avoid judgments of being unclean. As a woman I am expected to perform certain aspects of femininity. And good luck if I can muster the executive function to maintain that.

I can now look back on so much of the bullying I faced in school and directly tie it to my ADHD. A diagnosis I didn't receive until I was thirty-two. The last four years I have been able to understand myself better, but it doesn't make it easier. The clutter in my apartment and inability to do housework still haunt me and fill me with guilt. It doesn't send me into a full depressive spiral the way it used to, but it certainly doesn't keep me in the headspace I truly need to be in, either.

—A.M.

> I'd be happy to share my experiences as a queer and trans Chinese person with ADHD. It essentially boils down to being seen as a lazy burden on the family, plus a gender failure who's always making excuses for not being a productive, successful Daughter™. Chinese culture is very communal and generational, which means it's seen as shameful and disgraceful to not "pull your weight" by a certain age and gender demographic. Instead of the parents supporting you, you should be able to support your parents, which is obviously compounded by the struggles of being "productive" while having ADHD. There's also less knowledge and legitimacy around ADHD being "real" in the first place, especially among older Chinese folks, who think you're just being lazy and making excuses instead of dealing with a very real thing.

—C.C.

> Each time I have to find a new provider to talk to about my mental health, I panic. I am already someone who is not taken very seriously due to some of the diagnoses I've been given over the course of my lifetime. But being queer adds an entire other layer to that. Although I'm someone who is very comfortable with their sexuality and gender identity, there is always the fear that the provider who I am talking with does not accept people like me. Because of that, I have withheld a good bit of information from many different providers over the years, especially regarding mental health symptoms. If I do not feel safe, I am not my authentic self or completely honest with others. Ultimately, that has hurt me in the long run and has heavily impacted my treatment.

→

It took well over ten years to find a provider who I felt safe enough with to dive into the topic of ADHD. Many people who are not in marginalized groups do not relate to this. But for people like me, it's fairly common. Without feeling safe with a provider, I could not receive proper care, leaving me to struggle, alone, for quite some time.

My ADHD has always been very intertwined with other mental health issues, especially OCD, so when I finally found somebody I felt safe with, I was able to get treatment for everything I was struggling with at the time. Having safety in those appointments was absolutely life-changing, but also frustrating that it took ten-plus years to get there. It is imperative to provide a safe space for all clients, no matter what they bring to the table. Inclusive healthcare has saved so many lives, including my own, and for that I am so grateful.

—B

> What I want people who are not marginalized to understand about my experience with ADHD, particularly in relation to my identity as a nonbinary trans-masculine person, is that ADHD intensifies how I navigate the world. I love my gender identity and feel no shame in it. At the same time, I recognize that it doesn't fit into societal norms. Navigating that, along with ADHD, adds layers of complexity.

For example, ADHD heightened my experience in the gender transition process. Decisions like whether to have top surgery or start testosterone became all-consuming because of my tendency to hyperfocus. This can be empowering but also overwhelming, as these decisions carry significant emotional weight. ADHD also brings perfectionism into play—constantly striving to be everything at once yet feeling overwhelmed by that pressure. The combination of hyperfocus and perfectionism can be extremely time-consuming and leave me emotionally paralyzed and burned out.

Even in safe spaces designed for gender identity, my ADHD can make things more challenging. While these spaces can be empowering, they can also become exhausting or even crippling. I often find myself in a place of contradiction—feeling a sense of belonging because of my gender identity, while at the same time feeling different because of my ADHD. This dual experience can lead to anxiety and depression.

However, I've finally found a professional space where I not only feel like I belong but am celebrated for who I am. Working as a teaching artist, I use my musical talents and my background in elementary education. As a roster artist for an incredible organization, I teach in various schools, and I'm appreciated for my full self—nonbinary, transmasculine, ADHD, all of it. It's a stark contrast to my experience as a student teacher in the late nineties, when I didn't feel comfortable or safe being myself. Now I feel supported, encouraged, and advocated for, which has made all the difference in how I show up in the world.

Something else I've come to appreciate about myself is being a highly sensitive, deep feeler and thinker. This trait is something I now value, especially in my work as a songwriter. But in earlier years, I felt pressured to suppress this part of myself. When I did show my emotions, I was often labeled "such a girl" or worse, hearing derogatory comments linked to femininity—remarks that left me with dysphoric feelings. What does that even mean, to be "such a girl"? And hey, girls rock—I just don't identify as such. Many people with ADHD are deep feelers, and having those feelings dismissed or mocked has been especially difficult for me.

—Jamie G.

> Without feeling safe with a provider, I could not receive proper care, leaving me to struggle, alone, for quite some time.

EXPERT TAKES
ADHD AND BIPOC

GUEST EXPERT
Monica Johnson, PsyD

Black, Indigenous, and Persons of Color (BIPOC) are often underrepresented in research studies. For example, the National Institutes of Health (NIH)—the lead federal agency for healthcare research—reported a median of 10 percent African American participants in its mental health studies, while this population represents closer to 13.5 percent nationally.

More specifically related to ADHD research, the data suggests we still are missing groups and underdiagnosing ADHD for many. Recent findings indicate that ADHD continues to be less frequently diagnosed in youth who are BIPOC and female, compared to those who are White and male, even after controlling for potential confounders such as socioeconomic status and adverse childhood experiences.

I wish I could report that BIPOC individuals being left out of the ADHD conversation is an isolated event. However, we have a long-standing issue in mental health of historically marginalized populations being under- or misrepresented in the research, diagnosis, and treatment of a multitude of disorders.

GUEST EXPERT
Dr. Karen I. Wilson

▸ Cultural Barriers and Stigma

In many BIPOC communities, mental health can be a bit of a taboo topic. Take Latino families, for instance—behaviors linked to ADHD might be seen as just needing more discipline. The common belief is that stricter parenting is the answer, not medical help. Gender roles and family values also play a part. In many Latino cultures, traditional gender roles can affect how symptoms are perceived and managed. For example, boys might be expected to be more active and less disciplined, leading to a delay in recognizing ADHD symptoms as problematic.

Similarly, in Black communities, there's often a strong stigma around mental health issues. ADHD might be viewed as a sign of personal or parental failure rather than a medical condition that can be treated.

▸ Historical Mistrust and Bias

There's a long history of mistreatment by the medical community, which has fostered deep mistrust among many BIPOC families. This isn't just ancient history; it's shaped how communities view healthcare today. For African Americans, past exploitation and neglect, like the infamous Tuskegee Syphilis Study, have made many understandably wary of seeking medical help. This historical context creates a barrier where families might avoid or delay seeking diagnosis and treatment for ADHD, fearing biased or inadequate care.

▸ Socioeconomic Challenges

Access to good healthcare and education often depends on socioeconomic status, and unfortunately, some BIPOC families face financial constraints. Children from these communities often attend underfunded schools that might not have the resources to identify and support kids with ADHD. Additionally, without good health insurance, getting a diagnosis or treatment can feel out of reach. Families might also struggle with transportation, time off work, and other logistical barriers that make accessing care more difficult.

→

▶ Language and Communication Barriers

For families who don't speak English as their first language, finding a doctor who can communicate effectively is a big hurdle. Hispanic families, for example, may struggle to find Spanish-speaking healthcare providers who understand their cultural context, which can lead to misdiagnoses or no diagnosis at all. This language barrier can also make it difficult for parents to understand medical advice, follow through with treatment plans, or feel comfortable asking questions.

▶ Implicit Bias in Healthcare

Implicit biases among healthcare providers can play a big role in why BIPOC kids don't get diagnosed with ADHD as often as white kids. Studies have shown that Black children, in particular, are more likely to be labeled with behavioral problems rather than ADHD, which means they don't get the right kind of help. Physicians and educators might misinterpret behaviors due to their own unconscious biases, leading to either underdiagnosis or misdiagnosis.

▶ Educational System Shortcomings

Schools are crucial in spotting ADHD, but they often miss the mark with BIPOC students. Again, teachers might mistake ADHD symptoms for bad behavior, especially in crowded and under-resourced schools. Plus, many teachers aren't trained to recognize and support students with ADHD properly. For example, a child who is fidgeting or unable to focus might be seen as disruptive rather than as a student needing help.

▶ Lack of Representation and Advocacy

Lastly, there's a real lack of BIPOC voices in the ADHD conversation. When you don't see people who look like you talking about ADHD, it's easy to feel like it's not something that affects your community. Representation matters because it helps normalize the conversation around ADHD and mental health in general.

So, what can we do to change this? Here are a few ideas:

- **Education and Awareness:** Increase understanding of ADHD in BIPOC communities with culturally sensitive outreach. Community leaders, schools, and healthcare providers should work together to provide accurate information about ADHD.

- **Cultural Competence Training:** Ensure healthcare providers get training to respect and understand cultural differences. This includes understanding the specific cultural contexts and challenges faced by different BIPOC communities.

- **Community Engagement:** Work with trusted community organizations to spread information and provide support. Churches, community centers, and local groups can play a key role in reaching families and reducing stigma.

- **Policy Changes:** Advocate for policies that guarantee everyone has access to the healthcare and education they need. This includes better funding for schools in underserved areas, improving access to mental health services, and ensuring that insurance coverage is adequate for diagnosis and treatment.

> There's a real lack of BIPOC voices in the ADHD conversation.

What about TRANS and NONBINARY people with ADHD?

 Trans and nonbinary people are woefully underrepresented in studies about ADHD. That's frustrating for a number of reasons, but in particular, because a lot of important medical questions come up about "How might my hormone replacement therapy affect my ADHD?" and we don't have a lot of scientific answers for them.

What we CAN tell you is that this is a place where community matters. As much as people like to complain about "the rise of ADHD on social media," what's happened is that people are finding one another. **Trans folks with ADHD are finding community, starting important discussions, and sharing information about their own lived experience.**

We encourage you to seek out those resources and to find community with other LGBTQIA+ people—not just because they might have great suggestions for managing ADHD, but because local and online communities are deeply important for support, guidance, acceptance, and really cementing the knowledge that you are not alone.

> As much as people like to complain about "the rise of ADHD on social media," what's happened is that people are finding one another. Trans folks with ADHD are finding community.

EXPERT TAKES

ADHD and Trans and Nonbinary Folks

GUEST EXPERT

Katie Leikam, MBA, MSW, LCSW, LISW-CP

Unfortunately, there's not much research about the trans and nonbinary community as an identity. When we add another subject or another topic in with research about someone's gender identity, the research is woefully lacking.

When I logged in to the *International Journal of Transgender Health* for all articles published and available online since 2005, a search of *ADHD* and *attention deficit hyperactivity disorder* led me to eleven entries, *and only two of those* mentioned ADHD comprehensively.

As someone who listens to trans and nonbinary clients every workday, I think they are left out of the ADHD conversation because most people already don't know how to treat trans and nonbinary people considerately, in medical care, in psychiatry, and in society.

More frequently than I have heard a positive interaction, my clients report that their healthcare professionals either ignored they are transgender or, even worse, caused further harm with misgendering or using misinformation to treat them.

→

When we ask this same group of people to add the trans community to their research, they often think the research isn't needed because there aren't enough transgender people in America to warrant including them in the larger study. Or the researchers themselves at worst are transphobic, or at best just can't be bothered with learning how to sensitively include the trans community in their research.

This leads to the trans community being left out of a lot of research topics, particularly ones that have a narrow focus. I know some researchers may feel like getting through the institutional review board may be more difficult if they include the trans and nonbinary community as a research topic in their papers, because they believe there may be more rules or hindrances in studying the community. I have seen researchers nix other research topics that are sensitive due to this reason.

Trans and nonbinary folx may also be left out of ADHD research because there is already so much more research needed with the transgender community, and ADHD is not a high priority. When I was looking for ADHD research, what I did find lumped ADHD with anxiety and depression or with Autism. Each of these topics is so important that it needs its own separate research papers. At the moment, I believe researchers are still trying to catch up with all the affirming, nonbiased research that the trans community needs for their medical treatment. In doing so, they are overlooking a lot of research needs for mental health and day-to-day surviving that the trans and nonbinary community needs as well.

I find myself explaining to others that a transgender person is a whole person, and they have most of the same needs anyone else does. They need to discuss and talk about their mental health, speeding tickets, which theme park is their favorite, or getting through the mental exhaustion of living with ADHD just like any other person. A trans or nonbinary person does not always and only need therapy about their gender identity or transitioning. As a whole person, they need to process other aspects of their life just like cisgender people do. I think too many people see a trans and nonbinary person and automatically think it's just their gender identity or transition they want or need to discuss.

We know that transgender and nonbinary folx are far from burdens in research, and they absolutely deserve to and should be part of any conversation, but especially one like ADHD, where it is so important to the community that they should be included in all research. I hope that this message gets clearer and louder in the years to come.

GUEST EXPERT

Amariah Love, MS, NCC, LPC (she/they)

Systemic marginalization can affect every aspect of a transgender person's mental health journey. **In my experience, there are four common issues that arise for trans folks with ADHD:**

 ### Ableist Language Shaping Diagnosis and Treatment Options

The language used to describe ADHD in the fifth edition of *The Diagnostic and Statistical Manual of Mental Disorders* (the *DSM-5*) is deficit-based. This means that both the name of the diagnosis itself ("attention deficit hyperactivity disorder") and the criteria listed to guide the diagnostic process (e.g., "Often fails to give close attention to details or makes careless mistakes in schoolwork, at work, or during other activities") are all described in terms of deficiencies. As a result, clinicians are trained to assess patients' ADHD-related traits as shortcomings and their behaviors as disordered and problematic.

When mental health practitioners pathologize patients with ADHD, they label these neuro-specific traits and behaviors as abnormal and unhealthy— rather than normal, adaptive, unique, and valuable in their own right. For example, a counselor may note that a client meeting the *DSM* criteria "often talks excessively" during an assessment. Judging a client's talkative communication style as "excessive" can lead to discounting the valuable strengths that are usually on display when clients with ADHD are, for example, deeply passionate about a topic or interest, or when their minds generate an incredible number of thoughts and ideas in a very small amount of time.

This can be especially damaging to transgender individuals, who are already inundated with messages that there is something fundamentally wrong with who they are because of their gender identity.

One of the major challenges I've encountered as a therapist is figuring out how to discuss diagnoses such as ADHD with clients in ways that are accurate, affirming, and validating . . . even when the *DSM* criteria remain so largely deficit-based. ADHD has two of my least favorite words for describing how minds work—"deficit" and "disorder"—right there in the name. In order to validate a client's experience as a person with ADHD without reinforcing the idea that they are deficient and disordered, I have discussions with them about these issues and how they're inherent within the medical model of mental healthcare that utilizes the *DSM*. We also discuss how, despite this, a diagnosis of ADHD can be practically useful and emotionally validating for some people. →

Effects of Socioeconomic Status on Diagnosis and Treatment Options

Transgender people disproportionately experience more homelessness, limited work opportunities, and underemployment than the general population. As a result, they are particularly vulnerable to financial barriers to obtaining mental health services such as diagnoses and treatments, due to

- the high costs of health insurance,
- often expensive or ambiguously priced co-pays,
- the time and money involved with routine doctor visits, and
- access to and cost of medications.

Additionally, the high cost of gender-affirming medical care often puts transgender clients in the difficult position of choosing between medical care and mental healthcare.

 ## Lack of Transgender-Competent Clinicians

It can be difficult for transgender folks to find safe and affirming clinicians. It is doubly difficult to find clinicians who both meet this criterion *and* do not pathologize neurodiversity. This dearth of trans-affirming mental health practitioners often leads transgender people to choose not to seek mental healthcare, even when that support could help them cope with their ADHD-related challenges.

Accreditation standards for counselor education programs don't require courses specifically on working with transgender clients, either.

The Lack of Transgender-Identified Clinicians in Mental Health Fields

Many people prefer clinicians whose gender matches their own. Cisgender people (people whose gender identity matches their gender assigned at birth) do not have to worry about clinicians lacking a basic understanding of their gender identities. For trans clients, especially in rural areas, finding a therapist or psychiatrist with a gender journey similar to theirs may be impossible.

Socioeconomic barriers (as discussed above) often mean that gender minorities cannot access the expensive undergraduate and graduate degrees required to become licensed counselors, social workers, psychiatrists, or psychologists. They can also prevent graduates from completing postgraduate licensure requirements for supervised clinical practice. Most jobs available to clinicians during this part of their education are low-paying, highly demanding, and often lead to burnout.

Check-In

We know this chapter in particular may have brought up some strong feelings, so we want to offer you some space to reflect and process. Take a moment to breathe, drink some water, maybe eat a snack or take a walk if that feels right in your body. Then ask yourself the following questions in your own time . . .

- What intersectionalities or identities do you carry that impact your thinking about yourself and your ADHD?
- How do you think about ADHD in other people?
- Are you more likely to grant grace and forgiveness to other people than yourself? Why or why not?
- What are some positive affirmations or thoughts about yourself that you can name in this moment? Examples might look like "I am doing the best I can," "It's okay to feel this way," "I am worthy of care and kindness," or "I am not a fuckup."

As you move forward in this book and in life, we want to encourage you to intentionally commit to being a little kinder toward yourself. We cannot control the unkindness we face out in the world. We CAN control the way we speak to and think about ourselves.

PART 2

Getting the HELP YOU NEED

Asking for Help

A**sking for help** is hard. It can be even harder when you've been made to feel like an inconvenience, or that there is something fundamentally wrong with you. (How do you get help with THAT?) It's even harder if you're made to feel that you're bothering someone because you should be able to do all this by yourself, or that you shouldn't NEED to get assistance, or that you're just going to mess it up anyway, so what's the point?

> We're here to tell you that all that is bullshit.
> Asking for help is an act of profound bravery.
> Asking for help is an act of vulnerability.
> Asking for help is an act of self-love.

This book wouldn't exist if we hadn't asked for and accepted help. The very pages you are reading were a group effort between me, Erik, and our collaborative writer, Rennie Dyball. When we first started the process of speaking with publishers, a lot of them had reservations about hiring two people with ADHD (who'd never written a book before) to produce a finished manuscript in a timely manner.

It was suggested that we find someone to work with who could help us gather our thoughts, coordinate a reasonable schedule, and—most importantly—help us have something to turn in at the end of the process.

At first, I balked. To me, accepting that help meant that I was a failure as a writer—the thing I've always wanted to be. I romanticized what it meant to be a writer: REAL writers finish what they start. REAL writers power through distraction and self-doubt. REAL writers lock themselves away in a garret and write great tomes by candlelight with a quill and ink.

In reality, writing is a job, just like any other one. You have to show up for work and get stuff done, and you have to navigate deadlines and scheduling issues and feedback and meetings and what the cover should look like.

The more I thought about it, the more I looked through the dozens and dozens of unfinished short stories and plays and notes of novel ideas I'd scribble on Post-its at 3 a.m., I realized that if I wanted this book to become real, accepting help was going to be the first step. At the start of this process, Rennie sat and interviewed us for hours and created transcripts and then drafts that we added to and edited. As we got further along, she provided industry insight into the publishing process when we got overwhelmed and helped us maintain an editing schedule that made room for our ADHD and occasional schedule delays from meltdowns and depressive episodes that came with working on a project this big and important.

It also turns out, for those of you wondering, that a LOT of authors use collaborative writers and don't mention it—we've chosen to talk about it because the experience was a vital part of the journey, and asking for help and getting the accommodations we needed were part of making this book a reality. Rennie's work stopped being a question of "Am I a failure as a writer if we let her help us?" Instead, her support and guidance have become part of this book's story and the way we accomplished the goal of finishing it.

—Cate

What kind of HELP can I get?

"Help" can look like many different things. Asking for help may also depend greatly on where you are in your ADHD journey.

Help can look like support from partners, friends, or relatives, assistance from a service professional, or accommodations from a workplace or academic institution. It can look like taking the step to get a formal diagnosis to get therapeutic or medicinal support. It can look like scheduling body-doubling sessions (when someone keeps you company while you work on a difficult task) or joining an online support group.

There is no one-size-fits-all modality for getting help, but help is out there.

 For more on work accommodations, turn to page 303.

 ## Is it okay to PAY FOR HELP?

 Hell yeah. Of course it is. **Treat the people you employ fairly and pay them fairly, and then you have nothing to feel bad about.**

Can I ask for **HELP** with _____ ? It feels **WEIRD**...

Yes. You are allowed to ask for help/support/assistance/accommodations in whatever capacity makes sense for you.
There is no such thing as a silly ask or a weird ask when it comes to advocating for yourself.

Ascribing a moral judgment to the things that you need is not only unhelpful, it can also ultimately convince you not to bother. (Whether you GET that help or support is an entirely different question.)

It's important to remember, however, that whenever you ask for help from a partner, friend, or other unpaid individual, there is a PERSON on the other side of that equation.

"It's hard for me to choose a restaurant, because I never know what I want or if I'm even hungry. Can I ask my partner to choose?" Yes! That is a totally reasonable way for a partner to support you—but it ALSO means that your partner is signing up for a lifetime of having to handle that task every time you want to go out to eat.

For some partners, they might be totally stoked to plan date night. For others, that might be challenging with their work schedule or own neurodivergence. Perhaps a better support system might be taking turns or writing down a list of restaurants you've been wanting to try, then doing a quick rock-paper-scissors in the car to decide where to go.

"But sometimes asking for what I need feels WEIRD!"
It felt really weird when I got the training wheels taken off my bike. It felt really weird buying my own shampoo for the first time. **Things feel weird when we first do them, but over time, they start to feel normal.**

Asking for someone to repeat themselves because you spaced out might feel weird at first, but as you continue doing it, you will normalize it—both for yourself and for the people in your life. Pretty quickly it will start to feel like just another thing that can happen in conversation. After a while, you'll think nothing of it.

Can you tell us about a time you felt supported by a partner, family member, or friend in dealing with your ADHD?

> My partner is amazing at helping me deal with making sure I get paperwork-type tasks done—taxes, mail-in voting, making sure I send in my passport application in time, things I would probably have completely forgotten about otherwise.

—Mina E.

You WILL have to use your own discretion, however. If your friend has had to restart a story three times, and on the third retelling you missed the beginning *again*, you may want to just let it go so they can finish their story.

You don't have to ask for everything all the time; it's okay to let stuff go. There are probably certain things you're willing to ask of your best friend that you may not be willing to ask of your Uber driver, and that's just fine.

I'll also point out: as important as it is for you to feel comfortable asking your partner(s)/friends for support, it is as important for them to feel comfortable SAYING NO.

This may sound harsh, like I'm giving permission for the people in your life to neglect you, but just as support is essential to your mental health, *consent* is essential to the health of your relationships. **You always have the right to *ask* for support, and the person you're asking always has the right to not give it to you.*** **They have their needs to worry about, too.**

---

* Except in the case of accommodations you are legally entitled to. See page 164.

You might personally benefit from a friend who always meets every one of your support needs, regardless of how much they are willing to do so, but it can put strain on your relationship over time. Make it clear to anyone in your personal life whom you may ask for support or help that they are always allowed to say no, and that it's okay if they do.

"How do THEY do it?"

One of the easiest ways you can get help from other people is asking them how *they* do things. For whatever reason, it's just assumed that we will all figure out how to handle certain day-to-day stuff, without anyone actually teaching us. So there ends up being a lot of stuff we simply never learn how to do.

Ask your friends how they remember to pay their bills, keep up with their car registration, or schedule doctors' appointments. Sometimes people won't have anything useful for you, but sometimes they'll say something simple that is life-changing, so it's worth asking.

> **An Erik Note:** I had a friend a few years ago who would always schedule their annual checkups the week before Halloween, so they knew if they were getting ready for Halloween, they also had a doctor's appointment. So simple, yet so smart and effective. Apply this to any sort of annual appointment that you need to remember and associate it with a holiday of your choosing.

Can you give me a big, disorganized LIST OF LITTLE WAYS I can ask for HELP and support in my PERSONAL life?

Yes!
YOU CAN:

- Ask people to repeat themselves when you space out and miss something.

- Request that if you're going to have a long conversation with someone that you do it at your preferred location. (E.g., a café, outside, while taking a walk, or on a park bench)

- When you're about to start doing a big boring thing, ask your person/roommate/etc. to check on you in an hour to see how you're doing/hold you accountable.

- Give your person/roommate/etc. permission to ask you if you have your phone/wallet/keys any time you leave the house.

- Ask your person/friend/roommate to keep you company while you work on a thing that sucks. (Also known as "body-doubling.")

- Ask your person to help you with a chore you struggle to complete.

THE
BUDDY System

 Here are some ways two or more people can support each other with a task:

- **Tag-Teaming:** Take turns doing a set amount of a task. You do five minutes of dishes, I do five minutes of dishes, repeat until done. Alternately: you do half, I'll do half.

- **Divide and Conquer:** Dividing a task into parts and each handling one part. You unload the dishwasher, I'll load.

- **Maxing Out:** One person does as much of a task as they can before they're sick of it, then hands it off.

- **Hungry Hungry Hippos:** Both/all people attack the task at once, and whoever does the most in a set time wins. This works best with tasks that can be quantified in some way, like whoever fills the most leaf bags in the time it takes to clear the yard.

- **Fast and Furious–Style:** Similar to Divide and Conquer, but it's a race. Works best if both/all people can be working at the same time. A benefit of this one is that you can pit two unrelated tasks against each other, allowing for some creativity. E.g., "I bet you can't finish mowing the lawn before I get back from the grocery store!"

- **Put Your Money Where Your Mouth Is (Alternative for Fast and Furious):** If each person's task can't be done at the same time (like loading/unloading the dishwasher), the game then becomes "I bet I can unload the dishwasher faster than you can load it!" Stopwatch required.

In closing . . .

Before we move on to the next subject, dear reader, let's check in. Consider how you are feeling after reading this chapter by asking yourself the following questions:

- How do you feel when you have to ask for help?
- Why do you think you feel that way?
- What emotions come up for you around the idea of asking for help?
- What emotions come up for you around the idea of ACCEPTING help?
- Is there anything in your life that you could use help with?
- Have you asked for help? Why or why not?

Making It Official:

ADHD and Diagnosis

In a perfect world, we'd be able to give you a neat and tidy checklist of every part of an ADHD assessment, but the real truth is that experiences may vary WILDLY.

For some people, getting their ADHD diagnosis is a multi-month, multi-appointment process with lots of standardized tests. For others, it's going to the doctor and saying, "I think I have ADHD," and the doctor says, "Yup" and makes a note in your chart. Rather than set you up with false expectations or stress you out about tests that you may or may not wind up ever encountering,* we'd like to share some suggestions on how you can prepare and what you can think about ahead of your ADHD assessment to best support yourself on the journey to diagnosis.

Here is a very useful journaling exercise you can do. Google the adult ADHD self-assessment survey at home, before any doctor's appointment: https://add.org/wp-content/uploads/2015/03/adhd-questionnaire-ASRS111.pdf.

The next step is to think specifically and intentionally about each item and ask yourself two important questions: **WHEN** does this show up in my life, and **HOW** does it affect me?

So as an example, my journal for Assessment Question #1 would look like:

---

* If you are keen on seeing the actual tests you may encounter, turn to the appendix on page 380.

How often do you have trouble wrapping up a project after the challenging parts are done?

My answer: OFTEN!

WHEN does this show up? As I write this, I'm literally staring at the built-in bookcases I started building a year ago that still need trim and paint. This happens at home and also when I'm working. I have many unfinished videos and scripts and projects that I want to finish. I have several outstanding invoices and other administrative things to do.

HOW does this affect me? Living in a house of unfinished projects is frustrating to my partners. I have lost deals and contracts due to not finishing projects on time, and that has affected my income and my reputation as a reliable person to hire. I have hurt people by committing to things and then leaving the project before completion.

You can write as much or as little as you'd like for each one. Personally, sometimes my answers are only a couple of sentences; other times, examining things like this will suddenly click a few pieces into place and I'll wind up with ten pages.

This can be a useful exercise not only for providing conversation points with your doctor, but also to reveal how much and how often ADHD is impacting your life. For me, I was honestly surprised at how much it was happening, because I'd gotten used to shrugging off frustrations and downplaying and minimizing them instead of just acknowledging that completing tasks is actually really hard for me.

It's also totally valid to use this self-assessment survey if you're not super certain whether you have ADHD, or if you are wondering whether you're living with *just* ADHD or also with other comorbidities. As you go through each question, you can start to see where your life is negatively impacted and whether things like depression and/or anxiety are exacerbating the problem. Fun fact: Doing work like this is how I found out that I have rumination OCD. My writing about my constant worry cycles was what tipped my therapist off, and she helped me get the diagnosis I needed to get support.

—Cate

❓ What is the POINT in getting DIAGNOSED, and how can it HELP me?

Getting a diagnosis means you can formally request accommodations. In a perfect world, in an understanding and respectful workplace, you wouldn't have to pull out your official paperwork to be like, "Hey, can I wear headphones?" Or "Hey, can I do this so I can more effectively do my job?" Unfortunately, in a lot of workplaces, you have to have a doctor's note. You have to have a diagnosis.

The diagnosis is often going to be handy in requesting accommodations.

You can say, "I have ADHD. Can I have more time on my exams, or can I get the lecture as notes?" A lot of times they will require some kind of paperwork that says you're not just making this up. Much more on accommodations in chapter 12.

If a friend came to you and told you they'd just been diagnosed with ADHD, what would you say to them?

> Welcome to the club! We say we wanna meet, but it may never happen. I'd offer to listen and share advice if wanted.
> —Bailey C.

A diagnosis is a great ace to have up your sleeve when dealing with people who deny your ADHD. If someone's giving you crap about "not really having ADHD," you can say with confidence, "Well, a bunch of highly educated medical professionals have proved in a laboratory setting that I do. So you think what you want, but I'm going to believe them."

The other point in getting diagnosed is that you can't get medication without an official diagnosis. As we've said, medication isn't a fix and it isn't everything, **but for medication to even be an option for you, a diagnosis is necessary.**

What WON'T a (FORMAL) DIAGNOSIS do for me?

When you get a diagnosis, nothing about your life changes. Not a single thing. **It won't magically organize your house or change your life.** You walk into the doctor's office or you sign in to your Zoom meeting and then you get the diagnosis, and that's it. **You remain who you are, with the same struggles and frustrations and strengths and weaknesses.**

Now, what does sometimes happen is then the whole dam of trauma and regrets and sudden self-understanding, that can open up and . . . that's where I'm at in my life. And **for some people, a diagnosis can be the first step to self-acceptance. It can be the stepping stone to accessibility or accommodations that are needed. And for some people, honestly, it can be a stumble back.** It can be a moment of really having to do some self-reflecting and introspection and work on self-acceptance, plus working through the trauma of How did nobody notice this for the last thirty-five years of my life?"

And it's okay if you're feeling any of those things. **You can be excited, regretful, optimistic about the future, and angry about the past—all at the same time. There is no one "right" way to receive and process a diagnosis.**

MORE ON **EVALUATION APPOINTMENTS**

How do I handle getting through the evaluation appointment itself?

 A psychologist diagnoses, a psychiatrist prescribes.

BEFORE THE APPOINTMENT
- Gather important documents: ID, insurance card, etc.
- Ask the office if there is intake paperwork you need to complete before arriving.
- It may be helpful to compile notes/a list of things you specifically want to bring up at the appointment. It's very common to forget those things when you're actually sitting in front of a doctor.
- It is also TOTALLY ACCEPTABLE to bring a support person with you.
- If the process is entirely overwhelming or you're really struggling, consider looking into a patient advocate who can work with you. (This is a US thing, so if you live in one of those magical places where you don't have to worry about going bankrupt if you break your arm, your results may vary.)

DURING THE APPOINTMENT
- BE HONEST. Downplaying, deflecting with humor, or exaggerating because something is "typical" for ADHDers is not at all useful.

AFTER THE APPOINTMENT
- Make sure you know what the next steps are.
- Will you need another appointment?
- A referral to a psychiatrist for medication?
- Will they call you, or should you call them?

How do I get an **EVALUATION** for ADHD?

Think of landing yourself an ADHD evaluation as defeating a Gym Leader in Pokémon, where you have to beat each successive leader before actually being able to fight the main guy. In this case, however, instead of fighting Pokémon battles, you're making super-boring phone calls and going to super-boring appointments.

The first step is to find the first Gym Leader, who will then point you to the second, who will then point you to the third, and so on, until you eventually get an evaluation.

I'm **ABOUT** to go in for my **EVALUATION**. What will **HAPPEN**?

It can vary a lot based on your location, but **there are a couple things that are probably going to happen, like the Go/No-Go Test and the SNAP survey**. See the appendix on page 380 if you'd like to learn more about these—but no pressure. If it's too stressful to read about tests you may encounter at the doctor's office, skip it!

My evaluation was MUCH simpler—less of a Pokémon gym crawl and more like making a single phone call. I went in for the appointment, explained what was going on with me and how it had been affecting my life, and that was about it.

I had to do some paperwork/evaluations to make it "official," but the entire process took less than two hours. For some people, it's even more casual than that—I've known multiple people who go in for something else, like depression or anxiety, and the clinician will offhandedly say,

> A lot of late-diagnosed people are really good at not seeming like they have ADHD.

"And when did you get your ADHD diagnosis?" because it's just that obvious to a trained professional.

One common worry that we hear is "What if I can't get a diagnosis because I've gotten so good at managing/hiding my undiagnosed ADHD over the years?"

A lot of late-diagnosed people are really good at not seeming like they have ADHD. In particular, women with the combo platter of ADHD and Autism are *uniquely* good at masking their neurodivergence. That's how they've made it this far. Remember: The people evaluating you aren't interested in just your "on-paper" behavior and whether it lends itself to an ADHD diagnosis. They're interested in the rate and severity of your symptoms and how those symptoms are having an impact on your life.

I just got DIAGNOSED with ADHD and am FREAKING OUT a little bit. Help?!

First, nothing changed. You haven't changed. You've just measured something—like if it's really hot outside and then you find out it's ninety-six degrees outside, it's not hotter or colder now that you've checked. You just now know the specific temperature.

A lot of the concern about diagnosis is very much founded in ableism. So for people to get that ADHD diagnosis or to be at peace with the ADHD diagnosis, they have to get through all these layers of stigma.

Someone I know once came to me and said, "I'm a horrible parent. I got my kid diagnosed, and now he's gonna be labeled forever." I told her yes, he's got that "label," but now he can get help in school. Now he knows what to look up on Google. Now he has a lens by which to understand himself, build systems that work, and request accommodations to help him thrive. I had to talk her off the ledge, and it's because **there is a lot of misinformation about how a diagnosis can harm you or is somehow going to hurt your career prospects**.

There isn't a problem with getting a diagnosis. It's about taking somebody else's problem and making it yours.

If a friend came to you and told you they'd just been diagnosed with ADHD, what would you say to them?

> Nobody prepares you for the mourning period. There's the part where the diagnosis is like a weight off your shoulders. Like, "Oh my god, THAT's what's going on! I'm not lazy or broken! I'm just wired differently!" But then there's the part where you realize all the times you were yelled at and made to cry over your dirty room, or the friendships that didn't last because you "made everything about you" or "never paid attention." Nobody prepares you for that reality to hit you, so my most important advice to anyone is to pair it with therapy.

—Sabrina from Portland

> I've got twenty-five years of art supplies if you want to trade sometime. I'm looking for leather working tools at the moment if you have any.

—Leah from Chicago

I CAN'T AFFORD a diagnosis/meds/ therapy. WHAT should I do?

 Benefits.gov: This government website can help you find federal, state, and local programs you might qualify for, including health insurance, food, housing, and more. The Benefit Finder tool can create a list of government programs you may be eligible for based on your personal information.

Make the company pay for it: Some pharmaceutical manufacturers offer assistance programs or discount cards for medications. RXAssist, GoodRX, and (we hate this name so much) NeedyMeds can help you find coupons and financial assistance if you're struggling to pay for medication. CHADD (Children and Adults with Attention-Deficit/Hyperactivity Disorder) also has a discount prescription card!

The National Resource Center on ADHD (NRC): Funded by the CDC, the NRC provides information, education, and consultation about ADHD assessment, diagnosis, treatment, and health and well-being for children with ADHD and their families. For more information, you can visit the NRC website via CHADD.org.

Also remember that medication is not a "fix" for ADHD. It's a support system for ADHD, it's a tool in your tool basket, and it can be extremely useful, but a lot of people with ADHD live a perfectly happy life without medication. Medicated or not, the goal is building systems and structures that work within the means you have.

 A lot of information is free in the modern era. **You don't need a diagnosis or permission from anybody to learn about ADHD and realize it describes your experience.**

 One caveat: self-diagnosis is valid, but it's also important to recognize that, in some cases, depression or another comorbidity may be at play. So you can research and learn about ADHD while also knowing that if you do go for a diagnosis, you need to consider alternatives.

It may be that you have a number of comorbidities. It may be that you're dealing with anxiety or PTSD, which can look A LOT like ADHD without actually being ADHD. Not every doctor who suggests an alternative diagnosis is wrong—HOWEVER, it's important that the diagnosis come from an actual evaluation, not being dismissed offhandedly.

I'm SEVENTY-FIVE years old. Is there any REASON for me to get DIAGNOSED?

It's common to want to contextualize or understand your experience. **For some people it is a vital piece of understanding themselves to get the official diagnosis. Yes, you have ADHD, yes, you are Autistic. And for some people it's just an interesting factoid: "Oh yeah, it turns out I do have this."**

Again, I think it's a matter of access. If you are trying to access support, then yes, that diagnosis might be very important.

If it's a matter of really coming to terms with the life that you have led up until this point because of this thing that you didn't know about, then yeah, go for it. Again, it's not gonna change who you are. **It's not going to change anything except your understanding of yourself.**

FUN FACT: The current record for oldest diagnosis that we personally know of is a lovely woman who lives on a farm with chickens and a goat. She is eighty-seven.

What's often happening these days is that a thirty-five-year-old woman goes in for a diagnosis, and her sixty-five-year-old mom goes, "Holy shit, I might have ADHD, too." **Again, there's a hereditary component to ADHD. So sometimes the kid getting diagnosed can lead to the older adult getting diagnosed.** Or at least getting suspicious.

 Also, knowing more stuff about yourself helps the people around you in your life, too. Knowing that you have ADHD, that you have a tendency to be forgetful, that's not *just* for you. ADHD may affect others in your life. None of us lives in a vacuum.

MEDICATION FAQS

**The following was reviewed and edited by
Lesley Cook, PsyD, who specializes in treating ADHD . . .**

➤ How do ADHD medications work?

The most common ADHD medications are **stimulants (e.g., methylphenidate, amphetamines)**. They increase the availability of certain neurotransmitters in the brain, like dopamine and norepinephrine, which help improve attention and focus and reduce hyperactivity and impulsivity.

Dr. Cook adds: Norepinephrine is both a neurotransmitter AND a hormone, and it can act as both. It has roles to play in the fight-or-flight response, perceived fear, and motivation.

Non-Stimulants (e.g., atomoxetine): These work more slowly than stimulants. Atomoxetine increases norepinephrine levels in the brain, which can help with attention, impulsivity, and hyperactivity. They are often used when stimulants aren't effective or cause unwanted side effects like anxiety or headaches.

Dr. Cook adds: They can also help with anxiety because they can have an effect on fight-or-flight responses. These are different from stimulants because they build up in the blood and cannot be started or stopped suddenly. They may also have positive effects on blood pressure for some. There are different classes of non-stimulants that work differently as well.

Antidepressants (e.g., bupropion): Sometimes used for ADHD, particularly in adults, they can affect neurotransmitters in the brain, which helps control symptoms of ADHD, especially when a person also has depression or anxiety.

Dr. Cook adds: Because anxiety/attention/executive function/ short-term memory are all linked neurological processes, improving anxiety and depressed mood chemically can help break the links with ADHD and allow individuals more psychological "room" to develop coping strategies.

Important Note: If an ADHD medication doesn't work for you, it doesn't mean that you DON'T have ADHD or that you're untreatable. Every ADHD medication works differently for different individuals (much like medication for depression and anxiety), and it often takes time to find the most effective one with the fewest side effects. Things like dosage and time of day also make a big difference; so do the foods you eat while taking medication and other medications you take in finding the right fit for you.

➡ What do ADHD medications help with?

They improve focus, attention, and impulsivity control. They can also reduce hyperactivity, helping with daily functioning and task completion. Many people find that the changes that happen right away can also lead to longer-term changes in positive sense of self and improvement in work, school, and relationships.[1]

➡ What do ADHD medications NOT help with?

"Pills don't teach skills." ADHD meds don't cure ADHD or address non-ADHD symptoms like anxiety, depression, or learning difficulties directly. Social skills and organizational abilities are also not directly improved by these medications. (Sorry.)

➡ Will ADHD medications take away my personality?

No, they don't change your core personality. They may reduce some symptoms of ADHD, which can change how you express yourself, but you aren't going to stop liking Taylor Swift or lose your zest for mountain biking when you get medicated.

Dr. Cook adds: It may be important to note that sometimes early side effects can make someone feel less like themselves, but that usually resolves within a few weeks. If that feeling lasts longer, the person should talk to their doctor right away.

▶ Will ADHD medications take away my creativity?

No! This has been a topic of much misinformation online. It has been studied, and while some people report a reduction in spontaneity, others found their creativity enhanced due to improved focus and reduced impulsivity. Spontaneity can *feel* like creativity, but there is a difference between impulse—"I should make a painting RIGHT NOW"— and having a concrete IDEA for that painting.

▶ Are ADHD medications safe? Will I get addicted to them?

ADHD medications are considered safe when used as directed by a healthcare provider. The risk of addiction is generally low under medical supervision, but, like many medications, the potential for abuse and dependency exists, especially with stimulants. It's important to follow the prescribed dosage and discuss any concerns with a healthcare provider.

Dr. Cook adds: Also, several studies have identified that appropriately treating ADHD with stimulant medications can, in fact, lower the risk for addiction compared to untreated ADHD, especially the combined type in males.[2]

▶ Can I take ADHD medications if I've struggled with addiction in the past?

It's important to be honest with your doctor if you have a history of substance use disorder if you're considering ADHD medications, particularly stimulants, which have a higher abuse potential. That isn't to say that you can't or shouldn't use them, but alternative medications or therapies might be recommended first to see how those supports can help you. Many psychologists deal specifically with the interaction of ADHD and addiction, so you may want to seek them out for treatment informed by the latest addiction science.

I'm CONVINCED I have ADHD, but my doctor DIAGNOSED me with SOMETHING ELSE. What should I do?

 If your doctor is thorough and acts in good faith, you should accept the diagnosis they give you. Unfortunately, doctors aren't always thorough and don't always act in good faith, and it's up to you to earnestly make that distinction.

On some level, you have to trust this medical professional to do their job because you're not qualified to do that. That's why doctors exist. However, if you feel like your doctor did not give you a thorough, good-faith evaluation, you should seek another evaluation elsewhere if you are able.

 ## How does SELF-DIAGNOSIS work when it comes to getting medication?

 You cannot get ADHD medication legally without an official diagnosis.

 I also want to caution you, dear reader, about the wide array of online supplements that are often marketed toward the specific demographic of people who have or suspect they have ADHD but cannot get access to a diagnosis or medication.

A LOT of predatory brands out there will try to sell you their mushroom water or their vape vitamins or their fancy custom brain pills. *Please be careful.* Many of these brands also use messaging like "my brain on Adderall vs. my brain on this ALL-NATURAL SUPER-SAFE MAGICAL DRINK." Any brand that uses "*medication: unequivocally bad*" as their marketing does not have your best interest at heart.

What about SELF-DIAGNOSIS and accommodations at WORK?

 For the most part, you can't formally request accommodations at work without an official diagnosis. You might have a cool boss who's willing to work with your self-diagnosis, but this isn't always the case.

 Right—a lot of it has to do with where you are and what you're asking for. **If you're asking your boss, "Can I wear headphones?" you probably don't need a form for that.** However, if your boss says no, then you may have to go to HR with your diagnosis and say, "Actually, I really need this to be a good employee."

> **REMINDER:** much more about accommodations at work in chapter 12.

 ## I'm EMBARRASSED to tell people I have ADHD. Is that okay?

 Feeling any way, about anything, is okay. Of course it's okay to feel embarrassed. I would argue that you have no reason to be embarrassed, but feel how you feel. There can be a lot of internal conflict here, because you rationally know that you have this disorder and it's not your fault and it's nothing to be embarrassed by, but you still do feel that way.

The ADHD Field Guide for Adults

PART 2:
Getting the Help You Need

People tend to look at me and think, *Cate is so proud of her ADHD,* **when in reality, I TALK about my ADHD. I share my ADHD experience publicly. But the gnats in my office and the pile of garbage in the corner do NOT make me proud of my ADHD.**

You can think, *Hooray for my ADHD! I'm amazing!* You can also have times where you think, *My life is a mess, and I hate that I have this.* **You don't have to pick one emotion and stick with it. It is an ongoing process that changes as we move through our days.**

It's also okay to feel a sense of mourning, too: *Oh wow, it wasn't just that I wasn't trying. This is for real. This is forever.* Sometimes people tell you that you have ADHD before *you* know you have ADHD, prompting a feeling of *Fuck me, they were right.* It's all a process.

There can be a period of anger and resentment, too.
Why didn't anyone notice?
If I'd known sooner, I wouldn't have struggled for so long.
How did everybody in my life miss this?

In closing . . .

Many of my childhood memories are of me being shamed, embarrassed, even bullied by my (adult) teachers for struggling with organization and losing things. The biggest fights I remember having with my parents were about my "messy" room—but to me, it was organized, it just didn't look like it from the outside. Instead of learning to build systems that worked for me, I was taught to shrink myself, to conform, to look normal and pretend like nothing was wrong, all while spending five times the amount of effort and energy I needed to because I didn't know how my brain worked.

And then suddenly, at thirty, I learned that all that was actually part of my executive functioning. This entire time, I could have been learning to accept myself, to work with myself, to love myself as I was. Instead,

I was told over and over that I wasn't measuring up, that I wasn't good enough, that I was a Bad Kid (trademark pending) and a sinner.

It's angering. I feel a ton of resentment. I'm open and honest about that, because it's the lived experience of so many of us. There was no reason for my third-grade teacher to humiliate me in front of my class over and over, but she did. Instead of getting me help, instead of sitting with me and talking with me about what *my* needs were or *why* my desk was the way it was, she threw my stuff onto the floor in front of everyone to make an example out of me.

Even now, when I speak at parenting conferences, many parents make comments about their "difficult child."

"They won't clean their room! I've tried everything!"

"Have you asked them why they're struggling?"

"They're struggling because everything is in piles and they can't find anything."

"Have they told you that they're struggling?"

"Yes! I tell them to clean, and they just move everything around into piles and their room looks worse than it did before."

"Have you sat with them and asked them how they use those piles, or helped them identify places where they're struggling?"

"It's putting toys into a box, it's not that complicated, they just aren't applying themselves. They can sit and play video games for hours, so they clearly just don't want to listen to me about cleaning."

The thing I get most angry about these days is how so many parents ascribe malicious intent to their neurodivergent kids needing specific, clear directions and/or a different system that works better with their particular skills and struggles. Maybe you do, too.

Regardless of whether you're just getting diagnosed or entering your second decade of knowing you're neurodivergent, working through that anger will take time. You may want to consider talking to a professional about it. It's NORMAL. It's OKAY if you're mad. You have every right to be. You didn't get the support you needed, but now, today, you have the opportunity to support yourself and create a life that works with your brain, instead of against it. And that is an incredible opportunity.

—Cate

When I was working in kitchens, it took me YEARS to realize that I needed a more involved system for organizing my prep time than my fellow cooks, who could seemingly just scribble a couple of reminders on a piece of receipt paper and be fine. It took another year or so to develop the method that worked for me and another several years to stop feeling embarrassed about it in front of my colleagues. But I can say with confidence that despite my disability, by the time I left the culinary profession, I was a really, *really* good line cook.

It's frustrating to struggle with what seems like basic time management, especially while everyone else seems to do it so naturally and effortlessly. **It may not always feel like it, but managing time is something you can learn to do.** The hardest parts are convincing yourself that you are capable of finding a time management system that works for you and accepting that it's going to take time to get used to it.

Luckily, people have been struggling with time management since, well, presumably the beginning of time, so there are a LOT of off-the-shelf time management methods already out there. We will go through many of those methods in the next chapter. Try them out, tweak to your liking, and try to trust the process.

—Erik

PART 3

SYSTEMS and Organization

8

Time and Task Management

Every so often, as a person who studies ADHD for my job, I find a study that genuinely pisses me off. I get the "How did NOBODY ever mention this to me?!" rage, which is a very specific type of anger mixed with frustration and general annoyance. I have spent the better part of my life on an uncharted sea, feeling like I was this inept, irresponsible person, and generally like I'd missed some pivotal memo on how to be a human in this world.

Then I read a study about time, more specifically, how ADHD people perceive time, and I learned that ACTUAL SCIENTIFIC STUDIES have been done on this, and the way we relate to time is measurably different:[1]

> "[People with] ADHD have difficulties in time estimation and discrimination activities as well as having the feeling that time is passing by without them being able to complete tasks accurately and well."

It's right there, in black-and-white, concrete, peer-reviewed evidence. People with ADHD *feel* time differently. Study after study shows that we're bad at estimating how much time something will take, we're bad at estimating how much time has passed, and we're bad at finishing tasks in an allotted time.

Imagine how important and useful that knowledge might be for parents of kids with ADHD, or for teachers or partners. For understanding why some of us tend to run a few minutes late, why some of us tend to overcommit, why some of us live in houses with unfinished DIYs and crafting projects that "shouldn't take too long" to finish. I don't know about you, but this knowledge has made me a little kinder and a little more patient with myself.

Now, that's not to say that we as ADHDers have carte blanche to be late, waste people's time, or be irresponsible—like many things we talk about in this book, this research is not an excuse; it is an explanation that we can use to understand our unique challenges and learn how to build support systems that work for us. That's what this chapter is about—taking time and bending it to our will. Time Lord stuff. (Or, at least, getting-to-work-on-time stuff.)

—Cate

❓ I tend to FUNCTION better when I have STRUCTURE, but I also kind of hate structure at the same time. Is that normal?

I think ADHDers resent structure because we need it, but we struggle to create it for ourselves.

I submit that everyone functions better with at least some elements of structure in their lives. Sometimes those structures are external, like a school or work schedule, and sometimes they're internal, like a morning routine someone might follow without having to think about it.

A lot of the internal structures for others will have to be external for you. This can make it look like you need more structure than the average bear, when really it's just that more of the structure you need is visible to the outside observer. I sometimes think of it like doing math on paper rather than in your head.

The good news is that it will get easier the more you practice externalizing your structures. When I was training people to be cooks and we were making prep lists early in the day, I'd tell them, "You want to do all your thinking for the next several hours right now. What order you're going to do things in, what you want to grab from the walk-in, and what tools you're going to use." Doing all your thinking early and at once means that thinking won't get in the way when you're actually in the flow of doing stuff.

My suggestion here is to reframe how you think of structure. A lot of people with ADHD thrive in careers where they can change course very quickly—where there are a lot of different things happening from day to day.

But within that, there is still structure. **You get to the office, something happens, you eat lunch, something happens. There is a *framework*.** I think *structure* can be a scary word, because structure feels permanent. Unchanging. So I prefer the idea of framework.

The ADHD Field Guide for Adults

PART 3:
Systems and Organization

I have a framework by which I do my day . . . I wake up, I check my email, I have a coffee, I check my email again, and I do a cycle of social media. But I don't think of that as a STRUCTURE. It's a framework of key points. It's more effective for me that way, and it's flexible if and when I need to change it.

Make it fun.
It's your life. Have a good time.

A flexible framework in which to operate winds up being a lot more effective for many people with ADHD than a rigid system of "I must get X, Y, and Z done by 10:30." That introduces a whole host of issues like task prioritization and management, switching tasks, and so on.

I also like to think of it as a rhythm. **Having little protocols can help you remember what structure you've decided to follow at the time. Like wearing a fun hat while you're doing a twenty-minute laundry-folding session or a silly apron to do dishes, or lighting a candle while you're working in your office.** Make it fun. It's your life. Have a good time.

Lastly, it may help to figure out a way that the day visually makes sense to you. For instance, if a calendar view of hour-by-hour stresses you out, it might work better for you to create a block schedule or a task-based list.

Canva is not only an amazing resource for visualizing different formats and ways to lay out your schedules, it also allows you to customize EVERYTHING so you can create something that really works for you and your needs.

You can use a daily, weekly, or monthly planner. Personally, a monthly calendar with a block schedule every day works best for my brain, but that's me. I have a lot of Fancy and Important Friends who swear by their dailies. I just like having a big picture of my month whenever I agree to put anything else on my schedule.

 **Is there a task or chore that you used to hate doing, but you made some changes to how you do it that made it much easier?**

> I turned vacuuming into a race with the dog even if she doesn't know it. How much of the floor can I get done before she finishes her treat.

—Kelli from Kentucky

> I hate repetitive tasks—i.e., those things you have to do every day, several times a day. I try to bake in a reward system (I can only have my favorite chocolate while I do filing, I'm saving my next DnD show for the laundry) so I make it something to look forward to.

—Tsukino

> I hated meal planning/grocery shopping/cooking and how much time that all took. I'd procrastinate constantly and end up ordering in. But I made a weirdly strict schedule of doing a little food stuff each day, and it's a lot less painful now. Sunday through Wednesday I cook each night. Thursday is just leftovers, no cooking, so I make the meal plan for next week then. Friday I make the grocery list, and Saturday I do the shopping. A little bit each day makes it suck a lot less.

—Anne from Chicago

How do I NOT OVERCOMMIT to things?

Consider this: an *enthusiastic maybe*.

Oftentimes overcommitting comes from people-pleasing; you want them to feel like you're interested in whatever they're pitching and grateful for them asking you. **By being enthusiastic but not committing to anything, you're still communicating that you're interested and grateful, but aren't running the risk of having to go back on your word later on.**

It's tempting to say yes to all the things because saying yes makes people happy, and it's really nice making people happy! But you're going to make them *unhappy* if later it turns out the answer is actually no—more unhappy than if you had said no in the first place. So give them an *enthusiastic maybe* instead.

It's okay to have prewritten scripts for moments like this, especially if you're a person who struggles with saying no. You don't ever owe anyone an explanation, but explanations can sometimes help soften the blow while still maintaining your boundaries.

→ **You can be direct:**

- "Thank you for thinking of me, but I can't commit to this right now."
- "I appreciate the offer, but I'm going to have to pass."
- "I'll have to check my schedule and get back to you." (Use this only if you genuinely intend to check and respond.)
- "I have prior commitments that I need to stick to."

→ **You can be honest about your time:**
- "I'm currently swamped with other commitments."
- "I wish I could, but my schedule is packed right now."
- "I need to focus on my existing projects, so I can't take on anything new at the moment."

→ **You can offer an alternative:**
- "I can't help with that, but what if I [offer a different form of assistance]?"
- "I'm not available that day, but I'm free next week if that helps."
- "I know a guy who is AMAZING at [X, Y, Z], and I know he's looking for work—let me connect you two via email."

→ **You can just be honest, period:**
- "I don't think I'm the best person for that task."
- "I'm trying to cut back on my commitments to ensure I give my best to each one."
- "I've realized I need to prioritize my well-being, so I'm being more selective with what I take on."

→ **It's okay to request empathy:**
- "I hope you understand, but I can't take this on right now."
- "I'm really struggling with my mental health, and I don't think going would be the best idea for me right now; I know you know how it is."
- "I'm having a chronic pain flare-up today, so I won't be able to make it, let's catch up soon."

Remember that you don't have to OVERexplain. A simple "Thanks, but I can't" is fine—sometimes overexplaining can make things more complicated.

How do I **IMPROVE** my **TIME MANAGEMENT**?

Here is a grab bag of different schedule-keeping techniques and systems:

1. Time Blocking
- **Set aside specific blocks of time** for different tasks or activities throughout the day, like, "I check my emails from ten to eleven and six to seven, but that's IT." This helps create a clear structure and reduces the overwhelm of having too many tasks (and also compulsively rechecking your email thirty times an hour).

2. Theme Days
- **Dedicate specific days of the week** to specific types of work or activities. For instance, we always record the podcast on Monday, so we don't have to think about it the rest of the week.

3. The Pomodoro Technique
- **Work for a set amount of time** (like ten to thirty minutes) and then take a five-to-ten-minute break. After four cycles, take a longer break.

4. The Two-Minute Rule
- **Quick Tasks First:** If something takes less than two minutes, do it immediately. This helps clear small tasks that can otherwise add up.

5. The Eisenhower Matrix
- **Categorize tasks into four quadrants** based on their urgency and importance. Focus on important and urgent tasks first. It's okay if Wordle is important and urgent.

6. The ABCD-Z Priority System:
- **Assign Priorities:** assign each task a letter based on its priority or difficulty (A = highest priority/biggest pain in the ass, B = lower priority/less of a pain, etc.).

 I hate this one and I cannot do it. Prioritizing is really difficult for me, but a lot of people I know use this one a lot.

7. The Kanban Method:
- **Visualize Work:** use a kanban board to visualize tasks in columns (e.g., To Do, In Progress, Done).
- **Limit Work in Progress:** limit the number of tasks in the "In Progress" column to prevent overwhelm.

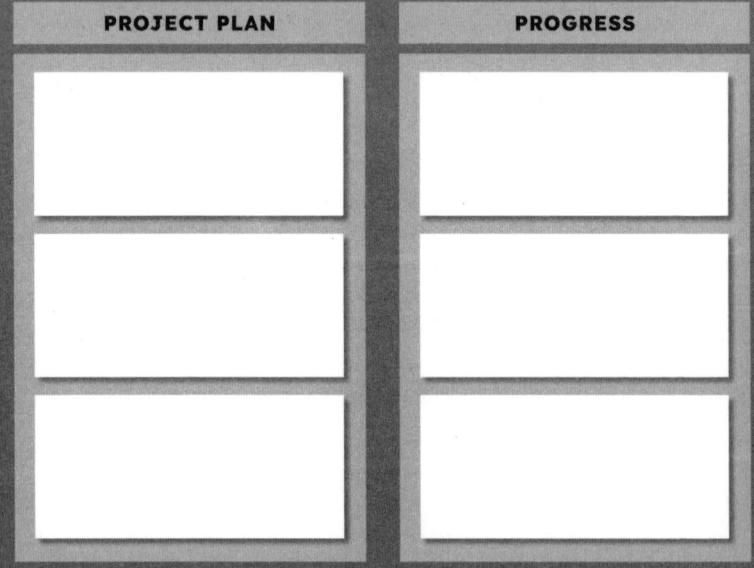

PRIORITY MATRIX

IMPORTANT, NOT URGENT
Decide when to do

_____

_____

_____

NOT IMPORTANT & NOT URGENT
Do later

_____

_____

_____

IMPORTANT & URGENT
Do immediately

_____

_____

_____

NOT IMPORTANT & URGENT
Delegate

_____

_____

_____

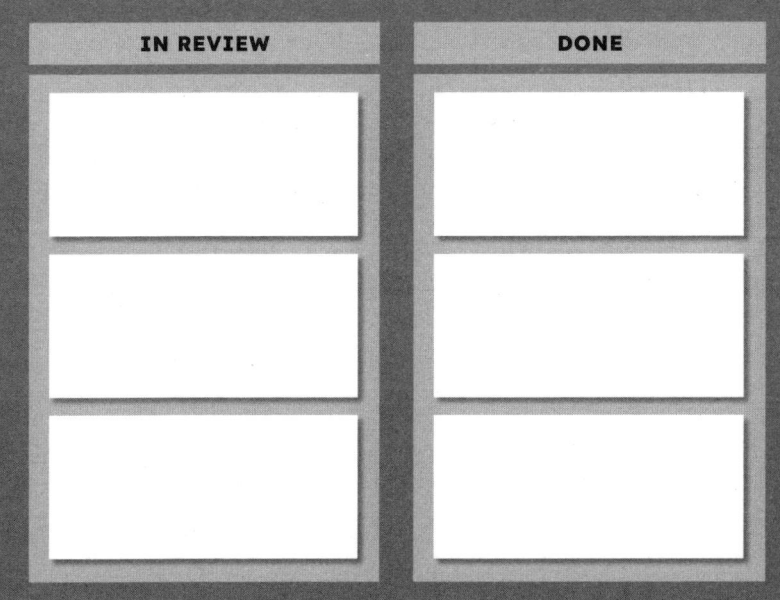

8. Time Auditing:
- **Track Time Spent:** Keep a log of how you spend your time throughout the day. Do this for a week or two, and then REALLY look at it to figure out where you can prioritize and organize to be more productive.

9. The Time-Boxing Method:
- **Allocate Fixed Time:** allocate a fixed amount of time to a task and stop working when the time is up.
- **Use for Unpleasant Tasks:** This method is particularly useful for tasks that suck. You'd be shocked at how far five minutes will get you with stuff like doing the dishes.

10. The 1-3-5 Rule:

I LOVE THIS ONE.
Each day, choose one big task, three medium tasks, and five small tasks to focus on.

11. The 80/20 Rule (Pareto Principle):
- **Focus on High-Impact Tasks:** identify and focus on the 20 percent of tasks that contribute to 80 percent of the results.
- **Eliminate Low-Impact Activities:** try to eliminate or delegate tasks that aren't as important or waste a lot of time.

None of these things needs to be set in stone, of course. A common ADHD struggle is the whole "But what if things change!?" Try out different techniques and use them while they're still working, but stay flexible enough to test out ones as needed, too.

❓ I need STRUCTURE and DEADLINES, but I can never follow them if I set them myself. What should I do?

Schedules do not exist to restrict you. They exist to *free* you so that you don't have to spend your entire day making decisions. You don't have to think about the amount of time you need to spend on any given task. With a schedule, you're doing your thinking all at once.

I was a cook for a long time, and when you make a prep list, you make all your decisions right then. You're doing your thinking at once, deciding exactly how you're going to get your tasks accomplished. So then, when you're actually doing the things, your brain is free to think about what you're doing now rather than what you're going to do next.

Don't think of a structure you made as an external thing that is now annoyingly telling you what to do. **Think of a structure as the result of favors "past you" did by making a bunch of decisions so "present you" doesn't have to.** It's not some authority telling you what to do. Remember that you're still the master of ceremonies here.

> Don't think of a structure you made as an external thing that is now annoyingly telling you what to do.

Another method is simply to pretend that it wasn't you who set the deadline. I often imagine my heroes are watching me, reading something I wrote, or providing commentary on what I'm doing. If I set a deadline for myself, I'll imagine that it was actually Stephen Fry overseeing what I'm doing, and now my goal is to make *him* happy by being on time.

One thing I like to do when setting deadlines for myself is gamification. **Making a game of meeting your deadline makes it feel more like something you've chosen to do for fun, rather than something you *have* to do.**

When I was a kid, I used "end of the world" scenarios. The world was going to end if I didn't clean the kitchen before my parents got home. I used to pretend that Tom Cruise was going to rush into the room with a cool metal suitcase with a big red light on it and be like, "All clear, team! Erik has cleaned the kitchen. Repeat: Erik has cleaned the kitchen!" and then the light on the suitcase turns from red to green and Tom pats me on the back and says, "Thanks, kid, I always knew we could count on you."

Okay, let's be honest, I still do that.

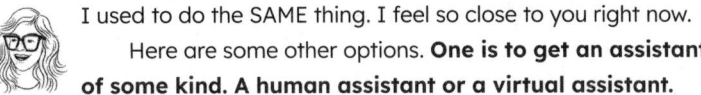

I used to do the SAME thing. I feel so close to you right now.

Here are some other options. **One is to get an assistant of some kind. A human assistant or a virtual assistant. I have an assistant not because I'm so fancy and famous, but because I couldn't handle everything myself and my business was struggling as a result. So I structured my budget such that I can pay someone to help me keep my business running.**

I had to realistically ask myself: *What do I need to make Catieosaurus Industries thrive?* The answer was to have somebody tell me on Monday, "I need this from you on Tuesday." And that has been really, really helpful. Visual prompts for things you need to do help, too. As we often say—if it helps you run your life, it's not silly.

Um, things can be silly AND helpful! Doing Pilates is the silliest thing I've ever seen, but I'll be damned if it doesn't help with core strength.

I also find this one to be completely delightful . . . **If there's a task that you need to do but you don't wanna do it, put on a really good song and do the task as though you are being filmed for a movie montage.** So maybe there's dancing while you're doing this task. Like performative cleaning. There's just something about it that's really fun and novel. **It's all about finding easy ways to create novelty, stakes, or rewards for yourself.**

The ADHD Field Guide for Adults

PART 3:
Systems and Organization

What do I do about CHOICE PARALYSIS?

ADHD brains are like sponges. If you dip a sponge into water really quickly, it's not going to absorb much liquid. The longer you leave that sponge in water, the more it's going to absorb and get bogged down until you have to squeeze it out and start fresh.

That is the process of making decisions when you have ADHD, because the more information that you have, the easier it is to get bogged down. And the easier it is to get distracted. With small choices, the more time you spend on it, the more information your brain is going to absorb, and that is going to result in a tougher decision.

> **PRO TIP:** If you're choosing between two things, flip a coin but don't look at what it lands on. You'll likely find yourself hoping that it's one rather than the other, and THAT is the one you should choose. (This isn't my original idea, but it seems the original source has been lost in the annals of the Internet.)

When it comes to choice problems, most of my favorite strategies have to do with limiting: limiting the amount of time you have to think about it, limiting the number of choices that you have, limiting the number of sources you can buy from, etc.

Outsourcing can be useful, too—i.e., having somebody else (who perhaps doesn't have ADHD) to help you decide. Externalizing the process can be immensely helpful because the outside person can remind you, "You just said five minutes ago that you hated that

> The more information you have, the easier it is to get bogged down. And the easier it is to get distracted.

restaurant" or "In the amount of time we've been deciding how to get to the restaurant, we could have gotten there no matter which route we took. Let's just get going." Having a mediator to keep you from going in circles can be really helpful.

One of my favorite things to do when it comes to choice paralysis is to **arbitrarily limit my options**. For example, if I'm choosing a couch for a room in my house, I'll arbitrarily go, "Okay, it's gonna be a blue couch." I don't necessarily want a blue couch, but it helps reduce the amount of information my brain has to contend with so I can more easily figure out what I actually want. "It's going to be a blue sectional." That narrows my options down even further. And then I can choose between blue sectionals.

This has nothing to do with my actually choosing a blue sectional, it's just that once I've narrowed my field, it becomes much easier to understand what my actual criteria are, so I can evaluate which couches will work in my space more easily.

It's about limiting your options so your brain stops freaking out about all the possibilities and you have something more specific on which to focus.

 ## Should I always use a PLANNER?

 Using my phone as my planner or calendar for regular use doesn't do it for me. 'Cause it doesn't exist unless I'm looking at it. But keeping a physical thing that you can write things down in, fucking great idea for me. **If the phone calendar or notes app works for you, great. If it doesn't, you're not alone. Try a more analog, physical thing.**

The ADHD Field Guide for Adults

PART 3:
Systems and Organization

WEEKLY PLANNER

Week _____

MON _____

TUES _____

WED _____

THURS _____

FRI _____

SAT _____

SUN _____

PRIORITIES OF THE WEEK

- [ ] _____
- [ ] _____
- [ ] _____
- [ ] _____
- [ ] _____
- [ ] _____
- [ ] _____

TO CALL/TO EMAIL

- [ ] _____
- [ ] _____
- [ ] _____
- [ ] _____
- [ ] _____
- [ ] _____
- [ ] _____

APPOINTMENTS

- [ ] _____
- [ ] _____
- [ ] _____
- [ ] _____
- [ ] _____
- [ ] _____
- [ ] _____

Fun little historical anecdote: When Agatha Christie died, they went through her stuff and she had all these planners and journals. She would start one and pick up another. There would be notes from May 1935, and then you turn the page and it's November 1945. She had ADHD! I can't prove it, but looking at her planners, I certainly recognize those patterns.

 Another option is those little field notebooks—the memo pads that come in a pack of three for a couple bucks. Cooks often have these on their body somewhere, and the front page is always blank and ready to write on at any given moment, because you tear off the pages when you're done with them. If you get a recipe idea, then you move it to your master notebook. For those in-the-moment things where you just need to scribble down a number or whatever, you always have a blank first page.

Think of it like scrap paper in a stack in your pocket, and you rip out pages when you're done with them. That's the kind of thing you can have on you at all times to jot down reminders.

In closing . . .

The ADHD life is one in which time management is liable to be a near-constant source of stress, but it doesn't have to stay that way.

We promise that you just need the patience and persistence to go through the various methods, test them out, and figure out what works best for you. This **will** change over time, so pack your flexibility while you're at it and be prepared to change things up as needed.

A Reminder/Cheat Sheet on the Methods:

- **Time Blocking:** I do *task* from *start time* to *end time*.
- **The Pomodoro Technique:** I do *task* for *x minutes* then take an *x-minute* break. Repeat.
- **The Two-Minute Rule:** If *task* takes less than two minutes, I do it right now.
- **The Eisenhower Matrix:** A chart that helps organize tasks by urgency.
- **The ABCD-Z Priority System:** Assign each task a letter based on its priority or difficulty level.
- **Time Auditing:** Keep a log of how you spend your time and look back on it after one to two weeks to reprioritize.
- **The Kanban Method:** Pin notes to a board for visualizing tasks in columns (To Do, In Progress, Done).
- **The Time-Boxing Method:** Allocate a fixed time for unpleasant tasks and stop working when time is up.
- **The 1-3-5 Rule:** Choose one big task, three medium tasks, and five small tasks daily.
- **The 80/20 Rule:** Focus on the 20 percent of tasks that contribute to 80 percent of the results.

And listen—don't be so goddamn hard on yourself. Even in the process of writing this book, we learned, we changed some stuff, we started to better dissect and understand the "whys and hows" of why we struggle with certain tasks, and why certain tasks are harder on different days. This takes time, even while you're learning to manage it. The goal isn't instant perfection. It never will be, and chasing that is going to burn you out. Instead, think of it like getting to know yourself from a different perspective—how you understand and appreciate linear time.

—Cate and Erik

9

Get Down with the Systems

We have two televisions in our living room. One is the main TV, and it plays whatever movie or show we happen to be watching at the time, and the other, smaller TV is just a cheap thrifted monitor hooked up to a gaming console. The idea is that we now don't have to choose between playing video games and watching TV, which we discovered was a source of stress and tension in our lives. Sometimes a system that works for you might seem strange compared to what you're used to seeing, but if it makes your life more functional, why not?

Behind our living room couch, there is a shoe organizer that has sat empty and unused for months. Directly next to it is a big ol' pile of shoes. Turns out, we love being able to thoughtlessly kick off our shoes when we come inside, and we find putting them into an organizer unnecessarily tedious. So we've decided to get rid of the shoe organizer, though we thought it was a good idea at the time, and get a shoe bin instead.

When developing systems, we have to get used to stuff not working and learn to let go of systems that don't work *without shame* or viewing the endeavor as a failure. We have to accept that as people with ADHD, our understanding of our needs and abilities is going to change over the course of our lives, and that's OKAY. You're not a fuckup if you really thought the shoe organizer was going to work, but it turns out that a bin or basket works much better for you and your brain.

> **To develop systems is to develop techniques for living more happily as yourself, so there is no one more capable of understanding the nature of your systems than you.**

Just past our shoe pile is a rolling cart that we load with dirty laundry throughout the week. It is kept in an accessible location so we can easily throw stuff into it, but close enough to the laundry room so that it can be wheeled next to the washer with little to no effort. As Cate's spine health has gotten progressively worse, she started looking for ways to make doing daily tasks easier. The laundry cart was an idea from KC Davis, author of *How to Keep House While Drowning*. Sometimes we discover our own systems; sometimes we learn about them from others.

Before we embark on this chapter, we'd like to clarify something: To develop systems is to develop techniques for living more happily as yourself, so there is no one more capable of understanding the nature of your systems than you. What works wonderfully for someone else may be a nightmare for you, and since every human is unique, there's a chance that the systems you need haven't even been thought of yet.

Endeavoring to build systems that improve your life is a deeply personal journey of self-discovery and acceptance. We would be honored to help you begin this journey by giving you some suggestions on where to start, a framework with which to consider problems, and tools to use along the way. But *nobody*, including us, can give you all the answers to all the deeply personal questions you're likely to encounter.

Those questions may include:

- Is this system not working because it's inherently flawed or because I'm just not good enough at it?
- Is this thing really a problem that I need to develop a system for, or do I just think it's a problem because everybody has always told me it was?
- Do I have the right to insist that others adhere to my systems, or would asking them be a violation of their personal sovereignty?

When it comes to systems, be fiercely honest with yourself about your priorities, abilities, and ambition. And as always, take from this chapter what you can use, which we hope is a lot, and feel free to leave the rest.

—Cate and Erik

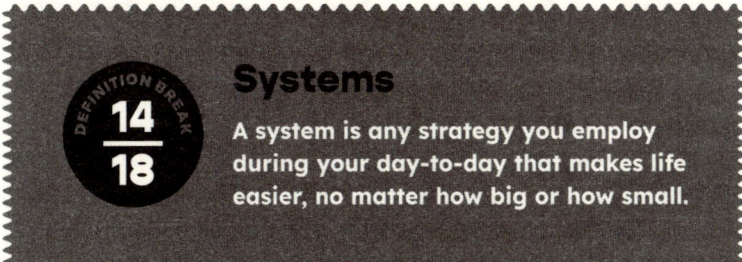

Systems

A system is any strategy you employ during your day-to-day that makes life easier, no matter how big or how small.

DEFINITION BREAK 14/18

What makes a GOOD SYSTEM?

 My own personal theory—and you can take it or leave it—is that a *good* system is sustainable, practical, and repeatable. **You must be within the triangle of sustainability, practicality, and repeatability for a system to work.**

Take your keys, for example. When you come home at the end of the day, maybe there's a little bowl on a side table and you throw your keys in there—that is repeatable, because the bowl is not gonna disappear. It's sustainable, since you don't have to buy a new bowl every single day. And it's practical, consisting of only one simple movement.

Now, if your system for never losing your keys was to have a hook screwed into the very top of your ceiling and every day you get up on a ladder and you put your keys on the hook so they can't possibly get lost, that's not sustainable or practical. And it's repeatable only until you fall off the ladder, Hans Gruber-style.

Systems can also develop organically. I started keeping my manicure set underneath my couch, which is a weird place to put it. But I realized that every time I was sitting on my couch, that's when I would be like, *Oh, I have a hangnail.* Or *I want to file my nails.* And so that system developed, and it's sustainable, practical, and repeatable for me to use my manicure set in that spot.

Systems are also deeply personal. What works for one person might not work for you. I just used a key bowl as an example, but what actually works for me is having a mail center, some key hooks, and a shoe bin all together in the same place. I need more support than a key bowl, but a key bowl was an excellent place to start.

 When figuring out a system, you might find it lacks practicality, repeatability, or sustainability. If that happens, tweaking is key—making small adjustments as problems occur. To make your system satisfy the Triangle of System Success, try making tweaks as needed in the following areas:

Accessibility

If your system isn't working because none of the other people who engage with it can consistently follow the rules, consider making your system more **accessible**. Make it easier for other people to learn and adhere to it—usually by simplifying.

Neediness

If your system isn't working because keeping up with it requires more maintenance and attention than you're willing to give, consider making it less **needy**. If your system works only if your kitchen sink is 100 percent spotless and it turns out cleaning the sink is your least favorite thing of all time, tweak the system so that it works even if the sink isn't totally clean.

Versatility

If your system isn't working because the situation it was built around keeps changing, consider making your system more **versatile**. If your comic book storage area works great as it is but needs to be dismantled and reassembled every time you get a new comic, so you end up just throwing them wherever, maybe add another shelf labeled "to sort" for you to put your new stuff. (I'm a huuuuuuuuuuuuge fan of "to sort" categories in general.)

The "Dopamine Factor"

If your system isn't working because the task involved intrinsically, irredeemably sucks for you, try upping the dopamine factor by adding things you like to it. This can be simple, like doing laundry while watching TV, or more involved, like throwing a rent party every month (see page 317). What does a spoonful of sugar do again?

Seriously, I can't remember. Someone call Julie Andrews.

It makes the medicine go down, Erik. Obviously.

Here are some examples of how the above qualities can affect your system's practicality, sustainability, and repeatability:

"My laundry system isn't **practical** because I hate doing laundry so damn much."

Your **dopamine factor** is too low. Add some fun to doing the laundry (podcasts, music, TV, or simmering a nice batch of Bordelaise).

"My rent-paying system isn't consistently **repeatable** because it involves all my roommates being home at the same time."

Your system isn't **accessible** enough. Maybe make a "rent slot" that your roommates can slide their check into if they're not going to be home on rent day.

"My system isn't **sustainable** because it requires me to keep my kitchen clean at all times, and I just don't have the energy to do that."

Your system is too **needy**. Try making it less ambitious so that it works even if the kitchen isn't spotless.

The ADHD Field Guide for Adults

PART 3:
Systems and Organization

sidenote

Other people are not obligated to use your system just because you want them to (unless they're your kids). You have the right to request that the people who share your living space adhere to your system, but ultimately, if you want others to use your system, you have to make it fit for them as much as it fits for you. I know that's probably not what you want to hear, but I'm just trying to save you an argument!

This is a huge soapbox for me, personally. A good partner will work with you and support you with reasonable accommodations in making your space more livable. If a partner saddles you with all the responsibility and refuses to participate in the facilitation of a living space, that's not a good partner. Sometimes issues like "My system isn't working," when you look REALLY closely, can actually be something closer to "My relationship isn't working because I'm receiving no support from my partner." That's a super-tough situation to be in, but it's also vitally important information to have moving forward. There are ways of communicating and negotiating and working through issues like this (couple's therapy and that kind of thing), but if your partner just straight up looks at you and says, "No, I won't help with the dishes, ever" or "I will not sort the mail like this," then it may be time to sit down and have a difficult conversation about why that is the case.

MUCH MORE on relationships in chapter 14.

How do I BUILD A SYSTEM?

 Former chef anecdote: In professional kitchens, we worship the concept of *mise en place*, which is a French phrase meaning "to put in place." So you've got the ingredients laid out, plus all the tools you're going to need, and the rags you'll use in their optimal locations, so that when you do the task, it's facilitated. And . . . language nerd moment incoming . . . *facilitate* comes from the Latin word *facilis*, which means "easy." This literally means *to make something easy*.

Just don't go overboard on the mise en place, because then you can never actually DO the task, because your area will never be set up PERFECTLY. **Perfect is the enemy of good.**

Before we embark on this next section, I want to mention that **systems don't have to be a huge deal**. Sometimes a system is just making sure you have the TV on when you're tidying the kitchen or keeping Diet Cokes around as a pick-me-up when you're writing emails.

The reason I still recommend thinking about these little things as "systems" is because it endows them with a deserved importance and hopefully makes them more likely to be remembered. **All systems, no matter how small, are your own personal techniques for existing happily as yourself and deserve to be appreciated.**

When building a system, start by identifying the part of the larger task that's tripping you up.

If you think, *I hate doing laundry,* take a moment to dissect how you engage with laundry and find the part of it that actually isn't working.

Maybe the plastic laundry basket digs into your hands, which stops the whole flow.* Maybe your laundry basket is too big—more clothes fit inside it than your washing machine can hold, so when clothes come out of the dryer there's no bin for them to go in, and they end up all over the floor.

---

* Wrap a pool noodle or piece of pipe insulation around the handles. Kaboom, now it's comfy. Once you've done that, maybe find some cool fabric and make upholstered handles, and suddenly your laundry basket is something you love to use. But do the pool noodles first!

→ **On Sharing Systems**

Run through the task in your head:

- What is your least favorite part of the task? Why?
- What is the most physically/mentally strenuous part of the task for you?
- Are there any times during the task when you're physically uncomfortable? How so?
- If you often don't finish the task, when do you usually stop?
- During the task, do you ever find yourself frustrated for lack of space?

Answering these types of questions will help you more effectively brainstorm ways of making the task more agreeable.

Erik Example . . .

About four years ago, I just started hanging all my laundry, except for socks and underwear.

I noticed that deciding whether to hang or fold something freaked me out, and that was why I was avoiding laundry. So one day I decided to get four hundred hangers for two dollars and just hang everything. Pants, shirts, whatever the thing—hang it up.

That was the problem area for me. It wasn't washing the laundry or gathering the laundry. I was fine with all that. I just hate having to make decisions while doing boring, repetitive labor. I'd rather turn my brain off and let my hands work. So I made the decision once and for all: everything gets hung up.

TL;DR: Figure out what part(s) of the task you hate the most. You likely don't have to completely destroy and rebuild how you do the task. Just tweak the parts that are broken.

Next, brainstorm ways to address the problem areas.

This is really good to do with somebody without ADHD if you can. Because it can be easy to start "Pie-in-the-sky-ing."

> **Pie-in-the-sky-ing:** getting distracted from your immediate needs by brainstorming elaborate new systems that require a lot of setup time and cost. If you're trying to figure out what to do about the massive pile of dirty laundry in your living room, and you start shopping for a sledgehammer to tear down a wall in your closet, you're pie-in-the-sky-ing.

It's important to keep your eye on the ball, and the reason it helps to have a non-ADHD person around is to remind you, "Hey, the goal right now is to get this pile of clothes that Sir Edmund Hillary would have a hard time scaling out of the living room.* Then we need to figure out next steps."

Remember, you're not trying to reinvent the wheel here. You're thinking of ways to make the parts of the task you struggle with less . . . struggle-y.

→ Some questions to ask yourself while brainstorming:

- What are some ways I can make the parts that suck the most a little more pleasant?
- How can I make myself more comfortable during the task, both physically and mentally?
- Is there a more suitable location for doing the task?
- Is there a more suitable time for doing the task?
- Are there ways I can ask other people to support me in doing the task?
- Remember: there's no such thing as a bad idea, just start throwing stuff out there.

---

* Erik thinks this is a very funny joke, but for the rest of us, Sir Edmund Hillary was a mountaineer, explorer, and philanthropist. He gained international fame as the first climber, alongside Tenzing Norgay, to reach the summit of Mount Everest on May 29, 1953. Cool joke, Erik.

TL;DR: Think of ways to make the suckiest parts suck less, preferably with a friend to help keep you on track.

Try It Out

Give your idea a go! If you need to get stuff, get the stuff. If you need to move stuff, move the stuff. If setting up the system is going to take some time, make sure to install a "rough draft" solution while you set up the real one (e.g., your fancy coat hooks aren't being delivered for another week, so pop up some Command hooks in the meantime).

Use the system for a few iterations: Do a few loads of laundry, have a few email-sending sessions. Pay attention to how things are working.

TL;DR: Do the thing.

Tweak

Tweak things as you see fit. What worked about the system? What didn't work? Can you think of any ways you can make your system even 1 percent more suitable to you?

→ **Some questions to ask yourself:**

- What worked about the system? What didn't work?
- Did it at least suck less than before the new system?
- Were any of the problems technical, like a headphone cord getting in the way?
- Are there any objects/tools that could make the system work better?
- How easy was the system to adopt? Do you think you'll get better at it over time?

This can be a pretty annoying process, and you might be tempted to completely abandon the system out of frustration. If you're deciding whether to abandon a system and start over, **always wait another week** and commit to adhering to the current system 100 percent during that week. If it still needs to go at the end of that week, feel free to scrap it, but don't write a system off immediately.

TL;DR: If it doesn't work immediately, that doesn't mean the system is doomed. Try working out the kinks.

And finally, just *do* the task with your new system.

Sorry, but no matter how awesome your system is, you still have to supply the activation energy yourself. You have to decide to get off the couch.

A lot of stuff we have to do as humans just sucks. Doing laundry, answering emails, getting your car registered, all of it sucks. Systems, no matter how simple or complicated, are ways of compartmentalizing and minimizing the "suck" so it doesn't start to invade more of your life by being left undone.

You have to practice overriding that initial *I don't wanna* or *I can't*. You're never going to want to, and yes, you can.

How do I get OFF the COUCH and GET STARTED?

When trying to muster up the will to get started on a thing, don't think about starting the *entire* thing. Think about starting the *first* thing.

Starting a "whole thing" can be daunting, so don't. Just start the first step. Then the second, then the third, until suddenly you're done! It can help to break things down into the smallest actual iterations of what you're doing—for example, laundry:

- Gather the clothes, even if some might be clean.
- Put clothes into the hamper.
- Walk hamper down the stairs to the laundry room.
- Load the clothes into the washer.
- Start the washer and set a timer on your phone so you'll know when it's done.
- Switch the clothes to the dryer; set a new timer.

The ADHD Field Guide for Adults

PART 3:
Systems and Organization

- Unload clothes from the dryer when the timer goes off.
- Fold clothes (or hang!).
- Put clothes away.

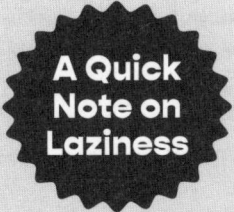

 There is a big push in the online ADHD community to reject the idea of laziness altogether, claiming that what we call "laziness" is just misidentified executive dysfunction.

I firmly disagree and find the notion counterproductive at best, and actively destructive at worst. I accept that, for a person with ADHD, a lot of what is commonly considered to be "lazy" behavior really is the result of legitimate executive dysfunction, but a lot of it isn't.

When you justify avoiding a task for long enough, your brain starts to think you're simply incapable of doing it and quietly admits defeat. Remember, defeat can be comfortable. It doesn't ask you to do anything. It doesn't expect anything from you, but it also has ZERO interest in helping you.

There are some things you'll never *want* to do, so if you wait to do them until you want to, you'll never do it. Practice doing things when you *don't* want to.

 The idea isn't to punish yourself, hate yourself, judge yourself, or give yourself the "If you just tried harder and applied yourself" speech. That's not helpful. **What IS helpful is learning how to recognize when you are feeling defeated by a task and finding systems that help you through those moments of difficulty.**

→ **Some more tips for getting started!**

- **Micro-Timer Method:** Set a timer for the shortest amount of time you can *force* yourself to do the thing, even if it's only ten seconds (make it shorter than you think), and then do it.

Congrats! You've succeeded in your stated goal of doing the task for ten seconds and can totally stop if you want, unless, of course, you think you can do another ten seconds. After a couple of reps, the timer starts to feel annoyingly short.

- **Don't think about starting. Think about *finishing*:** People with ADHD tend to have difficulty conceptualizing prospective time, so when we think about starting the dishes, our brains think we're going to be doing dishes for the rest of our lives and never doing anything we like ever again. To get around this, ask yourself, "If I start *right now*, what time will I be *finished*, and back to watching the Winchesters murder demons and stuff?"

What do I do if I STRUGGLE with a TASK purely for sensory reasons?

Much like laundry, we're taught that something like doing the dishes is a singular task. Even taking a shower is presented as a single task, but it's not!

ADHD-related executive dysfunction shows up in task organization, prioritization, and management. It's not that you suck at showering, it's that your brain recognizes it as a series of many tasks, and those tasks are trying to process all at once, so your processing system freezes up.

Personally, when showering, I've done things like forgetting to condition my hair or forgetting to rinse out my conditioner, shaving only one leg, or getting halfway through the shower and feeling too overwhelmed to wash my face. These things are very common.

What can help here is to build a support into each one of those "subtasks" that allows you to better slide to the next one. So rather than it being like an obstacle course, it's like a track that you're on and you go for the ride. Leaving a clean (or clean enough) towel in your bathroom at all times. Showering when you have the energy for all the steps. Not leaving the bathroom until you complete the final hair tasks, etc.

Keeping in mind I spent a long time as an undiagnosed AuDHDer, I have a "shower list": I take my showers in the same order, every time.

It's far more likely that you don't "hate showering" (the complete list of tiny tasks). You hate certain parts, like when the cold air hits you when you get out, or how your feet feel on the bathmat, or how the water feels on your face, or that you only ever remember to shower when it's 2 a.m. and you're already exhausted, or the way your arms hurt when you're washing your hair because of your chronic pain, or using the same shampoo for six months, or how you always are running late and hate leaving with wet hair, etc.

Breaking tasks down into steps provides much more clarity on where the problem actually is, which will also give you insight into what you might be able to change/do to fix it.

What if I DON'T KNOW what kind of SYSTEMS I need?

When designing a system, don't try to make the best possible system; aim for the most *suitable* system for you and your temperament.

Give yourself permission to let go of the imaginary, future perfect version of yourself. It's not about doing things the "right" way. It's about figuring out what parts of your life you truly care about and making adjustments as needed.

Above all, YOU DO YOU. All of us have been taught from an early age that if you're messy, that's bad, and you should feel bad about it. A lot of us have had our desks dumped out in front of the whole class because they were too disorganized. **If *you're* okay with having a messy desk, and you can come to terms with not having a consistently clean and organized desk, then you're golden.**

That just hit me right in the childhood trauma. I remember being seven or eight, and my parents would get on me about having a messy room. I knew even then—this is me, and this is how I have my space.

This continued to be a problem for my entire adolescence. I share this bit of personal history to highlight that a lot of times messiness is punished out of you as a kid. **You may have been taught that it's an embarrassing or shameful thing to be messy.** *Close your door when guests come over, lest they see your toys strewn across the floor.* This circles back, yet again, to the fact that I've spent a lot of time not knowing that I had ADHD, which makes it harder to accept. **But you can give yourself permission to be messy if that's what works for you and your living environment.**

I think ADHDers often think of themselves as being extremely organized and efficient if only we could just . . . fill in the blank. Try to let that go.

 It's a mixture of acknowledging that you have agency—that you can amend your behavior if you choose to do so—and accepting who you are. You struggle with this kind of stuff, and that is fine. **Stop comparing yourself to who you wish you were and start working on wanting to be who you already are.** I think the goal should be to know and to accept yourself without ridding yourself of the ability to aspire to be more.

FIX IT FIRST!
Put a coat hook on the wall, and THEN go shopping for the perfect antique coatrack.

SYSTEM Suitability

Lets talk about chef's knives. I promise I'm going somewhere with this.

Early on in my culinary career, while I was putting together my first knife roll, I was given some advice that I think about all the time...

Your first knife should be a beginner's knife: forgiving and cheap. A beater. You're going to mess up a lot as you learn, so you need a knife that can really take some punishment. You need an eight-inch Dexter-Russell chef's knife.

Your second knife should be intermediate. Nothing handmade, but something on the higher end of mass-produced stainless-steel chef's knives. A knife worth maintaining but that will forgive you if you don't. You will take better care of this blade, learn to sharpen it, hone it often, and store it carefully. You need a Mercer Genesis eight-inch chef's knife.

Your third knife should be advanced. Still mass-produced, but one that is a delight to use when well maintained and frustrating to use when it isn't. You need an eight-inch Global chef's knife.

Your fourth knife should be the last knife you ever have to buy, an absolute triumph of human craftsmanship that you'll have for the rest of your life. Single-bevel, carbon steel, probably Japanese. This knife will not forgive you. If you don't rinse and wipe it down after every cut, it will rust. If you don't hone it, your edge will break. If you don't store it properly, it will slice clean through your knife roll.

Note that this way of thinking about knives—and systems—does not deal in *quality*, but rather *suitability*.

The **ideal knife** isn't necessarily the best knife. It's the knife most suited to the user. When building a system, focus on making it forgiving and functional first, then making it better if you want. If you need a place to put your jacket, get a shitty coat hook first, then get a nice coatrack.

Can you tell us a task or chore that you HATE doing?

> I despise cleaning the clutter that I inherently create as a result of having ADHD.

—Rachel from Iowa

> Laundry. It's a multistep chore that's all done in big clumps. Multiple steps with at least an hour of wait time means I'm much more likely to forget that it's there. It's also done in big loads, so I get past the overwhelm of a big pile of (dirty) laundry, do said laundry, and end with a big pile of (clean) laundry, which is just as overwhelming to put away as it was to start washing.

—Miranda from Denver

> Dishes—takes forever, it's a task that's never truly done, it's Sensory Bad, and it can exacerbate chronic pain, too.

—Lux from Massachusetts

> Cliché, but it's the "boring" things. Dusting and vacuuming being at the top of my list. They usually only get done when I'm fed up with the dust or whatever, and even then it'll only be in the spot that I've noticed.

—@siarlas

> Showering/bathing. Unless I'm too exhausted to care, it's like stepping into a room filled with thick gas and being tapped/tickled by a hundred tiny toddlers for the fifteen minutes it takes me to get clean.

—Dominic from Colorado

What if my **SYSTEMS FAIL?**

 They WILL. No matter what systems you have, there are going to be times when your life becomes a disorganized mess again. It's just going to happen. Accept it, and realize it's not a commentary on whether you're a good person. Winter to spring. Summer to fall. Clean house to messy house. It's just about the cycles of life.

When you have ADHD and your systems are failing, and you're not doing the stuff that you need to do to keep your life together, and everything's awful again . . . that's actually a profoundly useful **self-research opportunity**.

Treat your lowest moments like you're the focus of a nature documentary rather than using them as an excuse to hate yourself. Just observe: What is the hardest part about this for you? Why is that so hard? Is there anything you can do to make that easier?

You may think, *Oh, wow, this really does suck. This is why it's so important for me to keep up with my systems, because when my desk is really dirty, I get restless. When the kitchen can't be cooked in, I just don't eat.*

It's frankly quite useful to have your systems fail every once in a while, to remind you of why you need them.

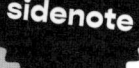

> **Not every system is an all-the-time thing.**
> You may interact with some systems only during certain times of the year. It might make sense for you to keep your winter clothes out of the way during off-season to save closet space. The answer may be simply "chuck them into a bin and take them out when it makes sense." Or it might help to structure things more: "On November 1, we pull out the holiday decorations and put out the winter coats."

 ## What is the hardest part about having ADHD?

> The executive dysfunction: getting overwhelmed with tasks others can do easily, losing track of things, the disorganization, the difficulty maintaining routines, falling behind on paperwork, the classic "ADHD tax." That last one led to my car being repossessed because I thought I'd had auto pay set up and then got overwhelmed with mail and didn't read closely enough.

—Lux from Massachusetts

> I, for the first time in my life, am living alone. I keep forgetting to eat and take care of my body.

—Connor Lynch

> Everything? It changes from day to day. Some days the hard bit is staring at the pit of despair that's suddenly too messy for my brain to function, and yet it's so messy that to even attempt to clean it is overwhelming. Some days it's the complete lack of memory, both of what I did six months ago and what I did six seconds ago. Other days it's a complete inability to process anything that's said to me. I know you're speaking English but I'm hearing gobbledegook. It's the mindset born from a lifetime of being told I'm lazy that now means that I will work myself to the bone, through injury and illness, ignoring my body screaming out for rest because I can't let myself be seen as lazy, or skiving, or letting the team down (thanks, RSD). The list could go on forever, and what's hard about ADHD for me just goes in endless cycles of me temporarily obsessing over things I just can't change.

—Emma from Shropshire

> Having to write all thoughts down or forget them then go crazy trying to remember what I just forgot three seconds ago. I have to have Post-its and pads and pens within arm's length at all times. Typing them in my phone is useless because when I pick it up to add a reminder or note I wind up in twenty different places and apps and actually forget why I got out the phone or pad. Debilitating and infuriating and I hate that I'm like this but powerless to correct it. It is so difficult when I am staked with a task and have all good intention, then it goes to shit and I disappoint because I totally forgot to do the task because I veered off trajectory.

—Stevie Mes

> Knowing I'm smart but feeling like there is this invisible barrier preventing me from accessing that potential, no matter what I do.

—Jenna from Denver

> The hardest part is to feel so alone and never understood. Almost nobody gets or even believes that some things are incredibly hard for me. Because I look function-able and not very ADHD-like on the outside, have tons of coping strategies, and actually excel in some areas, my struggles are often not taken seriously, even by some professionals. That adds to the shame. Sometimes I feel so stupid for not being able to function in the way others seem to do—what if I'm just lazy or making it up?

—Marlene from Germany

> The hardest thing about living with ADHD is having moments where knowing something needs to be done isn't always enough to keep my attention on a task. It's frustrating living in a society that responds to this with "You'll just have to put on your big boy pants and power through" as though I'm not doing that every day by default.

—Nitari Windrider

What are some of the most USEFUL SYSTEMS in your own lives? And can we BORROW them?

 Even on my worst days, I always use my pants hook (a hook I hang my pants on that requires no thought, no folding, and no decision-making) and place my toothbrush on the edge of the sink where I cannot miss it and thus usually won't skip using it.

I have a default type of socks and underwear (Hanes boxer briefs, bay-beee) because I hate thinking about socks and underwear. I have a type of socks that I like, a type of underwear that I like, and every once in a while I just get like forty of them and I'm set. I never have to find matching socks, and I don't have that one pair of underwear that makes me uncomfortable all day. They're all the same.

 I'm a big fan of **finder buttons. You can just tag stuff in your house like remotes, phones, keys. We use them ten times a day.**

It's like an AirTag, but instead of being hooked up to your phone, it's a physical box that's got corresponding buttons for each of the tags and you stick the tags on your remote, your phone, your keys, whatever you want. Among the best twenty dollars I ever spent.

 If you are able, buy a ton of phone chargers.

 I have one in every room and another prepacked for travel. No phone charger ever moves from any space that it isn't already in. And if you have a weird number of phone chargers, who cares? It's facilitating your life.

The ADHD Field Guide for Adults

PART 3:
Systems and Organization

Try putting one charger in every room, and then it never moves. Same goes for tape and scissors. You can get multipacks of scissors for relatively cheap. You can get twenty USB-C cables or ten toothbrushes or whatever it is you need to make sure you have the thing where and when you need it.

On the other side of the coin, since we know that systems are as individual as the people who use them, you may want to limit the amount of stuff you have rather than buying multiples.

I have thirty coffee mugs, and it causes an immense amount of stress, but I'm emotionally attached to them! If I had just two, then if my coffee mugs were dirty, I'd have to deal with it and they wouldn't pile up. You can also do that with clothes.

Something that I'm just starting to do is pulling a small amount of clothes. You wear those for a while, and then when you get bored of those clothes, you go to a bin in the basement or wherever and swap them out. Limiting your clothes to a week or a couple of weeks at a time means that you're not emptying your entire closet before you have to do laundry.

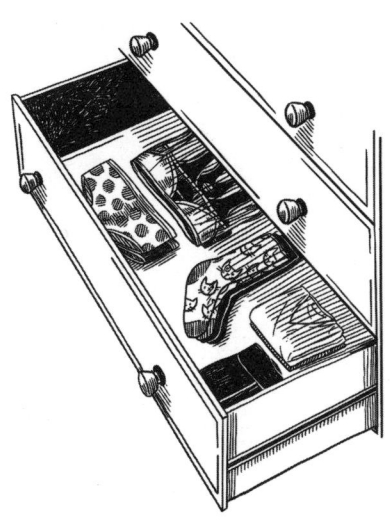

It increases novelty, so you're less likely to just buy a bunch of new clothes. It also helps with laundry scenarios: *Okay, I have twelve pairs of underwear. I know that on day ten I need to do the laundry.* So limitations can often sometimes be really useful, depending on your circumstance.

> **A lot of these systems** will be contradictory. You might think, *I can't buy in bulk and set limitations at the same time.* And that's okay. You *can* have ten phone chargers and just two pairs of shoes. **There are no laws. Do what you want. It's never silly if it makes your life easier.**

Other Systems We Use—and You Can Borrow

- **Keep a "Stuff I Always Lose" drawer in your kitchen.** Things like staplers, tape measures, an Allen wrench set, lint roller, fabric scissors, etc.

- **Keep an extra set of basic tools somewhere accessible** that's not in the main area in your house, **aka a "triage drawer."** Sometimes you just need a pair of pliers for like two seconds, and if you take the one from the shop, it's liable to get lost.

- **Get an accordion folder to store your important documents.** This one's particularly good for renters who may move around a lot. Label the frontmost compartment "to sort" and the rest "medical stuff," "car stuff," "insurance stuff," "taxes stuff," "receipts," and any other categories you might need. Be sure to leave at least a couple of sections blank for categories you may discover later.

- When you get a piece of paper you know is important and should be saved, pop it into a folder, and if you don't have the fucks to give to figure out what category it should go in, just put it in "to sort."

- **You can limit dishware to the number of people in the household, plus two.** If it's just you, you got one mug, plus another mug in case you have somebody over, plus another mug in case you shatter the first two. That's a great system if you struggle with dishes.

> When I first moved to my old apartment, I was living alone for a little while and using the limited dishware system (opposite), before my roommate showed up with a million dishes and it went all to shit. For a couple of glorious months, if I put every single dish I owned into my sink, it still wasn't enough to be overwhelming. That might not work for everybody and likely won't work for families. But for some people, it's a total game changer.
>
> **—ERIK**

- **You may also find it helpful to have "Museums" in your home for random stuff you want to keep but have no real use for.** For example, out of all the mugs you have, you probably have only one or two that you actually like to drink out of, but you still like the other ones 'cause they're cool. Like your mug that you got in New Orleans that you love but don't use for coffee. Mugs like those can go into a Museum—whether that's a shelf or a cabinet or any place you designate for this type of thing—rather than clutter the mugs you actually use.

- **Try to think of your stuff in two categories: the useful and the sentimental.** Useful things have tangible functions in your life, like the coffee mugs you actually use or a vacuum cleaner. Sentimental things don't actually serve a specific function; we just like having them around, like a broken gramophone. And if you have ADHD, you probably have a lot of those things.

- The Museum stores our sentimental items without tucking them away, because when those things start to get mixed with the functional things, it gets really frustrating really fast.

- **A helpful system for finding things you've lost around the house is to use a flashlight.** It hones the focus and makes the area look different, so it can get you out of that "I CAN'T FIND IT" rut. A flashlight physically changes how things look.

- **If you're prone to losing things, brightly colored duct tape and glow-in-the-dark duct tape are super useful.** People with ADHD gloss over things. We can stare directly at something that we're looking for and still not find it. Small, dark things, like a black phone-charging brick, can turn invisible at night. So anything that can help key items stand out visually, like neon-green duct tape, is great to keep around.

- **When you lose things, say the name of the thing you're looking for**—a study once showed that saying it out loud while looking increases your chances of finding the thing. If you're looking for your keys, you can gloss over them, but if you keep saying, "Keys . . . keys . . . keys . . . ," for some reason it puts your brain in the right mode to recognize the thing.

Cate's Final Thoughts

As I sit here, writing a chapter about systems, there are seven empty coffee cups on my desk. My laundry is unfolded, and there is a pile of boxes downstairs that have needed to be broken down for about three weeks. Writing a book is hard.

    I say this because what I'd like you to take away from this chapter is that systems can be slow going. Growth can be incremental. Putting a big "find it" button on my keys has helped immensely, but it doesn't negate the profound impact that ADHD (and depression, and anxiety, *and and and*) has on my life. I struggle with this stuff, constantly. Every day.

    I struggled with this chapter. Part of me felt like a hypocrite: *How can I write a section like this when my OWN systems don't work all that great? My house isn't perfect and I'm a big faking faker, acting like I know what I'm talking about.*

Then I realized that I **wanted to write a chapter like this not because I'm some expert with an immaculate, Pinterest-perfect house, but** *because I know what it's like to struggle.* **I know what it's like to be frustrated at yourself and your environment, to feel overwhelmed and frustrated and embarrassed and guilty. And I want to be here, with you, in those feelings, because I feel them, too. Every day.**

I ALSO know the absolute joy of building built-ins with a rolling library ladder like I've wanted since I was seven. I know the orgasmic satisfaction of knowing EXACTLY where that specific sewing tool is, EXACTLY when I need it. **There is joy to be found in systems. There is joy in accepting yourself.**

Learning how to create a system and how to support our neurodivergence is not a skill we're inherently born with, and for many people (myself included), it also wasn't something we were ever taught.

We were thrown into situations where we had to figure something out or ELSE. We were punished, we were embarrassed, we missed the deadline, or we lost the important thing and got mad, angry, or sad. *Unlearning* that and rebuilding from a place of love, support, kindness, and acceptance toward yourself—not shame, anger, frustration, or "if I just tried harder"—that's the goal.

What the system actually *looks like* isn't nearly as important.

Setting an Alarm to Pee

and Other Personal Hygiene Systems

Keeping up with personal hygiene is one of those things that we are never really taught in any substantive way. Maybe your mom showed you how to brush your teeth a couple times when you were little, but most of us don't go around having conversations with other adults about our strategies for consistently showering. It's just assumed that all grown-ups know how to integrate showering, shaving, and toothbrushing into their daily lives. Just like it's assumed that grown-ups can always tell when their body needs water, food, or to go to the bathroom.

For those of us who have ADHD and the executive dysfunction that comes with it, these monotonous personal care tasks can be very difficult to keep up with, and it can be even harder to ask for help with them.

For me, when I'm having a particularly bad time with my ADHD, my personal hygiene is the first thing to go. I stop showering and brushing my teeth. I wear dirty clothes from off the floor and am generally unkempt. This, in turn, makes my mental health worse, which makes it harder to get back into the swing of things.

It's good to have strategies for breaking this cycle—for getting your ass into the shower when your brain is really making things hard. So, let's talk about some! Remember: You're not alone, you're not a fuckup, and it's okay to talk about this stuff. Or at the very least, to read this chapter.

—Erik

❓ I often STRUGGLE to notice if I'm HUNGRY, THIRSTY, or need to go to the BATHROOM. Is that super weird?

No. Well, you might be weird, but not because of that. **We hear this all the time.**

Having ADHD means your brain is bad at assessing a stimulus to formulate and execute a plan. Having to pee or being thirsty is just another form of stimulus your brain sucks at noticing and doing anything about.

A good strategy to help with this is to set up visual triggers. Anytime you see a bathroom, pause, tune in to your body, and ask yourself if you have to go to the bathroom. If you see a sink or something that makes you think of water, ask yourself if you're thirsty.

Of course, the absolute best strategy for drinking water is to have water available to you at all times. Get a nice big container so cups don't pile up and you don't have to keep refilling.

However, once again, we come to a "why." WHY do you struggle with interpreting stimuli like thirst or hunger? For many people with ADHD and/or Autism (again, we remind you of the VAST overlap), struggles with interoception are part of the list of comorbidities that we deal with.

What is interoception?

Your perceptions of the internal states of your body, like hunger, thirst, needing to use the bathroom, and more.[1]

For me, I ALWAYS thought I was super weird because I struggled with regulating body temperature and moderating how much I ate. It wasn't until I learned about interoception and realized, *Oh yeah, I struggle with ALL these things!* Only then did I really start to unpack that I'm not weird or broken; part of getting through my day just means building structures that support my inability to recognize that I probably need to pee.

I STRUGGLE with remembering to do PERSONAL CARE tasks. And even if I do remember, I often get DISTRACTED and don't complete them. What should I do?

 I've always found personal care tasks uniquely difficult because they are so seemingly simple but also stealthily omnipresent.

→ **There are largely three goals here.**
- One, remembering to do the thing.
- Two, facilitating the starting of that task, which means having all the necessary things to do that task.
- And three, minimizing distractions, which may sidetrack you and derail the initial task.

You may have noticed that these are three things that people with ADHD are famously bad at doing. Cut yourself some slack!

 You can also have little personal care stations. I try to keep my meds by my coffeemaker, because in the morning, I go to my coffeemaker first thing to wake up for the day and I go, *Oh, medicine.* You can do that in any room with all sorts of different stuff, depending on what you're trying to remember.

 Say you REMEMBERED to shower and you've got the "let's go shower" energy going for you, but you don't have a towel within reach. Then, on your way to get the towel, you might remember an important email you have to send, so you do that first and then get completely derailed.

 You also have to look out for pitfalls, like how much you're going to hate washing and restocking towels, because that is simply a pain-in-the-ass task. But you can set up a system

The ADHD Field Guide for Adults

PART 3:
Systems and Organization

within your system here and make Sundays the day that you wash your towels, and then you'll know you have clean towels for the week. That hour you spend on Sunday washing and restocking those towels is going to set you up for the whole week. The more you do these boring prep tasks, the easier it gets.

As you practice any new strategy, you'll start to associate it more and more with the benefits of doing it and less with how unpleasant it feels to have to do it in the first place.

ADHDers will likely change the system even if the system is working, because at some point your brain needs novelty more than it needs a functioning system. Yes, this sucks, but it is a reality of life with ADHD. It can help to have little variations on your systems that still work just fine so you can inject some novelty without sacrificing functionality.

Periodically, you'll have to ask yourself: ***Do I change the system, or do I get better at the current system?***

How do I REMEMBER to BRUSH my TEETH?

Try leaving your toothbrush on the side of the sink so that you can't miss it when you're in the area. You see your toothbrush, you brush your teeth. Simple.

I have a magnet that sticks my toothbrush to my mirror, so visually I put it at eye level. Erik's way doesn't work for me. It stresses me out when his stupid toothbrush is over the edge of the sink, because *What if I knock it into the sink? Then it's gonna get dirty and gross.* And so I got my little magnet.

I also have a weirdly large number of toothbrushes. It's like changing your sheets. You know when you change your sheets and it feels really good? That to me is the same thing with toothbrushing, so sometimes, if it's like, *Oh, I don't want to brush my teeth*, then I'll get a new toothbrush. Novelty.

A friend of mine has ADHD and—I had never heard of this before in my life—she travels with a toothpaste buffet! She has all these different flavors like piña colada, strawberry, orange, mint, and vanilla. Every day she cycles through, so there's always a new flavor.

WEIRD ASIDE: People with ADHD have poor dental health compared to neurotypical folks, and science still doesn't know if it's a chicken-or-the-egg thing. Does our enamel suck, or do we just suck at taking care of our teeth properly? It's a real problem with real studies.[2]

We do know that shame-based practices do not work. And so there's a conversation with ADHDers that goes, "Every time I go to the dentist, I get yelled at because I don't floss." If you're caught in this cycle, advocate for yourself. Tell your dental health provider that you know you're not flossing or brushing your teeth enough, but you're doing your best and you don't want to talk about it. That may stave off a lecture.

Try to relish the benefits. After you brush your teeth, actively notice, *My teeth are clean. I had that weird taste in my mouth before, and now I don't. My teeth feel good, too.*

It may sound silly, but what you're ultimately doing is giving more weight to the good parts than the annoyance of having to perform the task. The point isn't to build personal systems—it's to get your teeth brushed and maintain your hygiene. And avoid painful dental procedures.

It helps me to remember that I can brush my teeth whenever I want. Did you know that? It does not HAVE to be in the morning!

Yup. I do not shower at a regular time, either. I always shower when the spirit moves me. Unless I'm on vacation, and then I always shower at the end of the day because it's convenient, and I feel gross at the end of a long day out. Speaking of showering . . .

The ADHD Field Guide for Adults

PART 3:
Systems and Organization

How do I REMEMBER to SHOWER?

 This one isn't quite as simple as remembering to brush your teeth or reminding yourself to pee. You're not going to take a shower every time you *see* a bathroom, the way you might try to do with peeing. To bridge the gap, **try putting a shampoo bottle in the doorway. Having an object in that transition space will help your brain go,** *Oh, that's right, I have to shower.*

You also want to keep ALL your shower accoutrements at the ready so when the mood strikes you to shower, there's less friction. If the linen closet is upstairs but you normally shower downstairs, that's enough friction that the shower might not even happen. Mise en place.

 As I mentioned, **I wait until the spirit moves me to shower. I love showering in the middle of the day, or even in the middle of the night.** I love showering in the dark . . . completely superior to showering in the light. I put on music, too.

Highly recommend lighting candles or adding a Bluetooth shower speaker—change your life.

 Having something to do in the shower can jog your memory to go take one, too. I sing in the shower. There are also a surprising number of waterproof instruments on the market!

 Yeah. I literally have a set list—a concert that I practice when I'm in the shower. Super helpful. I also started taping a piece of canvas to my shower wall, and I make little watercolor paintings in the shower. It's silly, but sometimes I get excited to paint, and then getting excited to paint means, *Okay, now I need to shower.*

What about MENSTRUAL HYGIENE? What about SHAVING?

 Changing your tampon—that's an uncomfortable one that we don't talk about a lot, but it's something people forget all the time. This is another great place for visual reminders. Where do you keep your tampons? I keep my tampons out and proud, I don't even have them in a box anymore. I keep them in a grab basket on the back of the toilet because then if I'm in the bathroom, it'll remind me to take mine out and put in a new one.

Tampons can get serious because you don't want to end up with toxic shock syndrome, so use whatever method is most effective for YOU here. Set an alarm (and actually label it TAMPON so you don't hit snooze or ignore it) or put a Post-it on your door so you don't leave without changing it.

 As for shaving . . .

 You don't HAVE to shave, it's your body, your choice.

 Sure. But if you are a person who likes to shave and you struggle to do it, either **get a really nice shaver that you enjoy using and won't lose or get two cheap ones so you have a backup when you inevitably lose or break the first one.** I can't tell you how many times I've grown a beard just because I didn't feel like spending an hour looking for my shaver.

To wrap up this chapter...

There are as many strategies for keeping up with personal care as there are people who need them. We are SO far from one-size-fits-all here.

As with every system or strategy for living with ADHD, what works for one person may not work for you. So, for starters, try out a couple of strategies mentioned in this chapter. Embrace what works for you and move on from what doesn't. Give strategies a chance even if they sound silly at first. And of course feel free to make up your own methods, too!

I encourage you to talk with other people about personal hygiene, to help break the stigma about struggling with it. It'll also serve to remind you that you are not the only one who has trouble with it.

Most importantly, you are not a failure or a fuckup for struggling with this stuff. I do, too. So do plenty of other people reading this book. You're not alone.

—**Erik**

> Embrace what works for you and move on from what doesn't. Give strategies a chance even if they sound silly at first.

10

So, You Need to Eat and Sleep, Huh?

I am exhausted. It is the middle of the school year, and I am in what actors call "hell week," the stressful period before a show opens in which rehearsals run late as technical difficulties and last-minute details are finalized for the performance. Last night, rehearsal ended at 12:30 a.m. because Romeo doesn't know his lines and Juliet got her period on her spotless white costume.

As I crawl into bed, despite my exhaustion, my mind will not slow down. It is 3:30 a.m. before I finally fall asleep. My alarm wakes me at 9:00, then 9:15, then 9:30. I open my eyes blearily and will myself—beg myself—to wake up, but everything feels like television static, my body aches, and I am so, so tired.

Despite the exhaustion that runs through me, I have perfected the art of getting up and being ready to go out the door in six minutes because being late gives me profound anxiety. I hate being late. I grab some clothes from the pile on the floor that I have been too overwhelmed to deal with and head to work, where I keep a never-ending mug of extra-strong coffee tucked behind the ice machine, topping it up every hour or so to get me through the day.

After my shift, I come home from a frustrating day of serving sandwiches and soup to a twenty-seven-top of demanding old ladies who make their orders particularly complex to feel "waited on." I smell like broccoli, and there is a light crusting of tomato bisque in my hair. I go straight to my computer without showering because I have a complicated paper on Shakespeare and textual culture due in a couple of days, and I have only a few hours before I need to leave for rehearsal.

I get home at 11 p.m.—a decent exit time for hell week. I finally shower and get into bed. It'll be another four hours before I fall asleep and a generous five hours after that before I am unexpectedly woken up by the sound of my mom's impossibly loud ringtone. I've always been a light sleeper, and like many nights that summer, I'd been pulled out of sleep every couple of hours as the slow rumbling freight trains passed the tracks near our house. My mother is on the phone making plans for some family event this weekend. She sticks her head in and puts her hand over the mouthpiece. "We need to be there at ten a.m. tomorrow; will that work?"

I groggily nod, trying not to be visibly upset—once I wake up, I have extreme difficulty falling back to sleep, and I've just lost the two hours I had before my carefully calculated alarm is set to go off. She turns back into the living room and continues with the conversation. "Catie says that's fine," she says with audible doubt in her voice. "We'll see if she wakes up on time. You know how she is."

I have never woken up ready to start the day. It doesn't matter if I get six or sixteen hours of sleep—waking up is extremely hard. I have never woken up refreshed and ready to go, and it wasn't until I was in my thirties that I learned some of the biggest issues and most common comorbidities with ADHD are sleep-related. I was judged constantly as a kid for wanting to sleep in. I have dozens of core memories of lying awake in my bed hours after bedtime, begging for God to help me fall asleep because I knew I had to be up at 7 a.m. for school. For years, I condemned myself. For years, I was deeply unkind to myself because I thought I was a failure for having a brain that needs a slow start and functions much better from 11 a.m. to 9 p.m. than from 7 a.m. to 6 p.m.

The thing that I want to stress, though, is that I DID get up. I am an ADHDer who is obsessively on time, usually compulsively early. I forced and fought against myself again and again for two decades to get to places when I needed to be because I had to be a responsible, professional adult. Sometimes we aren't in situations where we can make our own schedule. Sometimes our shift starts at 6 a.m., and it's show up or lose your job. The point is that you must internalize that you're not a fuckup if you struggle. You're not a bad person, and you're not lazy.

You *are*, however, 98 percent more likely to have sleep issues if you have ADHD. We'll cover sleep issues first, and then we'll move on to the eating part of the chapter, because feeding yourself is just as important as sleeping. Even though it might feel just as difficult.

—Cate

What's the LINK between ADHD and SLEEP problems?

While ADHD itself is not a sleep disorder, individuals with ADHD are more likely to have coexisting sleep disorders.[1] Conditions such as insomnia, sleep apnea, restless leg syndrome (RLS), and circadian rhythm disorders are more common among people with ADHD. The impact ADHD has on sleep could fill an entire book on its own, but some of the (again, not super commonly discussed) effects can be extremely difficult to navigate.

The relationship between ADHD and sleep difficulties is bidirectional, meaning that one can worsen the other. Poor sleep can exacerbate ADHD symptoms, while untreated ADHD can lead to sleep problems.

This is fun—did you know that **up to 75 PERCENT of people with ADHD have something called "delayed sleep phase syndrome"? People with DSPS usually take at least two hours longer to fall asleep when compared to individuals without DSPS.**

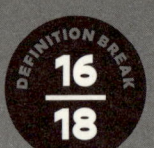

Delayed Sleep Phase Syndrome

Delayed sleep phase syndrome is a sleep disorder that affects a person's sleep-wake cycle, known as circadian rhythm. People with this sleep disorder have sleep patterns that are delayed two hours or more from usual sleep patterns. They go to sleep later and wake later. This makes it hard to wake in time for work or school.

GRIEVANCES GARGOYLE

If a neurotypical person thinks, *Oh, I'm getting a little bit sleepy*, they transition into going to bed and they close their eyes. Then it will take them, depending on the person, between five and fifteen minutes to fall asleep. For people with ADHD, *it can take up to three hours*. More on DSPS on page 241.

It's also really important to distinguish that **this is not a choice, no matter what people might say.** Physically and mentally, our bodies struggle with falling asleep. It's not that it's a party for us to be up until 4 a.m., and it's not that we're magical creatures of the night. Our natural sleep rhythm just looks different from other people's. (Which is why I will die on the hill that starting high school at 7:30 a.m. is inhumane.)[2]

More ADHD-related sleep issues...

- **Sleep Onset and Maintenance Problems:** Many children and adults with ADHD have difficulty falling asleep and staying asleep. Racing thoughts, restlessness, and the inability to "shut off" our brains can make it challenging to initiate sleep.

- **Sleep Disruptions:** People with ADHD may also experience frequent nighttime awakenings, leading to disrupted sleep patterns. These awakenings can be caused by factors like excessive movement, restlessness, or even periodic limb movements during sleep.

- **Daytime Sleepiness:** Are you usually tired when you wake up and tired during the day? Me, too. Daytime sleepiness can worsen attention and concentration problems during waking hours, making it even more challenging for people to manage their ADHD symptoms.
- **Medication Effects:** Some medications used to treat ADHD, particularly stimulant medications, can affect sleep patterns. They may cause difficulty falling asleep or staying asleep if taken too late in the day.
- **Sleep and Executive Function:** Sleep is wildly important for cognitive functioning, including executive functions such as attention, impulse control, and working memory. Poor sleep quality can impair these functions, making your ADHD symptoms more pronounced.

Do you have any TIPS for helping me FALL ASLEEP?

When it comes to sleep, I have plenty of suggestions, but the reality is that most of them are not much fun to institute. Tons of studies talk about the connection between ADHD and sleep, and best practices remain pretty straightforward across the board.

The first is practicing good sleep hygiene, which sounds like using a lot of hand sanitizer before you go to sleep, but it's actually physical and environmental factors that go into making sure you get a good night's sleep. Again, I know a lot of you reading this aren't going to want to hear it, but a regular sleep schedule that you stick to is one of the most important things you can do for yourself. Next up, like many things we've talked about in the book, is thinking through your needs and what helps you get to sleep. Some people need a white noise machine or background music, some people are very particular about lighting, some (like me) absolutely need a fan for moving air.

- Temperature and sleep are closely related. Part of the process of falling asleep involves your body temperature dropping slightly, and stimulant medication can make you run hot. Many sheets are microfiber or a polyester blend—those hold heat. I started sleeping my best when I shifted to linen sheets (so fancy) and a lightweight down comforter.

- Light is also an important factor in getting good sleep, as well as waking up. I much prefer an all-encompassing darkness like a cave, but I realized that my blackout curtains made it much harder to wake up with no natural light. If your bedroom is naturally dark, you might consider purchasing a sunrise alarm clock. I lived in a basement apartment for a year, and it ruined my sleep schedule. Getting an alarm that mimicked natural sunrise helped me reset. (You can also program smart bulbs to do this as a daily routine.)

- What you do before bed also matters, and I know you're gonna be mad, but doomscrolling through your phone immediately before trying to sleep goes against the physical and mental process of falling asleep. Wind down your night with yoga, tea, journaling, reading, or listening to an audiobook (yes, that might require your phone, but sleep timers are your friend). There are also lots of resources online for fall-asleep audios (including spicy ones).

- Speaking of, for some people, masturbation is an incredibly useful tool for falling asleep. We often treat masturbation like this self-indulgent, spicy thing, but it's a tool for self-regulation, and orgasm produces a ton of relaxing chemicals that can send you off to dreamland.

- As a last-ditch emergency button, introducing novelty can sometimes help if you're really struggling. Sleep the "wrong way," with your head at the foot of the bed, change your sheets, or get a relaxing aromatherapy machine. Sometimes our brains just need a smidgen of "newness" to get to the next step of falling asleep.

You will absolutely have to shift and change and adapt over time, which is why it's so important to start figuring out what really works for you and noticing if this changes during the year. One study referred to ADHD as a "24-hour disorder," and I think that is super important to keep in mind when we talk about sleep. What you do at 3 p.m. is going to impact what your mind and body are doing at 3 a.m. Take care of Right Now You, but also remember that Tonight You and Tomorrow You need to be taken care of, too.

 I use melatonin. Absolutely amazing. Going to bed can be pretty scary for people with ADHD because it generally involves some pretty high-octane boredom.

No matter which way you slice it, in order to go to sleep, you have to put down your phone, turn off the lights, and be bored until sleep happens. **Boredom can be painful for ADHDers. Having something to soften that moment is really helpful.**

How do you do that? You can try what Cate and I call screensaver thoughts. They soften the rough transition of waking to sleeping and give you that little bit of dopamine behind your eyelids.

Screensaver Thoughts . . .

- You have to rob a bank; how are you going to do it?
- If you could become invisible, what would you do?
- If you could make objects levitate, what would you do?
- If you could mind-control anyone, but you have to give them a high five in order to do it, how would you use this power to take over the world?
- What if you could fly, but only when wearing red?

 A lot of people with ADHD are more activated in the evening. There's a joke about people with ADHD not being morning people . . . That's not a stereotype. It's brain chemistry. If you work at an office job, it may be worth exploring

schedule adaptations with your boss. Getting to the office at 11 a.m. or noon and staying until 8 or 9 p.m. can be a better schedule for people with ADHD.

I know people with ADHD who have gone to their boss and explained that starting later and ending later is the best way for them to be the most productive employee they can be. And depending on the job and the circumstances, people have had success with that, and then they don't have to worry about waking up at 8 a.m. Not everyone will have the agency to design their life. If you do, take advantage. (More on this in the "Work, Work, Work" chapter on page 289.)

Your stress, anxiety, working to quiet your brain, and getting your body temperature regulated to the point of being able to fall asleep ... all that takes longer with ADHD. So even if you get into bed by midnight, you're not going to be asleep until 2 or 3 a.m. Then it's *Okay, well, if it takes me three hours to fall asleep, should I go to bed at 9 p.m.?* And so you constantly have to juggle that.

This has been an issue for my whole life. My entire childhood, I didn't get sleepy until 2 or 3 a.m. Consistently, ADHD sleep cycles are shifted forward from what is considered a normal circadian rhythm.

And it's wildly annoying.

What is REVENGE BEDTIME PROCRASTINATION?

RBP is the belief that you didn't have agency with your time during the day, because you were working or taking care of the kids or whatever, so when you finish at the end of the day and the kids are asleep and you're off work, you stay up super late in an effort to reclaim your time.

We also live in a culture of toxic productivity.

It's the valorization of pain and struggling. A lot of us think that if we're miserable all day and white-knuckling our way through a job that we hate, then we're doing it right. That leads to the "revenge bedtime procrastination" because you feel like your time is being taken away from you.

YOUR TURN: People with ADHD notoriously struggle with sleep. Do you have any personal tips on falling asleep or maintaining a (relatively) healthy sleep schedule/environment?

> Routine, routine, routine, and I make sure to get plenty of exercise during the day. Only use bedroom for sleeping, not hanging out / watching TV, etc., so you know it is sleep time when in there! No phone usage in bed.
>
> —H.F.

> I might be atypical for people with ADHD regarding sleep. I NEVER stop moving, so if I sit for more than thirty minutes (sometimes as little as five), I fall asleep. I fall asleep in the doctor's office, at the computer at night, etc. I have a very difficult time "winding down" at night and allowing myself to actually climb into bed, but once I do, I am usually out cold within minutes. I sleep like the dead for three hours, then my brain turns back on. The good news for me is that 2 a.m. is when I sometimes have my best thoughts: things I need to buy, problem-solving, etc. I solve a problem, then I can go back to sleep.
>
> —Laura from Maryland

> When I lie down and my head is like a hamster wheel of fleeting thoughts, I have to tell myself to stop. I take a few deep breaths, and I only allow myself to think of the great moments of my day/week/etc., not the insanity of what I didn't get done or need to do.

—Nicole Moran

> One thing I've noticed is that I crave novelty, even in my sleep environment. I'm always thinking, *I've finally found the one thing that fixes sleep! I'm going to be good at sleeping for the rest of my life!* And then a few weeks later, I'm accustomed to the item or the routine and I'm back to my shoddy sleeping ways. Little things that help: doing seasonal blanket/sheets, rather than an all-weather comforter, so every few months I have something new. Also, spending the money on a truly excellent pillow. Recently, I have noticed that my easiest mornings are the ones when I slept in pajamas more similar to day clothes (think: athleisure). It's easier to start my day when I am wearing clothes that allow me to start my day without being 100 percent aware that I have, in fact, started my day. If I'm wearing leggings and a T-shirt, I can answer the door, walk the dogs—just following my impulses as they emerge. It's kind of like the CEOs who wear the same thing every day to avoid decision fatigue. If jammies are just regular clothes, that's one less demand on your executive function.

—Karen Usher from Michigan

> I think for a lot of people with ADHD like me, endless scrolling on the apps ("doomscrolling," if you will) is very addicting. I have found that forcing myself not to look at my phone once I climb into bed helps me sleep better. I have also found I sleep better when I haven't had any alcohol before bed . . . makes a world of difference.

—Lindsay from Pennsylvania

How do I deal with **SLEEP-RELATED FATIGUE**?

 **First off, I'm a huge advocate of naps.** They don't have to be traditional, get-into-bed-and-fall-asleep types of naps. **You can rest during the day without actually sleeping.** I like to think of my brain as having two states. One is "up," the other is "down." When I am the type of tired that coffee just won't help, I close my eyes and try to get my brain into this "down" state for a couple of minutes.

 Erik, WTF are you talking about?

 Check it out, this is actually activating your parasympathetic nervous system: Take a deep breath in. Do you feel your brain sort of "turning on," like an engine starting up? Now exhale. As you exhale the last of the breath, do you feel your brain slowing down, almost like it's melting or deflating? That's the feeling we're going for.

Breathe normally, but every time you exhale, lean into that brain-melty feeling a bit more. Relax the muscles in your face and your ears and look at the weird blobs that you see when you close your eyes (called phosphenes). I like to imagine warm honey being poured over my brain. Think of it as lowering the frequency of your brain.

Even at work, you can just sit back in your chair for a few minutes and lower the frequency. **No matter how long you're resting or napping for, always set an alarm for the time that you want to stop. Even if it's for two minutes.** Because one way to make it really hard to lower your brain activity is to have to be thinking about the time. *Has it been five minutes? Is it one o'clock yet?*

It's a bit strange to get the hang of, but those little micro naps have saved me more times than I can count, and it's also a great technique for falling asleep at night.

One of the hardest things about managing ADHD is accepting that your brain works more effectively on a schedule that doesn't look like everybody else's. If you feel exhausted every single day when you're going to bed at midnight, maybe you need to go to bed at ten. Maybe you need to go to bed at nine. You may hate removing yourself from the world that early, but it may be worth it not to feel miserable and tired every day.

When I am exhausted, I think about what I've been eating. Sometimes I've had nothing but carbs for three days straight, and I know I'll feel better if I have some protein, some fat. What you eat can have repercussions for your energy level.

And drink water. I think "drink water" should be the default response to everything. Do you feel angry? You should drink some water. Tired? Drink some water.

 Whether you actually need to or not, you should probably still drink water, especially if you struggle to interpret your body's signals. My big issue is that I confuse thirst with hunger. A lot of times when we feel crappy, ADHD or not, it's because we're dehydrated. Whenever you feel bad—physically, emotionally, or mentally—drink some water just in case it's from dehydration.

 The right drinking vessel goes a long way if you're trying to be better about your water intake, too. I like a really big cup or bottle so I'm not refilling it ninety-seven times. I'm not going to do that. I won't drink water if I have to interrupt my day over and over to get more.

And you can jazz up your water with those little flavoring packets or just by adding a bunch of ice.

 On a related note, for waking up, try keeping your meds next to your bed. If I don't take my ADHD meds and my depression meds, then my brain doesn't work properly. And if my brain doesn't work properly, then I don't want to get out of bed.

Keep anything else that you might need to wake up right by the bed. I used to keep iced coffee next to my bed for a little while, just a small amount. Makes it that much easier to get up and get moving.

And now, the chunk of this chapter that's devoted to eating . . .

 ## How do I go SHOPPING?

 Before you leave for the store, **take a peek inside your fridge, pantry, and anywhere else you keep food to help avoid buying duplicates**. If you're shopping for a specific recipe, always go through the ingredients list and mark the things you already have.

Once you get to the store: Routes, baby! **Plan a route inside the store and take it every time (see illustration, page 252). Grocery stores are designed to overwhelm you so that you buy more stuff.** Plenty of non-ADHD people get overwhelmed at grocery stores—they're terrifying places. So first off, it's not weird that it overwhelms or bores you to death.

I highly recommend walking around the perimeter of the grocery store, dipping into aisles as you need to, and always coming out the same side of the aisle as you entered.

No matter how much or how little I need, I still go on this route. It's one less decision I have to make.

Grocery lists are helpful for many people because a list always helps simplify something that's overwhelming. Go into only the aisles you need and try to get an understanding of the general, default amount you spend.

Keeping a general amount of what you spend in mind can help you not overspend without having to rigorously set a budget.

 For some people, it's necessary to meticulously plan every dollar they spend. We are very privileged in that we can just go to the grocery store and put what we want into our cart.

I did not grow up like that. My mom would mentally round up to the nearest dollar in the grocery store to make sure that she had enough money, and sometimes we had to put stuff back.

Your individual economic circumstances will have a lot to do with how you shop. Curbing your overspending because you're impulse-buying cool new snacks is very different from trying to follow a strict budget because you have only $100 to stretch for a family of four.

How do I ORGANIZE my FRIDGE and my KITCHEN?

I'm just gonna lightning-round a few things here:

- **Keep backstock separate from items that are actively in use!** If you get a three-pack of dish soap, keep one by the sink and the unopened ones somewhere else nearby.

- **Use first!** Try to have only **one** of any given thing open at a time. One milk, one box of Golden Grahams, one jar of peanut butter. This will make it much easier to determine how much you have of each, so you don't run out abruptly or overbuy.

- **First In, First Out!** Make sure the *oldest* of a thing is the one that is opened and getting used (unless it's spoiled, of course) so you keep running through your stock. Otherwise, you run the risk of stuff sitting around and going bad.

- **If you rarely use it, tuck it away!** If you use an appliance less than twice a month, it shouldn't live on your countertop.

- **Get deli containers! Get rid of your Tupperware!** Deli containers are plastic food storage containers used by every kitchen from Denny's to Chez Panisse. They stack perfectly, are dishwasher and microwave safe (generally—you should still check), and most importantly, **ALL HAVE THE SAME LID**. Get a bunch of them in assorted sizes. You're welcome.

- **Get a container that can sit right on your countertop and put your high-use tools inside it.** Set the container to the right of your stove if you're right-handed, and to the left if you're left-handed. A bain-marie, a jar, anything. Don't put these items into drawers where you could forget that they exist. This is how you end up with five spatulas.

CHAPTER 10:
So, You Need to Eat and Sleep, Huh?

- **Anytime you can arrange things vertically and visually is a win. If you see it, you won't forget it exists.** Pegboards are not just for Grandpa's workshop.
- **If it's perishable, it's visible!** The shorter the shelf life of an ingredient, the more visible and accessible it should be.

One of my favorite tips (from the wonderful KC Davis) is to try **putting your perishables into the refrigerator doors**. Here's why:

People often put their condiments in their refrigerator doors—ketchup, mustard, salad dressing, etc. And then all the fresh produce and perishables go into the drawers. But for people with ADHD, if we're not looking at it, *we forget it exists*. This is called **object permanence**, and it's an issue that shows up with the ADHD brain.

How do I COOK for MYSELF?

The hardest part about cooking for yourself is thinking of yourself as someone worth cooking for.
> **YOU ARE.**

It's also easy to think, *Oh, I'm not a chef* and microwave another dinner for yourself. But you do not have to be a chef to understand some basic cooking principles and build on them. Cooking can feel more like a fun project rather than a chore.

> **The hardest part about cooking for yourself is thinking of yourself as someone worth cooking for.**

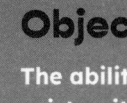

Object Permanence

The ability to know an object exists without seeing it.

In the kitchen example, if you can't see it to remember to use it, all the perishable food just rots inside the drawers.

Instead, **try putting your meats, cheeses, fruits, and vegetables into the refrigerator door shelves. This way, you look at them immediately when you open the fridge. Then move your condiments to the drawers.**

Erik used to work in kitchens, so one of the biggest game changers for us as a household was to start running our regular-person kitchen like a professional kitchen.

That looked like getting rid of a lot of the "extra" stuff that we had, like random duplicates of utensils and crusty old pots and pans from when I was in college. We really had to consider what we actually use, and when and how often.

For example, I'd been keeping my coffee mugs in a cabinet that's really far from the coffeemaker. It wasn't necessarily hurting anything, but in evaluating how I go about my day, I realized that it makes a LOT more sense to keep the coffee mugs above the coffeemaker.

Similarly, in thinking through how we cook and use our pots and pans, we started keeping some stuff readily accessible using pegboards or by stacking it in easy-to-grab locations. Julia Child had it all figured out. **Her entire kitchen was a pegboard, and she hung everything up so she could see it.**

As in many other places in this book, we have options that may or may not work for you. The best piece of advice I have is to really be mindful and think through how YOU do things.

Think through the "journey" your dinner plate takes from shelf to table, to the sink or dishwasher, and back again to the shelf. Is there a way you can streamline? Is there a way that you can make it easier to store, clean, and put it away? Maybe not, but once I started thinking about things like the best drawer for the knives or the best place for the paper towels, it really opened my eyes to how INEFFICIENT a lot of my kitchen systems were.

I'd just sort of set stuff there when we moved in and leave it there, rather than intentionally and specifically choosing to place stuff where it best worked for ME. Don't make this mistake!

What's it like dealing with family obligations—like feeding a family—with ADHD?

> Find your strategy early. For me, it's timers and calendar reminders. I use timers for everything. Get out chicken. Timer. Get out chicken. Timer. If you don't get out chicken, we won't eat. Timer. Start chicken. Timer. If you don't start the chicken, we will not eat dinner. Timer. Order pizza. Timer.

—@IconicTJB

> I never feel like I'm succeeding everywhere. If I'm killing it at work, dinner isn't getting made. If my kids are getting all my attention, my work is suffering (probably in ways that only I am noticing, but BOY am I noticing!!).

—Amanda from Texas

> Juggling ADHD became even more challenging as a parent because while I was breastfeeding, I couldn't take my medication. So now I was not only responsible for regular care tasks and adult responsibilities, I also had to care for another human while also trying to manage the overstimulation of parenting mentally and physically.

—Ashley Barajas

How should I **STOCK** my **KITCHEN**?

 Stock up on your shelf-stable staples. Get a ton of butter, because you always want to have it around. It'll take forever before it goes bad, you can freeze it, and buying in bulk will save you money because we all know groceries are ridiculously expensive right now.

 Costco! Buying in bulk can be really good for people with ADHD or neurodivergent people in general who tend to want the same thing a lot.

 PRO TIP: Most olive oil is the same level of mediocre. I always buy the huge, cheap bottle. Then you can siphon the oil into a smaller bottle at home so it's easier to use. Don't buy the smaller bottles. You can accidentally spend a ton of money that way.

Keep meal-makers around to get through leftovers. Anything that turns a pile of edible components into a cohesive *thing* I call a meal-maker. Got a pile of meat and rice? Add a tortilla, you got yourself a burrito. Got a bunch of random shredded cheese and sausage? Add pasta, you've got sausage mac 'n' cheese. One single egg and one single slice of American cheese? Add bread, and boom: egg sandwich. Meal-makers include, but are not limited to, sandwich bread, buns, tortillas, taco shells, pasta, and rice.

If you're into cooking for yourself, consider investing in a dehydrator. Dehydrators turn trash into something usable. Let's say you get a really good deal on steaks, but you're not gonna eat twelve steaks before they all go bad. Take half of them, cut them up into little strips, and put them into the dehydrator until they've lost most of the moisture. Kaboom, you're making your own jerky. It's fun to do with the kids, it's fun to do with the spouse, and you're preserving food the way that we've been doing it throughout history.

Or let's say you bought some fresh thyme at the store, used a little for a recipe, and now you've got a whole lot left. Dehydrator, and boom: you got dry thyme that'll last a billion years. You've got a bunch of onions going bad in the fridge and you don't know what to do? Cut them up, dehydrator, and boom: dehydrated onions.

With any cooking technique, it becomes a game once you start to see how the pieces fit together. It becomes less of a chore and more of a fun way to engage with the world. Kids love this stuff, too, and it affords you those valuable little dopamine pit stops.

Air fryers, too. Get an air fryer.

 An air fryer will change your life.

 On a less culinary note, your job with eating is to keep yourself alive, full stop. So if you survive on pizza rolls for a year, that's fine. You didn't die! Great. These tips are all for when you've got the brain space and the energy to dabble in cooking for yourself. **Gauge how much energy you have and budget how many fucks you have to give.**

On some level, all food is created equal. No matter how fancy you get. One of my old chefs, whenever he would see a cook get really stressed out about something, would say, "Remember: no matter what we make here, it all turns to shit."

 I have one thing to add when we talk about food, especially given the predisposition that people with ADHD have to eating disorders. **There's no such thing as good food or bad food. Food is fuel, and you can have really efficient fuel or you can have pizza rolls, but all food is still fuel.**

There can be this idea that you're immature or a bad person if you are picky. We don't know everybody's circumstances, sensory issues, or trauma that they hold around food.

Do what works for you.

 It's sort of a "keep your eye on the ball" thing. Remember, the point is to live a life that you enjoy. The point is to not be exactly the right weight. If your eating habits are causing you not to be able to live a life you enjoy, that's a different story. But **it's okay if you have the same food every day.**

If you're making something for dinner that can be frozen, make three servings, eat one of them, and freeze the other two. You're already making a mess in the kitchen, so do something nice for Future You by freezing additional portions. You're gonna thank me.

You can even cook pasta ahead of time. Just boil it like normal, then after you strain it, toss it in oil—more than you think you need—so it doesn't stick together. When it's done, pop it into Ziploc bags or deli containers, and it should keep for a few days. Then when you're making your mac 'n' cheese, you don't have to boil your water and look for your colander and *AGGGHH!*

So, if you have the energy on one random Tuesday afternoon, make a bunch of macaroni, and boom: macaroni for the week. **A lot of cooking with ADHD is in moments when you have the executive functions. Get it done then so that when you don't, you have options.**

 **What is a "weird thing" in your home that you love and works super well for your ADHD?**

> I joke about my bad object permanence, but it always means I get excited when I see Past Me made a cup of tea or a nice bowl of food. —**Bread from Colorado**

> I don't know if it's weird per se, but smart home devices. I automate the lights, the blinds, notifications for household upkeep, stuff like that. And I'm working on getting more. Especially the washing machine—I need it to tell me that the clothes are done washing and not stop until I go put them into the dryer. —**Leah from Chicago**

> I have a "trash can" next to the couch and in the kitchen. The one by the couch is for my socks when I'm sitting on the couch and I want to take them off . . . Instead of throwing them across the room, I put them into my trash can. And in the kitchen, instead of going across the house to put away the dirty hand towels, we put them in the li'l trash can there. Every week or so we empty the trash cans out into the dirty clothes. —**@foreverdre47**

> The "leave the house bowl." I have a bowl by the front door that always has my wallet and keys. On the floor by the bowl are my shoes. When it's time to leave the house, everything I need is right there, ready to go. The bowl is my single greatest weapon to being trapped at home all the time. I love the bowl. —**Connor Lynch**

> I feel like this is becoming more common for ADHDers, but I don't have doors on my wardrobes. If I could take the doors off my pantry, I would probably do that as well. —**@siarlas**

Is it okay to **THROW AWAY FOOD**?

Yes. It is a privilege to be able to do this, but keeping food in your refrigerator because you're trying not to be wasteful can ultimately create more waste and more mess. Frankly, it can be dangerous, because eating spoiled food could make you very sick.

I never bring home leftovers anymore. It used to be something that I carried a lot of guilt and shame about, but it made my life better. I know I'm not gonna eat it. I know it's just gonna mold in my refrigerator. So I figured out a system that works for me.

A lot of this conversation has to do with that societal shaming: *How dare you waste food or throw away plastic containers?!* Corporations are literally dumping tons and tons of plastic. Food is being wasted at an astronomical level. Do you want to contribute to that? Of course not, and you should do your best with your own personal responsibility.

Throwing away food feels terrible. Nobody likes doing that. But it's okay. I don't want to get all capitalist about it, but roughly one-third of all food that gets produced in America gets wasted for the dumbest reasons.[3]

If you're throwing away food for reasons other than it's going bad, the answer may be to clean out your fridge on a reasonably regular basis. Then try to figure out: Where's the waste coming from? It may well be a storage situation.

CHAPTER 10:
So, You Need to Eat and Sleep, Huh?

CHEF ERIK'S FAVORITE
Meals to Make

Cacio e Pepe

SERVES 3–4

Spaghetti
Black pepper
Unsalted butter
Grated Parmesan cheese
That's it. Really.

1. Melt a hunk of butter (about half a stick) in a large sauté pan, then turn off the heat. Do not brown.
2. Cook 4 portions of spaghetti.
3. Drain the spaghetti, reserving about a cup of pasta water, and immediately add the pasta to the melted butter.
4. Toss the spaghetti aggressively on low heat until a milky sauce starts to form. If a sauce does not form, add pasta water a teaspoon at a time.
5. Gradually sprinkle in the Parmesan cheese, preferably while tossing, until the sauce has reached desired cheesiness (note that adding cheese also adds salt!).
6. Gradually mix in coarsely ground black pepper, stopping when it's as peppery as you want it to be.
7. Give yourself a high five.
8. Plate and serve!

Tips/Shortcuts

- Taste frequently! This dish can get real salty, real fast.
- If it consistently comes out too salty, under-salt your pasta water.
- DO NOT add cheese before the butter sauce starts to form. The cheese needs an existing emulsion to incorporate into, otherwise it will end up as big lumps of melted cheese. (As a cook, I was never allowed to admit this, but honestly I like it that way, too. I mean, when are "big lumps of melted cheese" ever a bad thing?)

Pasta alla Carbonara

SERVES 3–4

Thick-cut bacon
Half a red onion
Spaghetti
2 egg yolks
Grated Parmesan cheese
Salt and pepper to taste

1. Dice the onion and ½ cup bacon (roughly ¼ inch pieces).
2. Add diced onion and diced bacon to sauté pan and cook on low until onions are completely soft (roughly 30 minutes). Turn off heat and allow it to cool.
3. Cook 4 portions of spaghetti (roughly one box).
4. Drain spaghetti, reserving about a cup of pasta water, and immediately add to the onion and bacon mixture, keeping the heat off.
5. Add 2 egg yolks and toss aggressively, gradually adding pasta water if the sauce is too tight/doesn't want to form. Once egg yolks are incorporated, toss in grated Parmesan until desired cheesiness is acquired (note that more cheese also means more salt!).
6. Plate, garnish with black pepper, and serve.

Tips/Shortcuts

- You don't have to use spaghetti. Use whatever pasta you want.

- In step two, you don't HAVE to cook the onions and bacon on low heat until the onions are completely soft. That's just how the pros do it. You can totally blast them on high heat until you feel they're done.

- Everything up through step two can be done ahead of time. You can just make a huge batch of the cooked onion and bacon mixture (aka sofrito) and freeze it for a rainy day. It's a great flavor enhancer for all sorts of stuff. Try adding some to your scrambled eggs sometime.

- While you wait for your pasta to cook, you can mix in the egg yolks with the sofrito, allowing you to skip step five, but ONLY IF YOUR SOFRITO IS NOT STILL HOT. If you accidentally cook the egg yolks, they will no longer work as an emulsifier. Warm is okay. Hot is a big no-no.

- Just a fun fact: Pasta alla carbonara is a relatively new Italian pasta dish. It is speculated that it was invented in Rome during the Second World War, since American GIs brought in a steady supply of eggs and bacon.

Is it okay to RELY on CONVENIENCE foods?

 Of course it's okay. It's your body and you're allowed to feed yourself whatever you want. You may want to take some sort of everyday multivitamin so you don't get scurvy, though.

 People love to use this as a point of attack on the Internet. "You don't make yourself a salad every day? You don't love your body."

A lot of the conversation is often framed around this idea of what you're *supposed* to do. But all that gets taken off the table when you consider that you have a disability. My ADHD makes it difficult to feed myself. It makes it hard to know when I'm hungry. It makes it hard to know what I want. It makes it hard to plan meals.

Instead of feeling guilty, reframe the conversation: You know what? **Today I ate peanut butter crackers and an ice cream bar, and I'm proud of myself because at least I remembered to do that.**

 ## Is it okay to use PAPER PLATES and PLASTIC cutlery?

 See mini rant above. YES. If you have the executive function and the patience to use silverware in your home, great. Do that. If you can't, it's okay. Maybe try to get the biodegradable kind so you're still being nice to sea turtles.

To close this chapter,

let's check in on the often tricky subject of sleep. Ask yourself the following questions and reflect on your answers . . .

- What is your relationship to sleep?
- How do you plan your mornings?
- What steps/tasks do you do for yourself to set yourself up for success?
- What is your ideal daily schedule? Can you adapt your current schedule to look more like the ideal one?
- Have you ever been called lazy? How does that impact you today?

The pursuit of "good sleep" is challenging. So, too, is "eating well." Like many ADHDers, some of this challenge is chemical, some of it is just simply part of the struggle of living with ADHD. Something that surprised me when writing this book was how attitudes on both—sleep and eating—can affect our ability to do either effectively. Only very recently did I realize that one of the reasons I hated going to bed so much was because I felt like I was "giving up."

One of the reasons I hate planning meals is because of the massive task load involved on the back end. Why would I cook a fancy meal when I know there are going to be a bunch of dishes afterward? Once I started filling in the implied blanks of what I was saying, it got a lot easier to understand why I'd been struggling and what I could do to change it.

—**Cate**

why Folding Socks Is Overrated,

aka the Household and Organization Chapter

AN OPENING RANT ABOUT SOCKS.

Fuck folding socks. Whoever invented socks made these tiny things that you're *supposed* to wear, and they're terrible anyway because your feet are hot and your toes are smashed and there's literally no wiggle room.

And then there's the expectation that your stupid socks MATCH. They come in pairs but then the mates disappear and they get separated in the laundry but somehow it's YOUR fault and your responsibility to rematch them.

THE EXPECTATION THAT WE MATCH OUR SOCKS IS A TOOL OF THE OPPRESSOR.

Fuck socks. Fuck folding socks. Fuck matching socks. That is all.

Well . . . not quite. One more thing . . .

In all seriousness, matching socks is an excellent microcosm of a LOT of the stuff that we can get hung up on with ADHD. It's not about the socks, per se, but about how we think about tasks.

There is a big difference between a mindset of "I HAVE to wear matching socks because that's NORMAL and APPROPRIATE and if I don't I'll be SHUNNED for being WEIRD" and "I keep my unmatched socks in a large bin and pull whatever two off the top every morning because I don't actually care about the socks I wear, people can't really see them anyway, and it makes doing laundry a lot faster and simpler."

Sometimes when we're talking about building systems, it can be really helpful to examine your attitude toward the thing. Do you actually NEED to do the thing at all? Or, somewhere along the line, did you internalize the idea that "NORMAL people do it THIS way," and now you're trying to constantly force yourself to be a "normal" person doing it in a way that doesn't work for YOU?

—Cate and Erik

 How do I ORGANIZE my house or apartment?

 Nobody is born knowing how to organize, manage finances, sweep the floor, or color-code the closet. So it's OKAY if you never learned or nobody ever taught you, or the way you figured out for yourself is actually not a super-functional way of doing things most of the time. If you're alive, you can learn new skills and develop new habits. In many cases, "disorganization" is code for "I never learned how to organize."

You're not a fuckup, you just never learned what you need. Now you get to do that.

Additionally, let's talk about the WHY. For a LOT of ADHD folks, disorganization, losing your keys, and struggling to finish tasks all come down to executive function. In particular, working memory and task initiation.

Our brains are wired to focus on the single most important task, and shifting from that task to something different activates a specific

The ADHD Field Guide For Adults

PART 3:
Systems and Organization

set of processes in our brains. Imagine walking in the door and immediately putting your keys on the special key hook—your attention was on the keys, and the process was not interrupted.

Now imagine that you walk in the door with every intention of hanging up your keys, but immediately your phone rings, the dog starts celebrating your return, and your partner tells you that you got a package. Will you remember to hang up your keys? Maybe. Or maybe you'll set them down in any number of places while your attention shifts from phone to dog to partner to package.

Again, it's not that you FAILED, you're inherently incapable of putting your keys on a hook, or you're doomed to a life of keyless hooks. It's that your task sequencing and working memory aren't built for those quick shifts, so you have to do things manually and with intentionality.

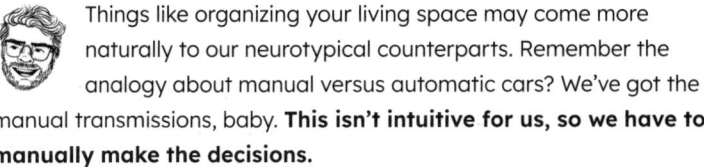

Things like organizing your living space may come more naturally to our neurotypical counterparts. Remember the analogy about manual versus automatic cars? We've got the manual transmissions, baby. **This isn't intuitive for us, so we have to manually make the decisions.**

- **When it comes to storing stuff, I recommend having a working storage and then a back-of-house, or backstock, storage. Your working storage is the stuff that you're frequently accessing and using all the time.** Stuff like plates and Windex and paper towels and dryer sheets.

- **Whatever you personally use on a regular basis—the stuff that is actively being used—should be stored as close as possible to *where* it gets used.** This inherently helps you remember where everything is. *Where's the laundry detergent? It's right next to the washing machine.*

- Don't store things too deep. If you have deep shelves or cabinets and you store layers of stuff, you are more likely to forget about the thing that's in the back. So try to always work side to side and THEN toward the back, only if you need to.

- **Now for your backstock storage. Find places for the stuff you rarely access that's totally out of the way. We're talking basement... garage... weird apartment storage cabinets that you need a stepladder to reach. This is where you can put the bulk paper towels from Costco since there's no more room in the kitchen.** Say you find a really good deal on Ziploc bags—put them in backstock storage. If you don't, that's where things start to get cluttered. You can also use your backstock storage for holiday decorations or other stuff that you take out only once a year.

 One thing that I have been learning is that you actively have to think about how you use stuff. It's really easy to go on Instagram and be like, *I'm gonna sort my pantry into a rainbow because it looks so pretty when I open the door!*

Be realistic about what is or is not functional for you. (No shade to The Home Edit—your work looks adorable.) **Think about how YOU like to get stuff and to use stuff. Do you like bins? Do you like baskets? Do you like boxes? If a magic organizational fairy came down, what would the ideal system look like? This answer is incredibly valuable information because now you can figure out how to organize your space.**

It also helps—silly as this may sound—to really slow down and think intentionally about where your things should go. Even if we're talking only about plastic wrap. *Okay, when dealing with leftovers, I go to the fridge, I take the thing out. Where would it make sense for that plastic wrap to go?*

And it's okay if it's a weird answer. I like to have things be grabbable, so I'll put it in a magnetic bin on the side of the refrigerator. **You don't have to use or store things the way you're "supposed" to.**

Adam Savage says to store things in the first place you'd think to look for them.* So if you get a new thing, a tool, or a wacky waving inflatable flailing tube man, imagine if you already had that thing—what would be the easiest place to find it? **Your first instinct is almost always correct. Don't overthink it.**

Whenever you're going through an organizational process of any kind, there will always be a bunch of stuff without homes. You think, *I'll address it later*, and then you get completely stuck because you're preoccupied with where to put these things that have no place to live. The best thing you can do here is address it NOW. If it's at all possible to find a logical spot, don't delay. **If you're truly stuck and find yourself asking too many questions about where a thing should go, create a "holding area" in a designated container to hold things that still need a home.** Then you can handle the more mindless stuff first, and anything that makes you go, *Fuck, where should this live?* goes in the holding area to be dealt with later.

For many neurodivergent people, there's this idea that there's a right way to do laundry or there's a right way to store your groceries or organize your space. BUT THIS IS A LIE. There is only what works for YOU and your circumstances and your household. If you need to keep your nail files on the coffee table because that's where you think about doing your nails, great. Just because you've never seen anybody else do it that way doesn't mean that it's wrong.

And if you live with other people and your placements don't work for them, that is a separate conversation. Hopefully you can explain to the person you live with that it's important to you to have X in Y location, and they'll understand that and support you. If not, there may be something else at play in the relationship.

---

* He may not have been the first to say it, but this is where I heard it first.

What is your number one tip, trick, or suggestion for someone who struggles with organization?

> Find the right partner for "body doubling." If someone is with you and is engaging you in conversation (or listening to you chatter)—especially if they are likewise occupied with something—instead of needing to sit still for the conversation, you can move and tidy all around the room while you talk. It works best for me if the person is in the room with me, but I've also had success with being on the phone with someone while they're cleaning at the same time.

—BE Bewley

> Sort things into different piles. Things may be a bit messy, but they will be manageable. Do the same with your notes: put them on a searchable folder on your phone. I find my main motivator and driver to be anxiety avoidance. I know I can get through a pile of work once I sort it into my own disheveled piles.

—Awkward Kev

> Don't ever let someone tell you that a system that works for you is "wrong." My office could objectively be referred to as an outright mess, but I know where every single thing is (usually—sometimes it gets out of hand) and can access it easily and quickly, which I would never be able to do if it was "put away" to someone else's standard.
>
> This is also important for parents. Nothing damaged my relationship with my father more than him throwing away my things because they did not meet his standard of "organized."

—Emylee O.

How do I keep my FLOORS CLEAN?

Have more than one broom and dustpan, because at any given time you're likely to know where only half of them are.
Roombas are a good time, if you can afford one.
Learn to sweep. Learn about it on YouTube—it's actually a skill that you can master. Most people are sweeping wrong. There's a better way.
Sweep whenever you think of it or you notice crap on the floor.
Mopping should be done with far less frequency than sweeping.

Oh, the Roomba. That thing changed my life. It sounds so silly, but get just a basic, plain, boring Roomba, or one of the off brands, and now you don't even have to sweep. Now you have a little robot who comes out while you're sleeping and does your sweeping for you.

How do I CLEAN the BATHROOM?

Any cleaning task is going to suck. For starters, it might help to identify what is the most gross or unpleasant part of it for you.
Is it kneeling on the cold floor? Touching the toilet? Smelling the cleaning spray in the air? Mitigate those issues from the beginning to have an easier time. You can get kneepads for the floor, rubber gloves to clean the toilet, and an N95 mask (we're all well-versed in those now) to avoid breathing in the cleaner fumes.
Your brain will say, *I hate cleaning the bathroom.* **But** *what do you hate about it?* **The smell of Windex? The act of scrubbing? Dissect it so you can mitigate the issue.**

Here's a totally free bathroom-cleaning hack: **Have an order in which you do things that make sense to you, and have that be the process that you always use.** For me, I clean the toilet, then the floor, then the sink . . . because by the time I get done with the sink, I can wash my hands and be done with the whole process. Find what personally works and makes sense to you. And if it doesn't work, change it.

 Keep paper towels in the bathroom . . . and every room of your house. In fact, try to keep a complete cleaning kit for that room, IN that room, even if it involves duplicates. So don't have one Windex and one Clorox underneath the sink in the kitchen. Keep those in each bathroom, too.

Do you have an unusual way of doing chores or tasks that makes them more enjoyable or easier to do?

> I do not fold my laundry. I have two laundry baskets (and a clean enough shelf), one for clean clothes and one for dirty. I do still hang up certain clothes and fold bigger things like blankets and towels and sweaters, but my average T-shirts, socks, underwear? That is only in my laundry baskets.

—Clover from Massachusetts

> I like to empty the dishwasher while boiling water for my tea or coffee. It's like a race to get it done before the water boils, and it feels sooo efficient!

—Marjolein from the Netherlands

A lot of keeping up with cleaning tasks when you have ADHD is just making it easy to catch the wind when it's there. So if you're in the bathroom and you go, *This bathroom needs cleaning and I actually have the energy and can imagine doing that right now,* BOOM! There you are. Don't add extra things, like having to go find the cleaning supplies that may be buried under the kitchen sink.

Many ADHD solutions will involve some form of simplifying so that in the moment, you can go, *Let's do this,* and start immediately without having to solve a million other problems first. It's weird how uncommon it is to keep paper towels in the bathroom. That little thing will go a long way because it bridges the gap from *I could clean right now* to actually having what you need to accomplish it.

 ## How do I do my LAUNDRY?

 YOU BECOME THE EMPEROR OF LAUNDRY, THAT'S HOW.
As the Emperor of Laundry, you are entitled to certain treatment:

- The Emperor's reign shall last for as long as they are engaged in laundry-related activities, concluding upon completion of the laundry.
- The Emperor may appoint members of their cabinet and delegate support tasks to them, which they are encouraged to complete lest they offend the Emperor.

CHAPTER 11: **Why Folding Socks Is Overrated, aka the Household and Organization Chapter**

- The Emperor may watch, listen to, or otherwise consume any type of content they would like for the duration of their reign.
- The Emperor is entitled to any food, beverage, or snack they would like during the duration of their reign.
- The Emperor shall not be inhibited from completing the laundry in any way and is entitled to carry out their duties in any location they see fit.
- The Emperor shall, upon conclusion of their reign, be applauded by all subjects for their fearless leadership.
- So go forth and launder.
- You are Oxy-mandias, queen of clean.
- Look upon your works, ye Tidy, don't despair!

Seriously, though:

Have a content plan for folding. Make sure you have something in mind to watch or listen to *before* starting the long boring parts so the boredom isn't as daunting.

Keep a roll of fifty-gallon garbage bags around to use as laundry hampers in a pinch. This will help keep unaddressed laundry contained and quantified.

Use colored tape to label bags as clean, dirty, linens, etc.

Consider storing linens closer to where laundry gets folded.

Try to fold laundry in the place you'd rather be. If you'd rather be on the couch watching TV than folding laundry, fold laundry on the couch while watching TV.

HOW TO
Store Your Clothes

After your default basics, have a deeper storage of clothes. Like with the other organizational topics we've covered, if you wear it a lot, put it shallow, right in front. There's no reason to have your three-piece suit just in the mix cluttering everything up. That should be far back in the closet. The same goes for that leather jacket you wear only once a year.

Getting dressed every day comes down to discipline allocation. If you can tolerate hanging everything up, getting dressed in the morning has very little friction. You know where things are, you put them on, you're done.

If you can't hang things up and you throw your clothes into bins, you'll have that friction in the morning when you're trying to get dressed. There's no right way or wrong way, but know that you're going to pay now or pay later. If you don't have a hanging-up or folding system for your clothes after washing and drying them, you'll have to pay later by finding what you want to wear.

ADHD people have to be a bit deliberate about where we're willing to have that discipline. Looking for clothes in a big pile or bin is not a big deal to some people. And it's worth it for them to not have to fold their laundry. Consider where you want to address the friction.

One final, related note on how to put clothes away. I can't bring myself to fold pants, so my pants would end up all over the floor. *Why would I put them away if I'm just gonna put them on when I wake up tomorrow morning?* So I came up with a pants hook system in my room, and the system shifted from (1) drop trou, (2) walk away, to (1) drop trou, (2) pants hook. **Sometimes the smallest things can make the biggest impacts in feeling like you've got a handle on your life and your living space.**

How do I DECIDE what to WEAR?

 This one is very personal. For me, I have "show" clothes and "non-show" clothes. There are certain shirts that I wear if I'm not planning to leave the house that day—I wear those when I don't want to burn one of my nice shirts.

And all my non-show shirts, or "shitty shirts," as I affectionately call them, are from one pack of large Hanes undershirts. I get a pack of them every once in a while, and they work just fine. **There's no reason to stress about what you're wearing if it doesn't matter that day. Pick a default. Cartoon characters wear the same clothes in every episode!**

You can also have defaults for your show shirts when you have to get out of the house and do something important. Having defaults for those is important because it's one less thing you have to think about.

 There's such a broad range of what clothing means to people. I have to wear clothes to be socially acceptable when I leave my house. Otherwise, I really don't care. For other people, it is a deep part of their individuality, their gender expression, or even their culture. **Sometimes a big part of figuring out what to do with anything has to do with your connection to it.**

It's also helpful to divide your closet or drawers into at-home clothes and going-out clothes so that you're eliminating another thing you have to think about.

 Break down *what specifically* you like and don't like about particular clothes. For me, I like shirts that are thinner and don't change colors when they get damp because I'm a very sweaty guy. I like them to be long enough that I feel comfortable. Boom, right there, if a shirt doesn't fit those two criteria, it's out.

Let's say you have seven button-up shirts and five of them are dirty. You've got a work thing and the only two show shirts you have left are weirdly tight in the shoulders, and it's going to make you uncomfortable and grouchy all night. Eliminate those types of shirts! You do not need the hellish distraction found in an ill-fitting piece of clothing.

Pay attention to how your clothes make you feel. For example, I used to be a medium T-shirt, and now I'm a large T-shirt. And that transition period was awful, because my shirts were slightly too small and I was miserable. It cannot be overstated how much better my day-to-day life got when I made the switch to the large.

I did that with underwear. I had good bras and comfy bras, and then one day I had the incredible revelation that I never wear the good bras, because they're uncomfortable, so why do I get them?!

I converted to comfy bras only, and it changed my life. **There is no rule that says you cannot design your life and your space and your physical environment and your clothing environment for comfort. If things are uncomfortable, you can get rid of them.**

If you're someone whose weight fluctuates like mine does, clothes can be a big source of frustration. I recommend having a bin for stuff that's too tight at the moment, because wearing too tight jeans is an AWFUL feeling and the quickest way to a bad day. But if I know I'll be down ten or twenty pounds by the summer, I put those clothes into a bin and go back to them when they'll fit.

There's also a benefit to having clothes that are easily findable, easily sourceable. As an ADHD person, you're going to lose clothes or spill stuff on them. You don't want them to be hard to replace, because that just adds stress. This goes back to having default pieces that you know will work for you.

Where do I put my SHOES?

 My rant about shoes is largely the same as my rant about socks, in that I fervently disagree that you should have to follow particular rules.

I used to just have a spot. I step inside the door, I take my shoes off, and there they stay. You've got a lot of other options here: shoe organizer, shoe rack, shoe bin, shoe rug. All those are valid, but it ultimately comes down to "What are you honestly and practically going to do?"

My shoe spot caused issues because our dog, Bailey, likes to steal shoes. So I got a shoe rack, but I realized I hate putting my shoes in a little spot. I don't know what it is, but it makes my brain scream. So I got bins and put shoe bins *on top of* the shoe rack. Now I throw my shoes into the bin so I don't have to get all precious about where they go, but they're up off the floor for the dog. And it doesn't feel horrendous to me, like, "And then I put my shoes in this special spot in slot 1A." I'd rather die.

 Work with what you're already doing. A lot of times the organization solution that would work best for you is very close to your current behavior, so perhaps tweak your behavior rather than starting from scratch.

Watch yourself like you're Jane Goodall observing an ape. *What do you already do? Can you nudge that process into something that works for you?* Growing up, we had a bin by the door that was low on one side, so it was easy to just kick your shoes into the bin. This worked well for me, as it's not super different from kicking them off and leaving them on the floor. **Figure out where your inertia is taking you and work from there.**

Remember the clothing tiers, too. If a shoe bin works for you, use it for the pairs that you wear every day. You don't need to have your nice dress shoes or your galoshes in there, clogging up the system.

If you have a lot of shoes, it can be easy to freak out about how you'll organize them. But you really just need to separate out those first-tier shoes. The two, maybe three pairs you wear most days. Have a system for them near the door and keep the others in boxes in a closet or somewhere different from the first-tier system. Think of about 20 percent of your stuff as tier one, needing to be in an easily accessible, working system. The rest can be stored.

What do you do with your shoes when you take them off?

> They go on or near the shoe rack, depending on how quickly I'm trying to get out of them.

—Cassady from Missouri

> Kick them off near the door on the little rug we have.

—@thatsexeducator

> Shoe pile! I have a shoe rack by the door, but there is always also a shoe pile right in front of it, my most frequently worn shoes.

—Jenna from Denver

> I put them in one of two places so I don't lose them. But that took years of work. They either go in the front hallway if I remember to take them off, or if I'm in the house they go under the couch. They are not allowed anywhere else in my brain. If they are not in those places they have been stolen. Ha-ha.

—Nk

What TOOLS should I have at home?

 If you want to make this as easy on yourself as possible, go to a hardware store and ask for a basic tool kit that will fit in a car. This way you'll get all the basics you need, packaged all together. No muss, no fuss.

If you're going à la carte: hammer, ruler, C-clamp pliers, needle-nose pliers (those will save you time—they're basically really strong tweezers), an Allen key set, a large flathead screwdriver, a large Phillips-head screwdriver, a small Phillips-head screwdriver, and a small flathead screwdriver.

 I strongly advocate for every human being to know how to operate a small drill or an electric screwdriver. If the idea of power tools freaks you out, IKEA has a little electric screwdriver that is perfect for most jobs around the home. It's nonthreatening, not scary, and costs like twelve dollars. Perfect for hanging up your pictures and such— you're not gonna do a major construction job with it. **Just a couple of basic power tools can significantly improve the quality of your life.**

 It's nice to have a portable shop. As a millennial who's rented his entire life, I need to be able to have a shop that I can pick up and just move somewhere else.

The ADHD Field Guide For Adults

PART 3:
Systems and Organization

How do I keep up with CAR MAINTENANCE?

This is a calendar thing more than anything else, but a great resource to get you started is *Mechanic Shop Femme's Guide to Car Ownership* by Chaya M. Milchtein.

It's a scheduling thing more than doing the task. Nobody wants to get their oil changed. A good incentive to get it onto the calendar and stick with the schedule is to plan on getting ice cream afterward or another little treat.

When the car place puts that little sticker with your oil change date on your windshield when you need to come back, add it to your planner or phone, too. That sticker is ultimately going to seem invisible to you. Put the date on your physical "year at a glance" calendar if you use one of those, or put a reminder in your phone two weeks before the oil change is due. When you get that phone reminder, make the appointment right then so it doesn't slip away and get forgotten. It never hurts to reward yourself with a little something when you schedule the thing when your calendar or phone tells you.

Any good mechanic will also tell you when your other routine maintenance (checking alignment, rotating tires, inspecting critical systems) is due. Make this a calendar priority like you do the oil changes.

How do I keep up with HOUSE MAINTENANCE?

Here's an important one that's easy to ignore—changing your HVAC filter. That's another note on the year-at-a-glance calendar or phone reminders. You should change that every three months or so. Go to the hardware store the first week of January, buy your four-pack, and you're set for the year.

Maintenance inherently favors your future self. Because it's not like if you don't keep up with maintenance, it's gonna break immediately. You wanna do a favor for Future You. And also try to consolidate whenever you can with big maintenance tasks. "March first is house maintenance day, when I'm gonna change the filter on the HVAC, mop all the hardwood floors, clean out the garage."

Sometimes you can't do that—if something needs to be done every three months and another thing needs to be done every five months. **Do your best to consolidate your maintenance tasks so you can have one painfully boring day.** People with ADHD are sprinters. So try to make a sprint out of it.

 If you're looking for a great resource, Mercury Stardust's book, *Safe and Sound*, has great tips and tricks for small DIY jobs around the house.

❓ How do I stop LOSING MY WALLET?

 A wallet has a couple of places where it's allowed to be. One is on your person wherever you keep your wallet. When you take it out of your pants to do laundry or out of your bag when you're in there looking for something else, there are a lot of places that a wallet can end up.

When it's not in its designated spot—on your person or in a purse or bag—identify one secondary place where it's allowed to be.

 Also, find a tiny moment of joy in the landing spot for your wallet, your keys, or other important items in your life. Go find a really cool dish that you like and use that dish for your keys. Or get a dorky little phone holder. Sometimes it's that little bit of novelty dopamine that will get you over the hump.

It'll also help you remember that the wallet system exists. Where does the wallet go when it's not in my pants/bag? In the Donald Duck mug by the office!

Are PETS good for people with ADHD?

Yes. Dogs, in particular, have been found to be quite therapeutic for people with ADHD. **Dogs get you out of the house. They force you to have at least some semblance of a schedule:** *I gotta get up to let the dog out, I gotta feed the dog, I gotta walk the dog.* So they make getting into executive functioning habits easier. They even have service dogs for ADHD.[1]

Completely agree. A lot of it is largely the same as car and house maintenance. **It's a scheduling issue more than a doing-the-thing issue.** But with a pet, **missing the maintenance things will have immediate repercussions on your life, because it is a living thing**. If you fall behind on car maintenance, it might start to feel funny when you're driving, but it's also not going to feel pain.

Whereas if you don't want to get out of bed but your dog needs to go out, your dog is going to go to the bathroom all over your floor. It's an immediate-feedback thing. You've got maintenance with any animal, but what you get back from them is also immediate gratification.

How do I keep up with PET CARE with ADHD?

Pet care is an area that you can, in many ways, simplify. I have dog food shipped to my house so I don't have to think about it and there are no moments of *Oh no, I'm out of dog food.*

Similarly, we go to a groomer with a monthly program. So once a month Bailey gets a bath, nails trimmed, and groomed, and I pay a monthly fee. I also have BarkBox, a subscription kit, so I don't have to go to the pet store and impulse-buy treats and toys. Or at least not as often! There are also services run by folks willing to clean up dog poop in your yard once a week or once a month.

On a larger scale, before you adopt a dog, remember that it is your responsibility to train them—whether you do it yourself or you hire a trainer. If you have a dog that is constantly misbehaving, that is not going to be good for your ADHD. We worked hard to get Bailey to a place where she can hang out and chill. You don't need to go out for a bit and worry that the sofa is going to be destroyed when you get home.

Still, pets are expensive, they're a time commitment, and if you

are at the height of your frustration tolerance and your dog poops on the carpet, that's not a great feeling. **Getting a dog is not going to cure your ADHD, nor is it going to particularly make your ADHD better. But living with a pet provides you a framework that gives you a little bit more structure and functionality.**

Also, have you ever seen a dog? Because they're the best thing in the whole world, and we don't deserve dogs.

We just want you to look at our dog.

Chapter 11 in short:

- **Don't wanna match socks? Don't do it.** The expectation that we match our socks is a tool of the oppressor.

- **You are not a fuckup for being disorganized.** Organization is not intuitive for people with ADHD. We have to manually come up with strategies and systems to keep our stuff in order.

- **Find systems and organization tips that work for you.** This is completely individual and does not need to be the way that other people do things.
- **Figure out what PART of household tasks (like cleaning the bathroom) sucks the most for you.** Then address that *part* and make a change to it, rather than writing off the whole task as something you can't or won't do.
- **Make a game** of boring, repetitive tasks like laundry.
- **Prioritize comfort** with your clothing, and store it in a way that makes sense to you and you alone.
- Shoe storage is a real pain for ADHDers. Don't force yourself into a traditional system. **If shoe organizers send you into a blind rage, find another system.** There's no shame in a shoe bin (or even a shoe pile!).
- **Schedule house and car maintenance tasks in a way that makes sense to you.** One idea is to consolidate these tasks into one very boring day.

Keep in mind: while you're learning and developing processes that work for you, you're simultaneously **unlearning** all the ways you were taught to do things that **haven't** worked for you and contending with all those inner voices telling you you're a fuckup for not being able to do things the way everybody else seems to.

To ease this process, do your best to maintain a sense of self-compassion and regularly affirm to yourself that you're doing good work, that you're worthy of a good life and capable of building one.

Your life is **your** life. There're no "adult police" who are going to show up at your house to arrest you for not folding your underwear, wearing the same type of shirt for ten years, or being too silly while folding laundry. Focus on tweaking the way you do household chores to make the process sustainable, practical, and repeatable (see page 204).

The "correct" household or organizational system is the one you're most likely to execute and complete, regardless of what those critical inner voices may tell you.

PART 4

WORK AND MONEY

Work, Work, Work

IT IS WINTER in the Midwest. It is snowing hard, nearly a blizzard, and I am in Big Trouble. I've once again made a mistake in Delphi: the tricky, complex booking software that manages the finicky day-to-day operations of which group has booked which ballroom, how many chairs and how many cheese trays they need, and whether they want decaf or regular coffee brought up at two-hour intervals. This time, I've realized only a few hours before two groups are scheduled to arrive that I've booked a huge $100,000-plus corporate holiday party directly against the Rat Pack Holiday Tribute concert.

My boss has sent me down to deliver the bad news personally, and I feel the familiar "I made a big mistake" stomachache starting to gnaw at me as I cross the hotel lobby and find Frank Sinatra, Dean Martin, and Sammy Davis Jr. huddled together near the fireplace. It'd be funny if I hadn't just been told that next time, I'd be fired.

"I'm so sorry, guys. There's been a double booking, we're going to have to move your show." Fake Dean Martin hugs me when I start to cry.

IT IS SUMMER, and I am scrubbing a vanilla latte out of the train of an eight-thousand-dollar wedding dress that's getting picked up tomorrow. I love my current job in bridal alterations, but the cramped sewing room is a terrible working environment for someone with spatial awareness and memory issues. This time, I forgot that I'd carefully set my coffee down outside the shop, as is protocol, but my well-meaning boss had brought it in for me. "You're a big girl," she says, "I trust you not to spill." Lucky for me and perhaps disconcerting for brides reading this, spills are common, and after three unpaid hours of careful scrubbing with special industrial-grade cleaner, the dress is no worse for the wear. My boss teases me about the coffee incident until I quit seven months later.

IT IS SPRING, nearly seven years later, and I am dressed like a pirate and crying. I am currently the entertainment director at a Renaissance festival, managing over one hundred entertainers, musicians, and actors. One of my employees has called because his paycheck hasn't arrived, and he needs the money very badly, right now. I feel the same familiar stomachache clench as I frantically double-check the check request list that I've sent to my boss . . . because I am not trusted to put in the requests myself . . . and my stomach drops when I realize his name isn't on it. I am racked with guilt and shame. Like many Ren Faire employees, he is living paycheck to paycheck, and my negligence is now the reason he doesn't have his next one. I explain the situation to the Big Boss, who screams at me and calls me careless and tells me he'll just have to wait. I quietly withdraw the money from my own account and hand deliver an envelope full of cash to him the next morning.

    This is life—and work—with ADHD.

—**Cate**

I have TROUBLE showing up to WORK ON TIME. What should I do?

 You can address this problem in two fundamental ways, and which way you choose is entirely dependent on your work environment. **You can make systems for showing up on time or request to change the time you have to show up to one you'll have an easier time managing.**

If you work at a small furniture shop, you might be perfectly comfortable telling your boss that you'd be a lot more productive from 10 a.m. to 7 p.m. rather than 8 a.m. to 5 p.m. Other work environments may be less flexible, requiring you to figure out how to show up at a set time.

 Asking for a little bit of flexibility in your schedule is totally appropriate if you're a person who needs that. Especially because time perception issues are a real thing for people with ADHD.

 Showing up to work on time is not a singular thing. To neurotypical people it might be, but to people with ADHD, **showing up to work on time is far from being a single task. It's the result of a successful completion of many tasks before it.**

Putting your feet onto the floor at a good time in the morning, getting into the shower promptly, not burning your toast . . . it all eventually ends with you arriving on time.

If you have to be at work at nine o'clock, reverse engineer your days to figure out when you'd need to wake up in order to arrive on time.

You also want to make sure your "leaving for work" routine can handle a decent number of unforeseen delays. If there's traffic or a car accident, your schedule may be thrown off. **So figure out what time you have to leave the house and then subtract at least fifteen minutes.**

The 15-Minute RULE

> **Always leave fifteen minutes before you think you should. For anything. Always.**

 I have *profound* anxiety about being on time. One of the reasons I thought "I couldn't possibly have ADHD" for so long is because all I'd ever heard is that people with ADHD are always late. In reality, a LOT of ADHDers like me have built structures and systems to ensure that we're on time (or weirdly early), and being late can trigger a lot of shame, guilt, and frustration. My biggest AuDHD meltdowns are always over lateness and schedule changes, so I've learned to work backward to ensure I'm on time.

If I have to be somewhere at 9 a.m., I'm not thinking about what I'm doing at 8 a.m. I'm thinking about what I'm doing at 9 p.m. the night before. And that can take a lot of brain space, but **if you get into the habit of doing things for your future self—like setting clothes out the night before or wearing the same shoes each day—then you have fewer decisions to make in the morning**. These are small choices, but they facilitate time management.

I also struggle with certain tasks, so I chose, a long time ago, not to wear makeup outside special occasions. I shower at night. I don't shower in the mornings, because it is really hard for me to wake up, so I structured my entire life around being able to roll out of bed ten minutes before I need to get into the car to go somewhere.

This is not to say you can't be into makeup or wearing awesome outfits every day. But if it's important to you and you know you're going to spend an hour or more getting ready and you also need to be at work at 6 a.m., there may need to be some give-and-take.

How does ADHD affect you at work?

> I'm supposed to have my shit together, and when I don't, it's really embarrassing. I hate it. Now that I'm the boss, I can laugh it off at work and make a self-deprecating comment, but we had to surround me with really organized and process-thinking people to make our business work as it got bigger.

—L.R.

> I tried to tell my last boss that since I got diagnosed with ADHD I was essentially learning how to be a whole person again, and it wasn't gonna change overnight. She kept telling me I was just lazy and didn't want to actually put forth any effort (the main issue was I was regularly two to five minutes late for work) and thus I don't care about my job, so why should she keep me? With her permission, I used her cane as an example to explain that asking me to "just be better" was kind of like asking her to walk to the conference room without her cane. Her disability was physical, mine was mental. I'm now in a place that is extremely supportive and understanding. I love my job now.

—Sabrina from Portland, Oregon

> I found a job that allows me flexible scheduling—I work from home and start around 9 a.m. I can work longer on days when my hyperfocus is engaged or flex to work fewer hours when my dopamine has hit rock bottom. It has been a game changer for me. My lack of personal executive functioning skills means that I am extremely reliant on outward systems. I have used this to my advantage as I specialize in implementing new tracking systems for the company I work for, while my attention to detail and pattern recognition are very helpful in data management.

—BE Bewley

What are GOOD JOBS for people with ADHD? What are BAD JOBS for people with ADHD?

I don't think that there are good and bad jobs for people with ADHD. We often hear people speak in generalities about this kind of stuff: "Being an EMT is a great job for people with ADHD because there's an immediacy to it." "People with ADHD make terrible lawyers." We aren't here to tell you to choose from a specific list.

What we *are* saying is that **there are good and bad jobs that highlight our individual strengths and/or weaknesses**. Some people would thrive in public service jobs with a built-in routine and structure; others would not be able to function in that system. I read an article that said everybody with ADHD should be stock traders because of the high pressure. But if you have impulse control and gambling problems, you're going to have a bad time.

A subset of people with ADHD are excellent under pressure. You might struggle in every other capacity, but the minute that the pressure is on and there's stress or an emergency, you instantly snap into leadership mode. Those people might make great EMTs or firefighters.

People often ask us this question because they're worried they chose the wrong career. Something along the lines of:

Hey, I'm in my second year of medical school and I've been struggling this whole time, but I really want to be a doctor. Did I screw up by choosing to be a doctor?

And the answer there is NO. **There is no career or job that cannot be done by a person with ADHD.** Some jobs require a lengthy period in which you have to learn how to do the job before you can actually start, like medical school for a doctor.

By my observation, people with ADHD tend to struggle with that learning period and often quit before actually doing the thing they wanted to do. It can be difficult to get excited about being a surgeon when you have to learn how to file charts first.

It's useful to consider what skills you already have that might shorten, or even circumvent, that learning period. If you're a really good carpenter or cook, great! Is there a job where you can frequently apply those skills in new and interesting ways? Maybe you could jump right into a company that builds cabinetry for restaurants?

And if you don't yet have any hard skills, **what skills would you be willing to learn, even if it gets hard?** There's a lot of sheer enjoyment and intrigue in having a skill, but sometimes you have to get over the tedium of being a beginner.

As another quick aside, getting rejected sucks. You may want to apply for a job or pursue a thing but feel haunted by the question *What if I fail?* **However, another question that can be terrifying for people with ADHD is *What if I succeed?* What if I'm really good at this and this is all anyone wants me to do for the rest of my life? And what if I get BORED!?**

Hey—don't do that. You're worrying about getting bored of a career you don't have yet. You basically just picked up a cello and are worrying about choosing between the Chicago and London Symphony Orchestras.* One step at a time, bud. Plus, **you can always pick up the saxophone later**. Plenty of people switch careers multiple times in life. Cate and I did!

Just remember: It's normal to get caught up in the mental game around jobs in general. Your life is going to be filled with all sorts of awesome weirdness no matter what career path you start on.

 There are also a lot of different, specific jobs within one category. Being a kindergarten teacher is a very different job from being a high school teacher, and both of those are very different jobs from being a tenured professor with a focus on research.

---

* This is (genuinely) common for people with ADHD—you realize you kind of like painting, and before you have time to really enjoy it, your brain has spiraled into imagining your super-successful Etsy store, merchandise line, New York gallery opening, and inevitably award-winning documentary. This can result in a vicious cycle of getting interested in something and then getting burned out because you spent the mental energy you could have spent actually painting or setting up a website and social media channels and designing merch. Sometimes, it's okay to just do a thing because you like it and work on being present in that. Not everything has to make you money, and not everything needs to be rushed.

Being a pediatrician is a very different job from being a podiatrist. When exploring career options, it helps to **start off broad. Then you narrow your focus until you find the thing that you actually want to do.**

I stand by the opinion that people with ADHD are not made to have one job for forty-five years. I think you absolutely *can* do it, but when you look at the evidence of job satisfaction in people with ADHD, it is typically very low. I have a lot of personal experience with that.

I was going to be a Shakespeare professor. I was bound and determined. I love Shakespeare, I love teaching, I love being in front of students. Every single part of that job is perfect for my interests, for my talents, for my skill sets.

You know what wasn't perfect for me? Grading papers and dealing with college admin stuff. I could not do it, and that made me feel like a miserable failure. **Is it worth it to be in a job you hate? You have one chance to live your most fulfilling life. It's not always going to be easy, that's a given, but if your job is making you miserable, why are you doing it?!** Yes, there's privilege at play here, but people deserve to be happy, too.

Don't necessarily think about the job that you want; think about what you want your individual days to be like. Do you want to sleep in? Do you want to get off early? Do you want to think about work when you're not at work or have work start and end at definitive times?

Another alternative to thinking about the scary question "What job do I want to have?" is to think instead about the types of *skills* you want to have and use. Steer yourself toward joy and satisfaction, not a specific profession.

There's also the great Alan Watts thought experiment: "What would you do if money were no object?" If you won the lottery tomorrow and never had to worry about money again, how would you spend your time? Would you be outside? Would you be hanging out with dogs? Would you be building things?

If you're really good at something, no matter what it is, somebody will pay you to do it. But you've got to get good at the thing first, and that can be hard. You'll probably have to keep your current job, or get a day job, for a while as you learn. **Focus on the skills you want to have and what makes you excited.**

It is also 100 percent possible to create your own job. We certainly did. There is no rule that says you *must* work for someone else. There are lots and lots of ways to make money. The thing to remember is that working for yourself means you are RESPONSIBLE for yourself. There is no "boss" to get mad when you don't post on social media, or forget to file taxes, or decide not to go to work for three weeks because you're burned out.

Many of my friends have unique, working-for-themselves jobs. Some are content creators but also jobs like . . .

- artists
- magicians
- circus performers
- Renaissance Faire musicians
- vintage clothing sellers
- dice makers
- candlemakers
- electronic repair people
- tool resellers
- lawncare workers
- full-time house sitters
- full-time pet sitters
- gig musicians
- food truck owners
- mobile pet groomers
- carpenters
- props makers
- record resellers
- movie and TV extras
- entrepreneurs

If you're willing to grind and commit to marketing and hustling for yourself, and understand that building a business from the ground up is HARD, not always fun, and not always super lucrative, you might thrive in making your own career.

❓ What are some of your own SYSTEMS that you use for WORK? And can we BORROW them?

I have learned over the course of writing this book that as a professional content creator, I am extremely bad at being a content creator. **For the better part of three years, I have entered a cycle of being *super* motivated, excited, and productive to . . . burned out, exhausted, and canceling things because I have ground myself down to a little nub.**

For me, the most important system I have is managing my workload. I know the following things about myself:

- I need a deadline. If I do not know when something is due, I will intend to do it, but it will inevitably fall between the cracks.
- I need a daily schedule that lets me know what I should be working on and when.
- I am likely to overcommit out of enthusiasm.

→ **Therefore . . .**

- I need to be careful not to burn out.
- Having the "right" pen/paper/environment is important to me.
- Checklists relieve my anxiety and give me confidence that I have remembered everything that's important.

→ **Therefore . . .**

1. Anytime anyone tells me, "Just whenever you get around to it," I ask for a specific date. I am very honest in saying, "If you do not get me a date, I cannot schedule this for you."

2. I use Calendly to schedule meetings, which I have automatically set up to generate a Zoom meeting and send a calendar invite, a reminder/confirmation email, and a thank-you note afterward. (Automation is incredible for handling small tasks.)

3. I have made a work schedule for myself that has set times for things like promos, podcast episodes, articles I'm writing, conventions I'm appearing at, etc.

4. The best way to plan for anything is to CBCB: Count Backward, Cover Bases.

→ **An example:**

Count backward from the date the Important Thing is due to fill in the schedule, whatever it is, like "pay this bill on Tuesday." As you're building the schedule, cover your bases and think through every aspect: *Do I need to buy stamps? Do I need to go to the bank to pay this bill? I should order stamps tomorrow to get them on time*, etc.

→ **An example:**

If I have a speaking gig coming up, I know that there is a very specific set of things that I need to get done, so one of my systems is running through this outline every single time, backward, to cover all my bases.

Arrange Travel:

- How do I get there?
- Once I'm there, how do I get to my final destination?
- Where am I staying?
- Do I need a car to get around?

What am I doing while I'm there?

- Do I need to prepare anything?
- What is the schedule for the event?
- If I am preparing something new, have I scheduled writing time?
- If I am preparing something new, do I need to rehearse?
- Do I have my notes/outline/slides ready to go?
- Whom do I send them to?
- How are they getting shown while I'm there?

What do I need to pack?

- What meds do I need to bring with me?
- Do I need to get any medications refilled before I leave?
- Do I need any specific outfits?
- Do I need to buy anything?
- Do I need any special props/costume/workshop supplies?
- Do I need to order anything?
- Do I need new supplies (business cards, pens, handouts)?
- Do I need to bring any tech with me?
- Do I need to mail anything ahead of time?

Do I need to promote this event?

- What do I need to do to promote it?
- Do I need to send them any materials?
- Where do I promote it?
- Do I have the right pictures, graphics, and information?
- Do I need to make content while I'm there?

Then, finally, I start counting backward and make sure I've scheduled all this out.

 WRITE. STUFF. DOWN. Carry a writing utensil and a burner notebook at all times. Use them to write down dates, times, and important figures.

ALSO: You can doodle on the back pages, rip out the paper and fold it during a meeting as a fidget, or make a paper airplane to de-stress. These aren't precious, just burn through them. I recommend those Mead spiral field notepads that fit into a breast pocket and often come in packs of three.

ALWAYS take notes when you're on a work call. It's harder to remember things people tell you when you're not looking at them. Try to have phone conversations in the same place and keep a pen and paper there. If you're driving, ask your phone robot to remind you what you talked about later. (We're already more likely to get into car accidents with ADHD; don't drive distracted!)

Make your plan for the next day the night before. You don't want to get to work and immediately have to make a bunch of scheduling decisions. Remember: the plan is not set in stone and can change as new things come up, but it will be massively helpful in building your momentum for the day.

Address the sensory environment you work in. You know that stressful background noise you don't notice until it turns off? Or the annoying glare on your computer screen from the lamp behind you? Look out for things like that in your work environment and address them. Small sensory annoyances add up and can lead to a chaotic mental environment.

Break things down into smaller deadlines. We ADHDers have a hard time conceptualizing time that is too far in the future. Break tasks down into smaller pieces, decide on an order to do them, and set deadlines for each of those pieces.

> Carry a writing utensil and a burner notebook at all times.

Delay your gratification. Want to get another coffee? Wait ten minutes. Reply to one more email. This takes practice and is frustrating at first, but it turns procrastination activities into rewards.

Hesitate. Take an extra beat before you get started on something, move from your workstation, switch tasks, or make a decision you can't undo (like sending an email). It's easy for our brains to start moving too fast, making it feel like we have to be in a huge rush to do everything, which can cause us to make unnecessary mistakes or make a bunch of trips when we could have made one.

❓ People keep JOKING about how ADHD DOESN'T EXIST. How do I HANDLE this?

There are a lot of interpersonal things you have to navigate when you're neurodivergent, and this one is a doozy.

It may not be worth it for you to try to get them to change their behavior. It might be best if you just put it to the back of your mind and move on, and that's fine—you're not doing a disservice to the ADHD community by protecting your peace.

However, if it's really bad and they're harping on it and making fun of you, that is obviously not okay. That's full-blown discrimination . . . like, the *illegal* kind. If you have an HR department, you would be completely justified in waging a formal complaint.

Always remember: **You have the ability and the right to pick your battles. It's never appropriate for someone to deny the existence of a disability. But this book is about *you* and *your* life. It's not about doing the most justice for the most people.** It's not your job to save the world, and if ignoring a jerk and moving on is what gets you through the day, it's okay to do that.

❓ What ACCOMMODATIONS can I ask for at WORK?

- Flexible work schedule
- Noise reduction (quieter workspace or noise-canceling headphones)
- Remote work options
- Structured task management tools
- Written communication for instructions

- Frequent breaks
- Regular check-in meetings
- Job restructuring
- Access to a quiet workspace
- Task reminders and alarms
- Access to support services (counseling or coaching)
- Flexible leave policies
- Mentoring or peer support
- Assistive technology (productivity apps, speech-to-text)
- Stress management resources
- Training and education (time management, organization)
- Conflict resolution support

It's important to note that some of these accommodations aren't viable for certain professions. If you're a heart surgeon, you're probably not going to be able to work remotely, or if you're an on-call EMT, a flexible leave policy might not be available to you.

In many cases, it's a great practice to figure out what you need *before* you start applying for jobs, because then you can eliminate those that don't provide accessible environments. For example, you might not want to apply for a job that boasts an "open floor plan" as a benefit of working there. Many of us NEED a door. See page 128 about disclosing neurodivergence.

REMEMBER, IF SOMEONE SAYS ADHD DOESN'T EXIST,

you can always remind them that everybody who is actually qualified disagrees by showing them the International Consensus Statement on ADHD!

Chapter 12 in short:

- Try **implementing systems to help you show up to work on time**, or explore a schedule that better suits your needs, if your job allows. There's no shame in being more productive from noon to 8 p.m. than 8 a.m. to 4 p.m.!

- **There are no "good" or "bad" jobs for ADHD.** And there is no job or career that cannot be done by a person with ADHD.

- **Think about your skills** . . . and the way you want your individual days to look . . . when exploring job options.

- **It's never okay for a boss—or ANYONE—to tell you that ADHD doesn't exist.** Pick your battles and remember, you always have the International Consensus Statement on ADHD in your back pocket.

- **You can request work accommodations** of all kinds, including a flexible work schedule, regular check-in meetings with a supervisor, noise reduction, or remote work options.

> There's no shame in being more productive from noon to 8 p.m. than 8 a.m. to 4 p.m.!

13

Money:
It's a Gas

A couple of years ago, I was mentioned in a *New York Times* article about how women with ADHD struggle with debt and finances. Specifically, I should say that my name was used as an example of someone who talks openly about my struggles with ADHD and how my transparency online inspired this person to seek out a diagnosis.

I broke the cardinal rule of the Internet and read the comments on the article. Hundreds and hundreds of people called me, and women like me: *Lazy. Stupid. Embarrassing for women. A conspiracy by Big Pharma. Immaturity. I feel sorry for their partners. Who would want such a useless woman? Take meds and deal with it. Making excuses. Adult ADHD isn't real. It's a fad. If you have the focus to go on spending binges, your ADHD can't be that bad.*

The comments weren't great, is what I'm saying.

What the *New York Times* didn't know was that this happened right around the time that I finally came clean about the fact that I was in a massive amount of debt. Whatever amount you're thinking . . . it was more than that. My name is Cate, and I am a compulsive shopper.

Whatever that makes you think about me, whatever judgments you just made about me, it's okay—I've thought of all that myself, and probably worse.

For a REALLY long time, I felt stupid. I felt ashamed, I felt embarrassed. I didn't want to tell anybody, let alone put it into this book for the whole world to see. It's a challenging problem to deal with, because not only is there the behavioral addiction component, there is also the absolute stigma of *Wow, what an entitled idiot who can't act like an adult* that stops a lot of people from getting help. I cannot stress to you enough how scary and overwhelming it is to feel powerless against something as ubiquitous as the Amazon "Buy Now" button . . . and in looking for help get told that you're selfish and incompetent and a bad person for struggling.

> My name is Cate, and I am a compulsive shopper.

No matter what I did or how hard I tried, I just kept messing up my finances. I'd swear to myself that this was the last time I'd buy some dumb thing I didn't need on Amazon at 3 a.m., only to find myself waking up the next night because I felt like I was going to die if I didn't buy new jeans right now. Important bills didn't get paid, and I routinely paid extra charges and fees for late payment . . . My finances were a mess, and I'm not proud of it. I had anxiety every time I checked out atced.the grocery store, wondering if my card would be declined.

Even as I write this, I know it sounds goofy. It's hard to understand. I wish there was a better way to explain how my brain will latch on to the wildest "need," which then becomes an all-encompassing obsession. One year after a particularly rough patch with my family, I found myself desperately speeding around town at 5:45 p.m. the day before Thanksgiving, trying to find the "perfect" set of dishes—the make-or-break, absolutely vital and necessary component of the dinner that would mean the difference between success and failure.

It wasn't until I learned about the connection between ADHD and impulsive/compulsive shopping that I started to understand it. For me, buying that thing I didn't need wasn't because I REALLY needed an entirely new set of dishes to throw a good Thanksgiving. It was because I was procrastinating on processing emotions and using the dopamine hit of getting a Fun New Thing to mask my feelings of sadness, boredom, stress, anxiety, and being SURE I'd screw something up and my friends wouldn't like me anymore. If I was a perfect dinner host with an immaculate tablescape, no one would know that I was struggling. I'd cover up and bury those feelings with literal, actual piles of stuff. (See page 75 about the connection between ADHD and hoarding, too.)

If you share these struggles, you are not alone. And you are not a fuckup for having them.

—Cate

I have **TROUBLE BUDGETING** money. Any **TIPS**?

Many people with ADHD struggle with impulsive spending, spending addictions, and even massive disorganization and hoarding. I have a spending problem. It's something that I have been embarrassed about, but I am a compulsive spender, and it can be very, very difficult to break out of that cycle.

And I want to be honest—a lot of this is still new for me. I'm not great at it yet. I went from being below the poverty line for most of my adult life to making a pretty significant amount of money. Nobody taught me how to handle it, how to make a budget, how to save for taxes, how to invest . . . but I'm working on it. Money management is a skill you have to learn, and personally, I had to learn the hard way.

Part of learning how to budget and how to control spending for me—your results may vary—was that I had to start unpacking how much my hyperactivity, my inattention, and my impulsivity combined when I hit that sweet, sweet "Buy Now" button on Amazon.

One of the big things that can happen is that shopping becomes, for a lot of people, dopamine-seeking and/or self-soothing behavior.

I recently woke up at three o'clock in the morning and was overcome with the impulse of *I want new jeans, I need new jeans, if I don't get the jeans now it's going to keep me awake all night.* I got out of bed, got on my computer, and bought like three hundred dollars' worth of new jeans. Then the jeans got here, and I was like, *I feel nothing. Why am I so unsatisfied?* That's because **it's not about the thing. It is about the future potential of the thing.**

This can be really challenging because for ADHD brains, reducing spending can start to feel like you're depriving yourself or missing out. The next time the feeling of wanting comes up, **one thing that helps is finding activities that are going to produce that same sort of dopamine**.

I've started going through **doom boxes (doom = didn't organize, only moved),** and it feels like, *I don't need to go shopping, because there are five things in this box that I forgot I bought!* Two birds, one stone: help with the disorganization while also not spending money.

We also recognize that not everybody has money they can just casually spend. **There can also be a lot of shame and embarrassment . . . *I've destroyed my finances, but I have the luxury to do that, so why am I complaining? I should just get my act together.* This is a real part of ADHD that's important to talk about.** In fact, the *New York Times* recently did a piece specifically on the phenomenon of late-diagnosed ADHD women struggling with compulsive spending and debt (NBD, but they mentioned me).

 Another thing about compulsive behavior, whether shopping or substance abuse, is that it gets worse the longer it remains a secret. It's good to acknowledge problem behavior with someone you trust. Just saying to a friend, "Hey, I'm spending way too much money these days, and I need to cut back" can make a difference.

Back to the hacks: try this trick for nonessential purchases. Say you're in a store and you see a cool Lego bust of Ruth Bader Ginsberg for fifty dollars. Imagine the fifty bucks in one hand and Ruth in the other. Which one would you rather have?

That can help money seem more real for each little purchase. It's easy to think that either you have money or you don't, but this brings money back to being a quantifiable thing.

One of the best things I ever did was having somebody help me with my taxes. First, I just went to the H&R Block guy who sits in a little cubicle at Target.

Then my dear, ever-patient, kind, reassuring friend Anne started helping me, and I'm not exaggerating when I say her help literally saved my life. I don't know how to do my taxes, and I'm bad with numbers. I have dyscalculia, so I get anxiety about it, and I got into a bad place with my mental health and my finances. That pressure started to build to a point where I was genuinely unsafe for a while.

Outsourcing to a tax person also means you get the benefit of their knowledge. If you are a person who does gig work or is self-employed, taxes can get really complicated quickly, especially if you're juggling a bunch of different forms and 1099s. And sometimes, as in this case for taxes, outsourcing the work to an expert is both inexpensive and incredibly helpful.

I have TROUBLE with IMPULSE SHOPPING. What should I do?

It was important to me that this chapter be included in our book, because for a long time I felt a lot of shame, guilt, and embarrassment about this. That is, until I realized that impulsive shopping is not only a coping mechanism for me, it is actually a direct result of my particular brand of ADHD.

LOTS of people with ADHD struggle with impulsive shopping.[1] They struggle with spending, saving, and/or hoarding. See more on page 75 about hoarding, but here's the short version: the desire to acquire stuff can be very much rooted in ADHD and, for me personally, in depression.

I get sad, so I decide that I know what will solve my depression—a new Roomba. And then the Roomba comes and . . . SHOCKINGLY . . . it doesn't cure my depression or make me feel particularly better. But now I have a five-hundred-dollar Roomba that I did not have before, and I'm in more debt than ever.

Impulsive shopping can be tricky because we need to buy stuff to survive, but our brains also do an incredible job of convincing us, especially if we have these tendencies, that the thing we want is the thing that we need to survive.

I have spent an embarrassing amount of money. I have not been able to pay bills because of the amount of stupid crap that I've ordered on Amazon at 1 a.m. It can be easy to trivialize this. It can be easy to say, "Well, just don't buy stuff!" **I know it's not that easy. But it IS okay, and you're not alone.**

Back to the Roomba you think you want to buy. What you really want is that dopamine you get from hitting the button and from anticipating its arrival.

- **HERE'S THE HACK . . . You can override this by tricking yourself into believing you'll get it. First, you're going to have to clean up all the spaces in your house that you want the Roomba to clean.** Every room, every hallway, every inch.

- **What you're doing here is harnessing the DELAY. Delay, delay, delay this big purchase that will put you into debt.** Tell yourself: *If I do all this stuff, when it's done two weeks later, if I still want the Roomba, I can get the Roomba.* **This plan will stop you from acting on that initial impulse.** Because if you give in to it, you'll end up with a box in the corner and a Roomba that you can't use yet because you haven't done any of that prep work.

- **Rather than buying the Shiny New Thing, whatever it is, pretend like you've already bought it and start the preparations for having it.** You can plan to buy the thing, but instead of hitting "Buy Now," start doing those other related things.

- Another thing to try is getting obsessed with researching which exact model or style of something to buy. That'll put it off another week or so.

You can also turn off your "Buy Now" button. Amazon makes it incredibly easy to just go impulse buy. They do NOT want you to turn that thing off, but it is possible.

Similarly, resist the impulse to save your credit card number into your computer or mobile device. Just that momentary delay can sometimes be enough to interrupt the impulse. If I want something at three o'clock in the morning, I have to get up and find my credit card to enter the number, and I usually won't do it. I also actively make the decision to put the phone down and give myself permission to buy it if I still want it at 1 p.m. No middle-of-the-night decisions; purchases only during work hours.

The Dollar Store is amazing because you can go and impulse shop and get your jimmies by buying a bunch of stuff, and it costs six bucks. Not great for clutter (avoid this tip if you have a clutter problem!), but it does scratch that spending itch. Just try to donate stuff once you've gotten your fun so it doesn't end up in a landfill.

For me, if it's only a dollar, I'm throwing fifty of them into my cart. So I actually utilize the *opposite* strategy, and I tell myself that I'm going to save up for the nice thing. So rather than going to the Dollar Store all week and buying five things, I'm gonna save that twenty-five dollars to buy myself something nice.

At the end of the day, it's just EASIER to buy now. Make that feeling go away. That's what you have to work through. That's the addiction. That's where the problem comes up. That dopamine may make you feel good in the moment, but the debt comes later.

A handy red flag: Do you feel the urge to keep it a secret that you bought THE NEW SHINY THING? Keep it from your partner or from the people in your life? That likely means either you can't afford it or it's just something that you need to further consider. If you ever feel like you need to hide it, pause, then choose a strategy to delay the "Buy Now."

SHOULD I BUY THIS THING?

STEP ONE
HOW DO I FEEL?

Y N

- ☐ ☐ Am I emotionally regulated?
- ☐ ☐ Am I hungry?
- ☐ ☐ Am I thirsty?
- ☐ ☐ Am I tired?
- ☐ ☐ Have I taken my medication today?
- ☐ ☐ Is it before 10 p.m.?
- ☐ ☐ Am I feeling shame/guilt/the need to hide this purchase?
- ☐ ☐ Is this purchase financially viable for me right now?

STEP TWO
TAKE TIME TO THINK

Y N

- ☐ ☐ Is this an impulse purchase?
- ☐ ☐ Have I thought about this for more than 24 hours?
- ☐ ☐ Am I reacting to an advertisement?
- ☐ ☐ Am I reacting to a trend?
- ☐ ☐ Do I have a place to put it?
- ☐ ☐ Will I keep it for more than a year?
- ☐ ☐ Does it negatively affect my ability to save?
- ☐ ☐ Does it impact my budget significantly?
- ☐ ☐ Can I find it used or borrow it?
- ☐ ☐ Would I still want this if I couldn't buy it for two weeks?
- ☐ ☐ Have I done enough research on this item to be informed of the best cost/brand/quality?

Something that really helped me was using a decision-making tool. I will be the FIRST to admit that it's going to feel like a monumental pain in the ass. I HATED it when I first started. I would get SO MAD at myself for having to use a dumb chart to buy a dumb sweater for a dumb trip, until I realized that avoiding feeling those feelings was why I was overspending in the first place.

STEP THREE
THE THING

Y N

- ☐ ☐ Do I *need* this?
- ☐ ☐ Do I *actually like* this?
- ☐ ☐ Am I buying for right now or an idealized version of myself that may or may not someday exist?
- ☐ ☐ Do I own something like it already?
- ☐ ☐ Does it create a solution to a problem I have?
- ☐ ☐ Is it made well?
- ☐ ☐ What is the "cost per use"?
- ☐ ☐ Is it a gift?
- ☐ ☐ Does the person actually want it or am I justifying spending by making it "not for me"?

STEP FOUR
FINAL CHECKS

Y N

- ☐ ☐ Am I honestly just bored or dysregulated?
- ☐ ☐ Does this brand or product support my values?
- ☐ ☐ Is there an immediate, emergent need for this?
- ☐ ☐ Can I live a fulfilling life without it?
- ☐ ☐ Is this an item that goes on sale at a certain time?
- ☐ ☐ Can I wait for that time?

Sit with this chart for a while. Then really, truly ask yourself: Do I need or really want this? Can I afford it? And am I being honest about these answers? From there, make your decision.

How do I make sure I have RENT COVERED?

OH, HEY! LOOK WHAT I FOUND ON THE FLOOR! IT'S A LIST OF STRATEGIES FOR PAYING RENT RANGING FROM OBNOXIOUSLY, BORDERLINE INSULTINGLY OBVIOUS TO OUT OF THE BOX AND SILLY . . .

- **Open a "Rent" Bank Account:** Most banking apps will have some option of opening another account, sometimes without even having to make a phone call. Open another account called "Rent" and put rent money into it as soon as you have it. It's much harder to accidentally spend money if you have to move it first. Just make sure you get a checkbook for that account and don't lose it. I used to put mine under my computer monitor.

- **Pay Early:** Some landlords will accept rent early. Find out if this is the case for you. If it is, pay rent as soon as you HAVE it, not when it's due. With this method it's important to have a place to note whether you paid rent for this month. I recommend a whiteboard marker on the fridge: e.g., "NOV. RENT–YES."

- **Cashier's Check Method:** This method works well if you can't pay early and if you have easy access to your bank. As soon as you have the money, get a cashier's check for rent. With a personal check, the money stays in your account until it gets cashed. With a cashier's check, the money gets taken out as soon as the check is written by the bank teller. You're essentially turning your rent money into a gift card that can be used *only* to pay rent. You still have to remember to send it, but it will stop you from accidentally spending it.

- **Credit Card Method:** This is a method of managing all your bills that was recommended to me by a neurotypical friend of mine.

    → Open a credit card with a limit that is higher than your monthly bills.

    → Set all your bills to be automatically charged to that credit card.

    → Pay off that credit card every month.

    → Do a fun little dance because look at you, doing such a good job.

    You gotta admit, it's elegant. It consolidates many separate problems requiring many different solutions into one problem with one solution. The VERY SCARY part of this method is that there is now an interest rate attached to your bills, so if you get behind on them, they don't just sit there, they get bigger. A lot bigger. So go for it if you want to try this method, but be careful.

- **Party-Time Method:** This method works best if you live with people, but can also be done alone. The Party-Time Method basically makes a holiday out of rent day. When I was in my early twenties, I lived in a house with six other people, and we each had to deliver our rent checks by hand. So every month, we would each set aside a small amount of money (twenty bucks or so) and use it to throw a little rent party. When rent day came, we would all hang out for a little bit, indulge in some things, play some *Mario Kart*, and then go to my landlord's house and slip our checks through the mail slot. I have a lot of fun memories from rent day! And I certainly didn't forget to pay rent, because I was looking forward to it.

    If you live alone, feel free to gather some friends or just have an absolute "treat yourself" day.

    TL;DR: Pretend your rent is slightly more than it is, then use the extra money to have fun on rent day.

You can also set calendar reminders, predate a year's worth of checks, and even (if you're able) save up and pay your landlord several months ahead of time. Some banking and budgeting apps will also allow you to set reminder notifications about bills coming up.

 ## How do I STRUCTURE MY FINANCES?

 The philosophy here is to try to reduce the numbers you need to think about; knowing how much money you need in your bank account on a certain day is clutch.

So on the seventeenth, or whatever, if I have at least $1,500 in my bank account, I'm cool. Try to reduce it to only a key number or two. The hard part here is you will need to have the discipline to figure out what that number is. This way you don't have to go, Okay, *what are my expenses?* month after month.

Have you ever found yourself doing this?

You: I have to leave in fifteen minutes.

Fifteen minutes later

You: I have to leave in fifteen minutes.

The same thing happens with money. Check your account more often.

RESOURCES: How do I make a BUDGET?

 Sometimes it's easier to start by looking. Not judging, not restructuring, just straight-up evaluating what you spend in a month to gather that data to figure out your strengths and weaknesses when it comes to spending.

Because making a budget is often difficult for a person with ADHD, it's easy to forget that some people can throw together a personal budget like it's nothing. It's worth it to reach out to money-savvy friends for help and advice.

There are many different ways that you can outsource without spending much money. Budgeting and savings apps have been super useful to us in terms of tracking spending and seeing where our money goes, and they are often color-coded and visual.

If you do have a little extra money to spend, hiring an accountant—even for a couple of hours to consult—can be life-changing for getting money issues under control.

Chances are, the thing that you've been agonizing over for months would take a professional about fifteen minutes to sort out. And it serves a dual purpose: you're sharing the problem so it's not a secret while also getting help actively solving the problem.

This is the part where we guide you toward people far more knowledgeable on the subject of budgeting than we are. Making a budget and managing your finances with ADHD are absolutely doable. Like everything else, it's individual, and you'll identify systems that work for you as you go. For budgeting in particular, we recommend you check out the following:

- **YouNeedABudget**
- **IUx: Introduction to Personal Financial Planning | edX**
- @HumphreyTalks
- Dasha Kennedy, @TheBrokeBlackGirl
- Tiffany Aliche, @thebudgetnista

DAILY SPENDING TRACKER

MONDAY	SPENDING	SPENDING	SPENDING	SPENDING	SPENDING
TUESDAY	SPENDING	SPENDING	SPENDING	SPENDING	SPENDING
WEDNESDAY	SPENDING	SPENDING	SPENDING	SPENDING	SPENDING
THURSDAY	SPENDING	SPENDING	SPENDING	SPENDING	SPENDING
FRIDAY	SPENDING	SPENDING	SPENDING	SPENDING	SPENDING
SATURDAY	SPENDING	SPENDING	SPENDING	SPENDING	SPENDING
SUNDAY	SPENDING	SPENDING	SPENDING	SPENDING	SPENDING

WEEKLY BUDGET   **WEEKLY SPENDING**   **WEEKLY SAVINGS**

I have a HARD TIME with having NICE THINGS because they always get RUINED. What should I do?

Try to have a home for them that is high up. Because if it's within reach, things are gonna fall on it. It's gonna get cluttered with other stuff.

Keep the original box. That new box feeling makes it feel special, like, *Oh, that's that nice thing.* Or get a cute case or something to hold it in. Anything that's visual or tactile that reminds you that this is a special thing.

How do I be FRUGAL without ridding myself of the JOY OF LIFE?

I like this question a lot. Fear not, dear reader, you can do both. **When you think about what brings you joy and how to stay frugal while doing that thing, you need to either do the thing less frequently OR find a similar thing that is less expensive.** So you're either reducing the cost or reducing the frequency.

Try thinking about it like this: Is it necessary for that thing you like to be expensive? For example: You love X restaurant because it's super nice inside and the waitstaff are friendly and the vibes are on point. So how about you go for a drink and an appetizer? If what you like is physically being there and not necessarily eating a whole big meal, you can still do that without spending a bunch of money.

What if the thing that you really like is the food, so it HAS to be expensive for you to enjoy that? Then you may want to look at other restaurants with food that you also really like but at a lower price point. Boiling down WHAT it is you enjoy about THE THING will help you choose which strategy to take with your joyful frugality—do it less frequently or find a cheaper way to do it.

Look at traveling as another example. Is the joy of traveling going a physical distance away and landing somewhere new? Or is it the destination itself that gives you the jimmies? Again, like with the restaurant example, **try to identify WHAT it is ABOUT the thing that you like**.

I love traveling, but I recently realized my favorite part about it is trying new coffee shops. And then I thought, *I live in Atlanta. I am literally less than twenty-five minutes away from like four hundred coffee shops. I'm never gonna have time to try all the coffee shops that are within driving distance for me. So I do not need to get onto a plane to New York to go try a new coffee shop.* I can get into my car and drive fifteen minutes to check out somewhere new. I'm not *depriving* myself of a trip to New York; I'm being realistic about my time and money and working within those constraints.

You can also use the concept of subtraction to identify what's important. What could you remove from the travel experience? Hey, Cate, do you wanna go to this cool, faraway place?

Yeah, totally!

Also, they don't have coffee.

Well, then not really.

So, it's about the coffee. That's the important piece. Now let's look at less costly options for you to find some joy at a new coffee shop without having to pay for airfare.

Final thoughts:

If you are really, truly struggling with finances in a way that is scary, out of control, or otherwise harming you financially, there is help available. There are some great resources through Debtors Anonymous.

I've used some of their suggestions and resources to help me reduce my compulsive spending. If you're not super comfortable with the God aspect in twelve-step programs, their workbooks and journals do a really good job of making it about money and finances, not turning your bank account over to a higher power.

—Cate

Questions to ask yourself . . .

Finances can be tough, especially if you're just starting to get them together. Here are some questions you can ask yourself as you read this chapter and consider how money factors into your own life . . .

- What feelings come up for you when you think about the state of your finances?
- What feelings come up for you when you're in a store or shopping online?
- Do you keep your spending habits to yourself or make purchases in secrecy?
- If you want to buy something but make yourself delay the purchase by three days, would you still want it?
- Would you buy as much stuff on Amazon if it weren't for that "Buy Now" button?
- Would you buy as much stuff online if you didn't have your credit card number memorized or saved on your computer?
- Is paying rent or mortgage a big stressor in your life? If so, would you benefit from a system for making those payments?
- How often do you check in on your bank accounts and credit card transactions online?

PART

5

Relationships, SEX, AND LOVED ONES

14

All About
Relationships

> "You shouldn't be in a committed relationship with someone unless you feel there's a good chance you're going to spend the rest of your life with them, otherwise you're just running out the clock."
>
> —ERIK GUDE at twenty-two, incorrectly and arrogantly

For the first twenty-two years of my life, I did not meet anyone with whom I thought I could spend the rest of my life. So, for the first twenty-two years of my life, I was never in a serious relationship. I dated around a little bit, but I never considered getting close to anyone. Until I met Danielle.

She was my roommate's coworker, who came back to the house one day after their shift. I was frantically practicing fine-dicing carrots in my kitchen (I was about to start a line-cook job that was so scary it made me almost break my fingers to get out of it) when she tapped me on the shoulder. She had so many interesting questions about what I was doing and why I was doing it the way I was. Her enthusiasm was raw and infectious. She asked me out a few days later. I could tell that we both had a lot to teach each other.

We did . . . just not the things I'd hoped.

Being in a committed relationship was scary new territory for me, and I quickly realized that supporting a romantic partner was a *skill* you have to *learn*. I didn't have this skill, and my ADHD would make it difficult to learn.

It felt like no matter what I did, I would inflict a million little injuries on her every day. I forgot important dates, showed up late to places, forgot her mother's name (like a weird number of times, even for me).

I had a hard time just sitting still with her or cuddling. I always felt the need to jump up to get something else, or change the lighting, or turn on music, or other dumb little things. I worried that made her feel like she wasn't enough for me. I think it did.

She was always so nice about everything, because she was wonderful. She would healthily bring up the ways I was hurting her and help strategize with me on how to be better. She gave me chance after chance, and every time I would fall short.

Perhaps most damaging, I hadn't yet learned to manage the nagging boredom in the back of my head. To be clear: Danielle was *not* boring, nor was I bored by her. She was a wonderfully curious and engaged person I loved spending time with. I just hadn't learned yet that I, Erik, have a little ADHD monkey in the back of my head who is bored all the time, and I have to be ready to entertain it lest I get frustrated/dissatisfied with whatever I'm doing, including spending time with my partner. The guilt I felt from feeling bored around her was immeasurable. I felt evil.

So I broke up with her. She deserved better than I was capable of being at the time, or at least that's what I told myself. I still get knots in my stomach when I think about what I put her through.

I wasn't equipped to be in a relationship the way I am now. I don't mean "equipped" in the sense that I have a vast catalog of "ADHD life hacks," or even that I have a more thorough understanding of the neuropathology of ADHD. What I have is **a much greater understanding of myself and the specific problems I have to address in order to be fully present in a relationship**.

So as you read this chapter, remember that there is nothing more necessary for managing your ADHD than *knowing yourself* and understanding how *your* ADHD shows up in *your* life. Tools are useful only if you have something to do with them. Solutions aren't solutions unless you know the problems you are trying to solve. Try to maintain a compassionate curiosity about your brain and always endeavor to learn more about your own mind. Above all, be honest with yourself.

—**Erik**

One of the biggest frustrations I have as a person with ADHD is that everyone talks about how hard it is to *make* friends, but I never felt like I heard anyone talking about how hard it is to KEEP them. I'm AMAZING at making friends. I make friends at every single event and party I go to. I love meeting people, I love listening to their stories and what inspires them and motivates them, and I am excited for a lifelong friendship, only to realize a week later that I forgot to text them back after the party, if I even remembered to get their number at all.

"Out of sight, out of mind" feels appropriate when we're talking about our keys or the moldy vegetables we forgot about in the fridge again. It's a lot less comfortable to acknowledge that for many people with ADHD, "out of sight, out of mind" applies to your grandma and your best friend. Sometimes in June, when the Father's Day advertisements start to go up in stores, I have a momentary rush of panic that I've forgotten to get my dad something. Then I remember that he died ten years ago and feel the same raw rush of grief and loss that I felt the week he died, and then I feel a secondary rush of shame and guilt for not remembering.

> I am not a bad person or a bad friend for struggling to maintain friendships—and neither are you.

I am hypercognizant of Internet comment sections when it comes to topics like this—how easy it is to accuse someone with ADHD of not caring, of not being invested in the relationship, of being a "bad" friend: "If they wanted to, they would." But I also know what it is like to live in my brain, how much I *want* to be a good friend, how much I *try* to be a good friend, but there is a whole lot of executive functioning involved in actually *making this happen*. I am not a bad person or a bad friend for struggling to maintain friendships—and neither are you. You are not a fuckup. You just need to take some self-awareness and some manual steps . . . perhaps a system or two . . . to improve your relationships when you have ADHD.

—**Cate**

I have TROUBLE LISTENING to PEOPLE when they TALK. WHAT should I do?

If you have ADHD, you've probably been told a lot in your life that you're not paying attention and you need to be. You might internalize the idea of *If I don't look like I'm paying attention, then I get yelled at.* That can get ingrained deep in your psyche, which can lead to a practice of pretending like you're paying attention.

It also depends on the person. If it's a friend, I would say, "Hey, just so you know, I can either *look like* I'm listening or *actually* listen. So if you're talking and I'm looking away or fiddling, that's what I need to do to be able to listen to you."

What if it's not a friend? Little strategies and stims that aren't noisy or distracting can help. For me, a good one is touching my thumb to each of my fingers and counting *one, two, three, four* as I touch each one, even under a table if I need to keep it to myself. And you can mix them up: *One, three, two, four. One, four, two, three . . .*

You can also make a little drum set that only you can hear in your mouth by GENTLY tapping your top and bottom teeth together. That little drum and percussion set got me through high school.

It might be useful to directly (either in person or via email) explain the situation to a teacher, colleague, or boss. Contextualizing in the positive—"doodling/taking notes/having a fidget toy helps me to focus, process, and retain the important information you're giving me to better succeed as your student/employee"—can go a long way.

Speaking of frustrating social norms . . .

CHAPTER 14: All About Relationships

❓ I have TROUBLE making EYE CONTACT in situations where eye contact is expected. Any ADVICE?

ADHD struggles with eye contact can be grounded in distraction. It can be difficult to stay focused on maintaining eye contact while also paying attention to what the other person is saying.

There is also the Autistic experience of eye contact. **Research has shown that eye contact can be physically painful or uncomfortable for Autistic people.**[1] **Then there is the overlap conversation—20–40 percent of people with ADHD are also Autistic.** So a little column A, a little column B.

In addition, there's this idea that if somebody doesn't look you in the eye, they're a liar or disinterested or a narcissist . . . the body language expert–type of pseudoscience. If you look to the right, you're telling the truth, and if you look to the left, you're a liar. Except maybe there's a spider in the corner, you know? The truth is, a lot of this stuff has been 100 percent debunked, but it's a way to put people into neat little boxes.

All that is to say that **the eye contact conversation is really tricky because for some people, eye contact is a mark of respect**. I've had bosses who feel very strongly that you look them in the eye when you talk to them. Me: "Great, I can do that, but then I'm not gonna be listening." Similarly, in some cultures—non-Eurocentric white American cultures—looking people in the eye can be considered disrespectful or aggressive. There is not one worldwide, unified way of "paying attention."

I would add that in a lot of situations you don't have to look people in the eye as much as you think you do. In those situations that really do require eye contact, you're going to have to either white-knuckle it or hopefully find a way to talk about it.

"Hey, friend, please don't pay attention to how much eye contact I'm making. It has nothing to do with how closely I'm listening to you." **You can also try what I like to call "park benching," or facing the same direction as the person you're talking to.**

 Or going for a walk or a drive.

 Exactly. So, rather than sharing eye contact, you're sharing stimulus. You're sharing what you're looking at. **Think about how many good conversations you've had in cars 'cause you don't have to look at the other person. You can just stare at the world while you're talking about stuff.**

If you have no other option but actual eye contact, like in a job interview, you can practice looking behind somebody. You're facing the person so that your eyes are pointed at their eyes but you are actually focused on the wall behind them. It doesn't make a conversation less boring, but it does make it less nerve-racking.

What is it like dealing with family expectations and obligations while also juggling ADHD?

 Pretty sure they all think I don't care because I struggle to reach out regularly.
—**Clint**

❓ I don't know how to have a CONVERSATION without INTERRUPTING people. What should I do?

Let's say you had a disorder that causes you to compulsively punch people in the face. Hopefully, the necessary people in your life are aware that you have this disorder and that you're doing your best to not punch their faces. Perhaps they can even be understanding if you do it sometimes despite your best efforts to suppress the urge. No matter which way you slice it, it's still a bad thing to punch people in the face, and it's your responsibility not to do that.

Interrupting people is the same thing. Hopefully, the people close to you understand that sometimes it's difficult for you not to interrupt them. But it is generally still rude to do, and it is your responsibility as a person with agency to curb your impulse to interrupt people, and to treat others with respect.

PTOUGH LOVE PTERODACTYL

If you're looking for this book to say, "It's okay. If your friends are not cool with you constantly interrupting them, then they're jerks. You're perfect," well . . . sorry.

So, when people are talking to you, dear ADHD friend, the communication goes both ways. **If you know what they're going to say, you may feel like you can just jump in and finish the thought because** *Efficiency! I already know what they're gonna say, so there's no need for them to say it.* **But it's important that *they* say it.** So don't interrupt somebody just because you know where they're going.

Accept that you're not going to get to say all the things. Sometimes you are gonna have a funny, interesting quip, but to get it in at just the right moment, you'd have to interrupt someone, so you've got to let it go. A lot of people do this automatically, but if you have ADHD, you may have to learn to do it manually. Luckily, when you do something manually for long enough, it starts to feel automatic. It gets easier.

 I think there is a big difference between struggling with impulse control and lacking empathy, and there is an important distinction there. One of the best pieces of advice that I ever got was that **it is far more useful to be *interested* than it is to be *interesting*.**

It is okay if you are a neurodivergent person who is excited and passionate and interested and constantly thinking great thoughts. But **it's part of our personal responsibility to give other people space. We have to let other people experience that joy and excitement. And we can't do that if we're constantly taking up all the space.**

Learning how to take a step back and hold that space for people is a great way to practice better listening skills and patience. Patience is important because people like having the chance to say something—everyone wants to feel included in the conversation.

 If we want people to be patient and accommodating to us and how our brains work, we must also be patient and accommodating to them and how their brains work.

There's also something to be said about the RSD component of communication (reminder: RSD is a common experience of ADHD that interferes with a person's ability to regulate their emotional response to *perceived* rejection and failure—refer to page 112 for more on the subject).

With rejection sensitivity, it can be easy to assume that everyone is judging you or being hypervigilant about body language, and let that affect your communication—*Tony looked over at the clock . . . Am I taking too long? Is my story boring?*—when in reality, maybe Tony just wanted to know what time it was.

> Everyone wants to feel included in the conversation.

CHAPTER 14:
All About Relationships

Similarly, there can be a danger in what I call "Mrs. Maisel-ing," which is where you turn normal conversations into full-blown performances and/or a stand-up routine because you feel like the only way for people to like you or to engage with you is to be "on" or to be "entertaining." That's not how good friendships are formed.

Ask yourself: Are you engaging in a conversation, or are you doing a routine? Are you *actually listening* to what is being said, or are you waiting your turn for your next witticism? Are you constantly slipping entire mathematical equations or quoting Nietzsche in your conversations *because that information is important/relevant to what you're talking about*, or are you doing that to prove that you're smart and interesting and know stuff and you're worth listening to?

People pick up on those subtleties, which can often read as pretentious, attention-seeking, or insincere. Doing this frequently can be an incredibly efficient way of establishing your presence in the conversation, but ask yourself—are you leaving room for others?

Again, people with ADHD and/or Autism often develop pattern recognition and pattern matching. This can be a really good thing and it can also be a really bad thing because sometimes, particularly in conversation, the ADHD brain can easily go from A to B to Z without having to expressly go through the rest of the letters.

It's a way that our brain processes information. But it can come off like you're rushing to the ending or interrupting—not because you're being malicious or because you think the other person is boring, though it can come across like that if you're not careful.

There are many ADHD memes about how we can watch the first five minutes of a movie and know what's going to happen or know who the bad guy is. There's a whole thing on social media about how people with ADHD are psychic. **We're not**, we're just really good at recognizing and processing patterns, especially in media, which often uses them to deliver information.

Can you share a personal story about a time when ADHD affected your relationship with someone?

> I've lost friends because I just didn't think to contact them. I'd go so long without saying anything and then be embarrassed that I lost touch.
>
> —Craig from Wisconsin

Why can't people ACCEPT that FORGETTING things, interrupting people, being LATE, etc. are just part of my ADHD and that I CAN'T HELP IT?

Because you *can* help it. You can figure out ways to remember stuff. You can learn not to interrupt people. You can develop strategies to show up on time. You are not doomed to inconveniencing other people for the rest of your life, and more importantly, **you're not entitled to do so**.

You are also not entitled to any more comfort than anyone else and should never **expect anyone to accommodate you at the expense of their own well-being**. That's not accommodation; that's a type of social theft. Accommodations exist as an attempt to keep people on a fair and level playing field, not to get you what you want.

I know we say it a lot in this book, but it bears repeating: **being neurodivergent is *never* an excuse to hurt other people**.

> **Your behavior affects other people.**

Erik is being the bad cop, so I'll be Cool Aunt Cate cop for a minute: managing RSD can be extremely difficult, and the fear of an awkward or uncomfortable conversation with a friend can be overwhelming. As a result, MANY neurodivergent people inadvertently become terrified of confrontation and/or conflict.

It's not fun to fight with your friends, it's not fun to have tension with your friends, but sometimes, if it's a friendship you're committed to, working through that is what needs to happen for the friendship to last. It doesn't mean you're a bad friend or you failed at friendship. Similarly, we can outgrow people. We can discover that a friendship isn't a good fit. Okay, back to Erik . . .

When you forget to show up for things, lose other people's stuff, or interrupt a friend's story, you are hurting them. Your behavior affects other people.

Now, you might be thinking, *WTF? Didn't these clowns just write a whole chapter about how I'm allowed to set up my life and my systems however I feel is best for me? Now they're saying everything I do affects other people?*

Do you wanna know a secret? **Learning how to build functional systems isn't just about helping you. Sometimes it's about minimizing the likelihood that your ADHD symptoms will negatively impact someone else.**

My FRIENDS say I'm ANNOYING. What should I do?

 This one is tricky because there are two major narratives that happen when we talk about neurodivergence. The first is "In a perfect world, I should be able to 100 percent be myself. I should be able to interrupt people. I should be able to talk for as long as I want. Because if those people were my friends, they would understand that I can't help it because I have ADHD."

On the other hand, if you consider your personal responsibility . . . is your interrupting people hurting feelings? Is your unwillingness to pass the mic to someone else in conversation causing issues in the friendship?

If your friends are annoyed that you breathe too loud, then okay, maybe you need to get new friends.

If they're annoyed that your favorite food is sushi and none of them like sushi, then maybe they're not good friends for you. Or perhaps you just decide, *Hey, I'm gonna stop bringing up sushi with these particular friends and go find a local sushi enthusiast group that meets on Thursdays.*

But if they're annoyed because you interrupt, you talk over people, or you're flaky, those behaviors still have repercussions, even if those behaviors stem from your neurodivergence.

It's easy to just lean into the "real friends will understand" narrative. But real friends are also allowed to have boundaries, like "I don't really want to be talked over every time I raise a point." Or "I don't want to be shot down every time I suggest something." Or "You've said you'll come bowling with us four times now, but you never show up."

It's tricky, but I think a lot of it is less about being neurodivergent and more about being a good friend yourself.

 HOT TAKE: if someone is annoyed by you, and you're not doing anything unreasonable, fuck 'em.

❓ What do I do if I like someone, but I know I don't have enough BRAIN SPACE to SUPPORT them in a way they deserve?

Every good relationship is based on a firm foundation of friendship. So be friends with the person. If you can't be friends with them, then you probably shouldn't be dating them in the first place. And friendships are like romantic relationships "lite." It can be easier to support a friend than to support a partner—it's lower on the relationship hierarchy. So be friends with them first.

I would also caution you, dear reader, to be careful of love-bombing, which can happen really easily for people with ADHD. The person you've met or the excitement you feel becomes a hyperfixation, so you get super excited and want to text and talk with them all the time. Then two weeks go by, the newness wears off, and then that person is like, "Hey, how come you haven't texted me in like three days? We used to talk for hours and hours and hours at a time." It's very common in the ADHD dating experience, jumping in with both feet.

Not everybody's ready for a committed relationship at any given time. That's why it's so important to be aware of where you are in life right now, what you want, and what you're able to offer another person.

It's so easy to overcommit with ADHD. You say yes to something, but then you realize you can't actually commit to whatever or whomever it may be. Do that self-reflection work *first*. **Are you being hard on yourself, or are you truly not in a place right now to give another person what they need?**

What can I do if my PARTNER says ADHD DOESN'T EXIST?

The International Consensus Statement is free online.[2] Basically, a huge group of medical professionals around the world wrote this paper that has a lot of really interesting stuff in it, but it also just says: *Hey, ADHD exists. It's not because of video games, goddamn it.*

Your partner's opinion on whether a medical disorder exists, unless they're a doctor, is meaningless. If you were sick and went to the doctor, who said you have cancer, and then you got home and your partner said, "Cancer doesn't exist," you'd tell them to fuck off.

If your partner is denying your reality to that extent, I want you to question whether they should continue being your partner.

This feels like the right time to bring up some very upsetting facts about ADHD that don't get talked about enough: Individuals with ADHD experience higher rates of sexual assault, rape, psychological abuse, and intimate partner violence than those without. And kids with ADHD are more likely to be victims of kidnapping and sex trafficking.[3]

I want to be clear: none of this is ever, ever the fault of someone with ADHD, but **abusers often use our weaknesses against us, to gaslight and coerce and manipulate us into accepting unacceptable behavior or staying in unhealthy relationships out of fear that no one else will love us.**

> If your partner is denying your reality to that extent, I want you to question whether they should continue being your partner.

CHAPTER 14:
All About Relationships

TO BREAK IT DOWN FURTHER:

Control and Manipulation

At the heart of many abusive relationships is the concept of control. When someone denies the existence of ADHD, it's often less about the medical condition itself and more about establishing dominance. By casting doubt on ADHD, they're subtly suggesting that those with the condition might be overreacting or not fully grasping their own experiences. This isn't just a casual dismissal; it's a calculated move to shift the narrative, maintain an upper hand, and position themselves as the more "rational" party. It's a way to make the person with ADHD feel like they're just imagining things. It's like saying, "Hey, it's all in your head, therefore you need me to guide you," or "I'm not paying for your ADHD medication, you don't need it." This tactic not only maintains dominance but also manipulates ADHDers into thinking our struggles are self-inflicted.

→ More information on how to escape an abusive partner:

- **National Domestic Violence Hotline (US):** Offers a 24/7 hotline, online chat, and other resources to anyone experiencing domestic violence: www.thehotline.org/ or 1-800-799-SAFE (7233)

- **Women's Aid (UK):** Supports women and children experiencing domestic abuse through helplines, live chat, and refuge services at www.womensaid.org.uk/ or via the National Domestic Abuse Helpline: +44 (0) 808-2000-247

- **ManKind Initiative (UK):** Provides a confidential helpline, practical information, and support for men experiencing domestic violence: www.mankind.org.uk/ or +44 (0) 808-801-0327

- **Anti-Violence Project (US):** 24-hour bilingual hotline, counseling, and advocacy for LGBTQ and HIV-affected communities dealing with intimate partner violence at avp.org or 1-212-714-1141

- **The Network/La Red (US):** Hotline, advocacy, and group services for LGBTQ+, polyamorous, and SM/kink survivors of domestic violence at tnlr.org/en/ or 1-800-832-1901
- **Women of Color Network (US):** Provides training, community outreach, and policy advocacy for survivors of color, with resources available at www.wocninc.org/

GRIEVANCES GARGOYLE

Ignorance and Misinformation

Some people genuinely lack understanding about ADHD due to misinformation, personal biases, or lack of education. They might see ADHD as a convenient excuse for certain behaviors or even as a modern, made-up ailment. In an abusive relationship, this ignorance can be weaponized, with the abuser using social misconceptions to further demean and control their partner. There is a difference between someone who doesn't know and someone who refuses to listen and learn.

Fear/Dismissal/Simplification

Beneath the surface of many "ADHD is fake" denials, you'll often find fear lurking. Recognizing ADHD might mean confronting deeply ingrained biases or challenging long-held beliefs. And while we're **all** for simplifying complex topics to make them more digestible, there's a fine line between simplification and reduction. For some, it's more comfortable to reduce or negate ADHD's complexities than to genuinely engage, understand, and empathize. Unfortunately, many parents also fall into this category, especially when they are undiagnosed neurodivergent themselves.

If you take nothing else away from this chapter, remember these two things:

1. You are worthy and deserving of love, of care, of compassion and kindness. You do not have to change who you are at the molecular level to be loved. Your needs, your systems, your supports, *those matter*, and you deserve to have a partner who validates them, respects them, and supports you without unkindness or judgment. WITH THAT BEING SAID . . .

2. Having ADHD is not an excuse for forgetting things, being late, or inconveniencing others. You are not entitled to any more comfort than anyone else. We don't mean for this to sound harsh. What we mean is that the sooner you figure out your own ways to remember things and develop strategies to show up on time, the more harmonious your relationships will be.

Relationships, even the best and healthiest ones, can be hard sometimes. They can be especially hard when one (or both!) of the people in a couple have ADHD, and simple things like "remembering to do the task" or "remembering what knives don't go into the dishwasher" get easily confused with "Are they listening?"; "Do they even care about me?"; "I've reminded them nineteen times and I'm exhausted."

Surviving abuse or neglect or manipulation at the hands of someone you trusted and loved is horrendous, but it unfortunately happens—and it happens more frequently to neurodivergent people. Be aware of that. Watch for red flags or concerning patterns of behavior. Having ADHD is not a "reason" you might encounter abuse, but some abusers will use your struggles to their advantage. You are worthy of kindness, you are worthy of love, and it is not your fault if you have found yourself in this situation or ever do. Please know that help is out there (see the list of resources on page 340) and you have options available to you.

Let's Talk About Sex

Neurodivergency and sex is my special interest because I spent a long, long time feeling like I was broken, that everyone else understood how to have great sex, and I'd just missed the memo. It took me a long time to learn that there was nothing wrong with me; it was just that 99.99999 percent of the conversations we have about sex and intimacy are predicated on the notion that everyone involved is 100 percent neurotypical.

That's not a functional way of discussing sex. Many people have issues and struggles that stem from their own experiences as neurodivergent people. In fact, I got so mad about how much I was left out of the conversation that I went back to school to become a certified sex educator, so when I say I know a LOT about sex and neurodivergence, I'm literally an expert.

This chapter could be a book on its own. Sex, intimacy, communication, relationships—these are all huge, complex topics on their own (about which many books have been written already). When you add something like ADHD or Autism or start stacking comorbidities, like we talked about in chapter 2, it gets incredibly complicated very quickly.

It's always seemed weird to me that we talk about ADHD like this thing that happens exclusively in school or at the office. We talk about it like it's completely separate from sex, and when you walk through the bedroom door, it just magically disappears, and that just isn't the case. How your ADHD manifests in sex and intimacy is going to be different for everyone, but it will happen.

Approximately 40 percent of people with ADHD, regardless of gender, struggle with sex in one way or another.[1] That's a huge percentage of the community who deal with frustration (and sometimes shame, guilt, resentment, anger, or embarrassment) about these struggles.

With ADHD as an added consideration, it can be difficult to get into the mood, to stay in the mood, to get an erection, or to keep an erection. Orgasm can be very difficult, or you might be hypersensitive to orgasm. Your mood and attention might shift easily. Many ADHDers oscillate between an extremely high (hyper) sex drive and an extremely low (hypo) one. Then there's the MASSIVE impact that rejection sensitivity can play in navigating sex and intimacy. All this is a common part of the ADHD experience.

I'm going to break down some of the larger concepts to give you an idea of how ADHD fits into the equation of sex and intimacy. But before I do that . . .

Intimacy and sex are not the same thing!

It is REALLY IMPORTANT to understand the difference between the two. We often conflate them, but they are fundamentally different. Some people are incredible at intimacy but get super hung up around sex. Some people really, really like sex but find that being intimate and vulnerable is scary.

In this chapter, I am going to discuss mostly sex, but I'll also talk about ways to create intimacy without sex. As a person under the asexual umbrella, creating intimacy without necessarily having sex is a super-important part of my own life.

Intimacy vs. Sex

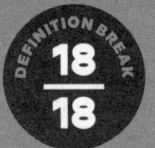

INTIMACY: The deep, personal connection we share with others. It's not just about romantic relationships or having sex—it's about opening up and sharing our innermost thoughts, feelings, and experiences.

This kind of sharing creates a strong foundation of trust and understanding. Intimacy is present in the bonds we have with friends, family, and partners. Intimacy is a mix of love, deep friendship, trust, affection, and caring. It's all about feeling truly connected and understood by someone else.

SEX: In simple terms, sex is about the physical side of relationships. It encompasses sexual intercourse and other sexual activities, focusing on physical pleasure, arousal, and often the pursuit of orgasm, though that's not always the case.

People engage in sexual activities for many reasons—it could be for the sheer pleasure of it, for reproduction, or just out of curiosity. It's important to note that sex doesn't always involve an emotional connection. People can have sexual experiences that are purely physical, without the deep emotional intimacy that might come with a romantic relationship.

> Approximately 40 percent of people with ADHD struggle with sex in one way or another.

❓ I get BORED or DISTRACTED during SEX. What should I do?

One of the most important things to understand about sex and intimacy is that, from an executive function standpoint, **your brain does not distinguish much between having sex and making a sandwich. It is still a series of tasks to organize, prioritize, manage, and (hopefully) complete.**[*]

At any point while making a sandwich and/or during intimacy, you can get interrupted, you can get distracted, you can lose focus, or your body or brain might be mismatched in its response. *I thought I was hungry, but now this sandwich seems unappealing.*

It's common to ascribe guilt and shame to these experiences. *I checked out during sex. I must not love my partner. My partner must not love me. I'm not doing a good enough job. I'm bad at sex.* None of that is true, and you're not a fuckup in this department. But because so much media and conversation are centered on this idea of "perfect sex, every time," it can be easy to feel like you're doing something wrong.

Even more than that, many, many people with ADHD have those stacking comorbidities. They might also be Autistic. They might also have depression, anxiety, OCD, or all of the above. All those things impact how we respond to intimacy or how we embrace pleasure—it's one thing to struggle with focus during sex, it's another thing to struggle with focus but also feel ugly and disgusting and unlovable while also dealing with sensory issues.

Before we get into tips and tricks, I want to talk about the different types of desire. This is based on the work of Dr. Emily Nagoski, who wrote the book *Come as You Are*, which I REALLY encourage you to check out.

---

[*] One time I got into a really big argument about this with one of my professors, who insisted I couldn't use this example because "Sex comes with emotions! Hormonal release! Dopamine! Seratonin! Oxytocin! A sandwich doesn't do that!" I said, "Clearly you just haven't ever had a really good sandwich."

Desire is often presented as one thing: you want your partner, your partner wants you. But it's much, much more complex than that.

People experience different types of desire in different ways.

- **Conditional Desire:** It's all in the name—conditions have to be right in order for a person to experience desire. That doesn't just mean candles and rose petals on the bed. It's things like being in the right mindset and headspace, not being worried about chores, to-do lists, or the stuff you've got to get to later. It can be extremely difficult to get into the mood (or stay there) if your anxiety about stuff getting done around the house or being late or even just orgasming is running rampant in your brain.

- **Responsive Desire:** Sometimes, for desire to initiate in our brain, we have to get a little nudge or reminder that we have the capacity to feel desire. Initiating might feel foreign to you because you need to feel wanted or desired before your own desire kicks in. As a result, sex can often feel like an afterthought unless you have a partner who enjoys initiating. (Most women fall into this category.)

- **Spontaneous Desire:** Some people just . . . get horny. It might be from seeing a particularly sexy person, it might be from thinking a particularly spicy thought, it might be because your hormones suddenly start screaming, "I NEED SEX RIGHT NOW!" but this kind of desire is usually sudden and swift. (It is also, statistically, how most men experience desire.)

- Do you see how important THAT is, right off the bat? If you have a relationship with one spontaneous and one responsive partner, intimacy is going to be a lot easier than in a relationship with two partners who are more the responsive type.

So, back to getting bored or distracted. Step one is that you've got to let go of those judgments because our brains are dopamine-seeking and engagement-seeking. The example I often use is this: You can be deeply in love with your partner and having great sex. Then if your neighbor starts mowing the lawn outside your window? Your brain is going to latch on to that because it's a new piece of information.

One solution is to **mitigate distractions**. For some people, that looks like being open with your partner and saying, "Hey, sometimes I'm going to get distracted. Don't take it personally. Can you do a quick check-in? Can you just ask if I'm okay?"

It is also VERY important to remember that checking in can be incredibly sexy.* A well-timed "Are you here with me?" or "Do you like how this feels? [listen for answer] Good. Beg for more" can be a very powerful addition to your sexy time.

Checking in also doesn't necessarily have to be a *question*. It can be a statement that prompts your partner to be an active participant: "Show me what you want," "Touch yourself for me," etc.

"Ew, that's so weird and awkward, I don't want to have such a clinical conversation with my partner where I say stuff like 'clitoris.'" Listen. I get it. I am a deeply, deeply awkward person.

PTOUGH LOVE PTERODACTYL

But at some point, you need to really look at yourself and your life and decide if your pleasure, your happiness, and the satisfaction and success of your relationship are worth an awkward three minutes.

There is no "right" way to have a tough conversation, especially when it comes to sex. Sometimes, having a conversation *about* the conversation can be useful.

Personally, I never want to do a highlight reel RIGHT after I have sex. That feels weird and puts me on the spot to come up with things. I always want at least a few hours to process. I want to be wearing clothes. I want to not be in the bedroom. All those are valid things to ask for! It can be REALLY helpful to make a rule to never talk about stuff right before you're about to have sex or right after. Other people might want to debrief right away. Also valid.

---

* It's also totally okay if your checking in is clinical and direct. Sometimes putting pressure on yourself to think of a smutty way of asking something can be much more distracting than just being direct and straightforward. Play around with it and discuss it with your partner.

"My partner likes to TALK right after sex, and I need time to PROCESS—what should I do?"

That's okay. In a scenario like this, sometimes creative problem-solving needs to happen—it may be that the partner who likes to discuss right away might mention some things they enjoyed a lot or maybe jot down notes so they don't forget what they wanted to talk about later on.

"YOU TAKE NOTES ON SEX??"

It's not silly if it makes your life easier . . .

I got distracted writing about being distracted. Back to it:

Other people might like to **incorporate something like a blindfold (it mitigates distractions!)**. One person might opt for turning out the lights to mitigate distraction, while another may want the lights on because it helps to know what's going on in their environment. It's very personal. **Similarly, you can use earplugs, put on music, pull the blinds, OR TURN OFF THE OVERHEAD LIGHT. Anything that makes you (and your partner) feel more comfortable and present and in the moment isn't weird, silly, or awkward. It's a TOOL. USE IT.**

I like to make the observation that when someone says, "Right there, don't stop," that's not the time to switch things up or get creative. However, when you have ADHD, if the sensory input is the same for too long, your mind can start wandering.

That's when you're noticing the ceiling fan clicking. That's when you're noticing your neighbor mowing the lawn. It can be very challenging.

But the boring, tedious truth here is that a lot of times it has nothing to do with sex, intimacy, or your relationship.

The ADHD Field Guide for Adults

PART 5:
Relationships, Sex, and Loved Ones

It's that the ADHD brain often needs everything around the moment of intimacy to be handled. This is conditional desire. *Did the dishwasher get emptied? Are the kids getting picked up from school? Boy, that pile of laundry next to the bed is making me feel a lot of shame about my mess while my partner is going down on me.*

If this kind of stress and guilt and shame starts to become so intense that it's stopping you from being able to enjoy intimacy, it might be a good time to zoom out and look at whether your partner is meeting your needs in other areas. If you're struggling or your needs aren't being met, it may be useful to open a conversation about building systems that allow your needs to be met.

Is being KINKY the same thing as being ADHD?

Nope!

There are kinky people who don't have ADHD and people with ADHD who don't enjoy kink at all, and both of those things are totally okay.

However, based on (this is important) *anecdotal, community-generated evidence*, it is probably fair to say that a fair number of folks with ADHD are also, in some ways, kinky. Perhaps not a majority, but quite a few.

Scientists aren't running to study the correlation between kink and ADHD, but the simplest way to explain it is to remove the "kink" from kink and evaluate what is left: sensory input and structure. The majority of your run-of-the-mill kinks—blindfolds, handcuffs, being tied up, impact play, power dynamics—boil down to adding (or subtracting) sensory input during intimacy while providing some kind of safe context in which to explore pleasure.

What do ADHD brains crave?

Input. Novelty. Sensory stimulation.

What's a GREAT way to make intimacy a little more exciting? Input. Novelty. Sensory stimulation.

What is something that a lot of people living with RSD (rejection sensitivity—see page 112) need to feel safe?

Direct communication. A safe container. Reassurance. Structure.

What is something that a power dynamic provides?

Direct communication. A safe container. Reassurance. Structure.

You see where I'm going with this?

It's okay if you're not into kink. It's important to remember that kink is not one-size-fits-all. You don't have to be super excited about wearing a collar or calling someone "sir" or "Daddy." (Not my thing, and I talk about kink on the Internet for my job.) You can take the elements that excite you and leave the ones that don't. At the end of the day, it's about healthy communication and negotiation with your partner to keep both of you safe. The rest is up to you.

So how do you navigate these conversations? How do you initiate that first "maybe you could tie me up sometime" conversation?

One of the best ways of coming to these conversations is to use something called a "yes/no/maybe list." These are basically master lists of a bunch of interesting and creative kink/BDSM activities that can range from the very basic to the very . . . unconventional. The idea is that you and your partner(s) sit down either together or separately and go through the list, and then you can compare notes and talk about what seems interesting, what you'd be willing to try, and what you're definitely not interested in doing.

It's totally okay to script/plan out what you want to say ahead of time, and if you're REALLY stressing, maybe write your partner a cute note or an invitation. "You are cordially invited to come tie me up."

Sometimes it can also help to define a specific "why," especially if your partner is a little hesitant or holds a bit of stigma or bias against kink. "I'd like you to tie me up" can sound intimidating, but "I really like deep pressure, and I think that not being able to move might allow me to stop worrying so much about what's going on and focus on sensation, rather than what my hands are doing."

Are some people with ADHD HYPERSEXUAL? Are some people with ADHD HYPOSEXUAL?

Hypersexual

Exhibiting unusual or excessive concern with or indulgence in sexual activity. —*Merriam-Webster*

Hyposexual

Hypoactive sexual desire disorder—also called HSDD—is when you're not interested in sex (have no sex drive or a low sex drive),[2] and—THIS IS REALLY IMPORTANT—it bothers you or is affecting your quality of life.

First and foremost, there is no one "right way" to have a sex drive, and any/all conversations about sex drive are based SOLELY AND ENTIRELY ON YOU AND YOUR OWN EXPERIENCES. There is no secret council that determines the international horniness scale upon which every human is judged.

This can get frustrating because we constantly hear something based solely on the individual experience referred to in the collective, so it can often feel like there's a way that we're "supposed" to be, and that's just not the case. We use the terms *disorder* and *dysfunction* to talk about low sex drive, but in reality many people simply just HAVE a low sex drive, and it's not problematic.

If you are 100 percent DTF all the time, every day, and then suddenly you're not, that might be something that you'd want to talk to a doctor about. If you have never been particularly interested in sex, that's *your* baseline; you don't need to try to force yourself to like sex more or in a different way.

For some people, sex has to do with dopamine seeking. For others, it's about providing more stimulation for your brain. And for others, there's less interest in sex because it becomes an overwhelming series of tasks. And for still others, having ADHD doesn't affect their sex life at all.

Sex drive also changes over time and is flexible—especially for people with monthly cycles. Some people go months without thinking about sex; some people want sex at least once a day. Both are valid. Some people start out very vanilla and un-kinky and wind up discovering that no, sex is GREAT when there are spankings or a power dynamic at play. It's okay if your understanding of yourself and your relationship to sex changes and flexes over time. You never have to just "decide."

It's not okay to decide that a person who isn't as interested in sex is somehow weird or broken or needs to change who they are to suit their partner's desire. Many couples simply have mismatched desires. It doesn't mean either of them is wrong. There may just need to be some discussion or compromise.

It is important to say here that many people with ADHD also experience things like sexual assault and a higher rate of sexually transmitted infections (STIs).[3] Many studies talk about this in the context of "risk-taking behavior," which always feels a little like victim blaming to me, but if you are a person who is experiencing a period of hypersexuality, it's important that you seek it out safely. I said yes when I meant no a lot when I was younger, and it put me into some very dangerous and very physically unsafe situations. This is another place where RSD can show up and create a lot of problems.

> For some people, sex has to do with dopamine seeking. For others, it's about providing more stimulation for your brain. And for others, there's less interest in sex because it becomes an overwhelming series of tasks.

Are a lot of people with ADHD QUEER?

Studies do show that there is a higher rate of queerness and gender nonconformity within the neurodivergent population.

However, this is a chicken-and-egg question because some people would argue that if you're a neurodivergent person, you're already used to living in a society that doesn't necessarily fit the way that you understand the world.[4]

Can people with ADHD be POLYAMOROUS?

Yes. Polyamory, "ethical nonmonogamy," or "open relationships" work for different people for different reasons. **For many people with ADHD, having an open relationship can ease that tension of *I have one partner and I can only ever be with this one partner*. That can cause a lot of fear, anxiety, and stress in some people.**

Other people who are neurodivergent and polyamorous may say that they just need different types of support from different partners. Personally, I get a very different type of support from Erik than I do from my husband, Chris. I love them both deeply, but our relationships are different. Polyamory can work for some people with ADHD, and for other people it can be completely overwhelming and not be the right choice at all.

I'm here not to tell you what is valid, but to talk about your options. I want things like polyamory, open relationships, ethical nonmonogamy, etc. to be part of this conversation, because for some people, they are a legitimate way of having their needs and support met and having generative and useful relationships.

And for other people who say, "Forget 100 percent of that," that's okay, too, as long as you aren't being a judgy asshat about it.

❓ I DON'T THINK about SEX. I don't even LIKE sex. Am I BROKEN?

NO. One of the biggest challenges in talking about sex is that there is an assumption that of COURSE you want to have sex, and if you don't, then there's something wrong with you that needs fixing. That is 100 percent not the case.

Asexuality and aromanticism are perfectly valid identities.[5] Period. Personally, I am demigraysexual. Sometimes people think that's weird: *You're on the ace spectrum, but you educate about sex?* To me, it makes perfect sense.

Sex is fascinating as a subject, especially when you pair it with the complexities of neurodivergence, but it's not something that I personally spend a lot of time wanting. (Until I do.) **Fun fact: recent studies have indicated that neurodivergent people tend to be asexual at higher rates than the neurotypical population.**

The asexual umbrella is huge, but in recent years, more specific definitions for a myriad of different relationships to sexuality have emerged. To highlight some of them:

1. Asexual (Ace)

DEFINITION: a person who experiences little to no sexual attraction to others.

This does not mean that an asexual person might not enjoy masturbating or cuddling or enjoying other types of intimacy with a partner. (Yes, asexual people can have fulfilling, loving, wonderful relationships.) Some asexual people are sex-repulsed, meaning that they have no interest in sex, and some asexual people really like having sex, they just enjoy it as a pleasurable sensation or endorphin-releasing activity. There is no "one right way" to be asexual, and what you do with your body to own your own pleasure is entirely okay.

2. Demisexual

DEFINITION: a person who experiences sexual attraction only after forming a strong emotional bond with someone.

3. Graysexual (Gray-A or Grey-A)

DEFINITION: a person who falls somewhere between asexuality and sexuality and may experience sexual attraction only under specific circumstances.

4. Aegosexual (Autochorissexual)

DEFINITION: a person who experiences a disconnection between oneself and the object of arousal, possibly enjoying and fantasizing about sex but not wanting to participate in it themselves.

5. Cupiosexual

DEFINITION: a person who does not experience sexual attraction but still desires a sexual relationship.

6. Libidoist Asexual

DEFINITION: an asexual person who experiences sexual desire but does not feel sexual attraction to others.

7. Akoisexual (Lithosexual)

DEFINITION: a person who experiences sexual attraction that fades upon reciprocation.

8. Fraysexual

DEFINITION: a person who experiences sexual attraction only to others they are less familiar with and loses that attraction as they get to know the person.

9. Reciprosexual (Recipromantic)

DEFINITION: a person who experiences sexual attraction only after knowing someone else is attracted to them.

NOTE: ALL these terms are JUST about sex. There is also the romantic part of it—you can be asexual and aromantic, or just aromantic, but still experience sexual desire for someone. Replace "sexual" with "romantic" in all the definitions above, and you'll get the idea.

What are ways to build INTIMACY and a CONNECTION with my partner if I'm NOT super excited about sex?

- **Cuddling and Physical Touch:** You can touch your partner without it leading to sex (and it's honestly important that you do). Activities like cuddling, holding hands, hugging, or massages without the expectation of sex at the end can build intimacy and trust through touch. For an added intimacy builder, practice synchronized breathing.

- **Shared Activities: DO STUFF TOGETHER.** This could be anything from cooking, hiking, playing a board game, *writing a book*, or working on a DIY project together. Create something together, whether it's art, music, writing, or even a garden. These activities create a shared foundation of experiences that you can build on together.

- **Intellectual Intimacy: Read Stuff Together. Watch Stuff Together. Learn Stuff Together.** The world is full of interesting books and movies and think pieces and documentaries and ideas about philosophy. Talking about them together allows you to connect on an intellectual level to understand your partner's thought processes and experiences, and how they see the world.

QUICK FIVE-MINUTE
Intimacy Builder

▶ (Eye Contact–Friendly Version)
Set a timer for five minutes. Sit across from your partner and place your hands underneath theirs. Look into your partner's eyes silently, without speaking, until the timer goes off. At the end of the timer, talk about what feelings and emotions came up. This can be a vulnerable and revealing exercise.

▶ (No Eye Contact Version)
Set a timer for five minutes. Sit on the floor or bed with your partner, back-to-back. Lean against your partner so you are using them as a support, but don't try to knock them over. Start the timer, close your eyes, and consciously try to feel your partner against you. Feel your partner resting against you and try to synchronize your breath with theirs. At the end of the timer, face your partner and talk about what feelings arise sharing this type of closeness with them.

- **Active Listening:** Turn off the TV, put down your phones, and really, truly talk to each other. Talk about your worries, your hopes, your dreams, what you ate for breakfast—whatever. The goal isn't to Win at Conversations. It's about taking time and space to listen to each other without distractions to show that your partner is important to you.

- **Establish Rituals:** Create small rituals like having coffee together every morning or reading to each other at night. Greet each other when you come home, no matter what you're doing. Text each other a "would you rather" during the day to talk about when you get home.

- **Affirmations and Appreciation:** Express appreciation for your partner AND ASK THEM how they like to be appreciated. Some partners like to hear verbal affirmations; for others it means far more to get a nice card that outlines things you love about them. Take turns sharing what you appreciate about each other for two minutes. Make a point of sharing three to five things you're grateful for every day. They can be about each other, your relationship, or life in general.

I have SENSORY ISSUES that show up in the BEDROOM; what can I do to ENJOY INTIMACY?

In many circumstances, especially if I'm stressed or feeling overwhelmed, I don't like being kissed. It took me a long, long time to admit that to myself. It doesn't mean that I don't love my partners, it doesn't mean that I don't find them attractive, it doesn't mean that I'm weird, it just means that in honoring my own needs and my own sensory issues, I am not a huge fan of kissing.

In the same way that we've been talking about systems and structures, you can also build systems and structures that support your sensory issues, creating an environment that allows you to relax and enjoy intimacy in a way that feels authentic and pleasurable to you. For me, a kiss on the neck or the forehead or getting a long hug from my partner makes me feel far more connected to them than mashing our faces together.

TOUCH

Finding the RIGHT touch for your sensory preferences can be a vital part of enjoying intimacy. Explore different types of touch. Show your partner how you like to be touched and ask them what they enjoy. You might find that one type of touch works better or worse for you—soft caresses; deep pressure; long, sustained contact; short, infrequent bursts; stingy or slapping; or thuddy and deep . . . there can be a lot of variation. (Especially if you bring kink/BDSM tools into the mix.) There are many other things you can do besides kissing to express intimacy, and there are a lot of ways to be touched that aren't necessarily sexual but can create a feeling of closeness and intimacy.

SOUND

If you're particularly sensitive to sound, you might want to consider putting on music. There are a LOT of different kinds of music that can work in intimate situations, everything from New Age Zen instrumental tracks to hard-core death metal. Play around with what makes sense in your brain. For me, personally, classical music really, really enhances the experience. If you're particularly bothered by outside noises (or even the natural noises made by bodies; it's VALID to not enjoy that), you can try wearing noise-canceling earbuds.

LIGHT

This is nearly the same thing as sound—play around with what works and doesn't. Color-changing light bulbs can be amazing for reducing visual noise and creating a different mood spatially in the bedroom (or wherever you're getting down). Blindfolds of varying degrees of opacity can also help cut down on visual stimulus. It's okay if you need to turn off the lights, and it's okay if you want to keep them on. This is about what works for you.

TEXTURE

I have a specific fuzzy blanket that is a Good Touch* for aftercare. Finding textures and touches that work for you can be as simple as shopping for sheets that you really enjoy or as complicated as playing around with jute ropes vs. silk ropes vs. cotton ropes—they all give a very different sensory experience.

---

* Good Touch is a type of physical contact that makes a person feel safe and secure.

SMELL/TASTE

Listen, I know that talking about smells and tastes in the sex chapter is about the most unsexy thing in the WORLD. But a lot of neurodivergent people are sensitive to smells, and the fact is, our bodies naturally make a lot of smells, both good and bad. If you are a person who is sensitive to smells, or worried about overproducing your own, sometimes simply showering before you do the deed (and paying attention to what products you use—mildly scented or unscented products may be best) can help mitigate. If you've got the space, you can also always shower *together* to lead into sexy time. There are also scented and flavored lubes and condoms. Some people like to have a specific perfume or cologne they wear or a scented candle they light during intimacy, which is awesome because it can also start to build an association for that smell meaning, "It's time to get turned on!"

In conclusion...

Over the past few years as my platform has grown, I have gotten thousands of heartbreaking emails and letters from people asking me for help with intimacy, sex, and relationships. Every time, I am just overwhelmed by deep frustration and sadness. *Why were so many of us undereducated and uninformed about our own bodies? Why were we taught that our bodies were shameful, that our sexuality was sinful, that masturbation was going to send us to hell, and that pleasure was secondary to procreation?*

I know that's not everyone's experience, but many of us, **ADHD or not, were raised in a culture of shame surrounding sex**. Even as a person who talks about sex on the Internet for my very public job, I still feel that same creeping shame and embarrassment come up sometimes. Unlearning those lessons can take years and years, especially when attitudes surrounding sex and intimacy are so polarized and politicized.

In so many places and in so many ways, sex and intimacy are still talked about in hushed tones and behind closed doors. Organizations out there are still fighting to take away access to information and education that can protect people and inform them about how their own bodies work, and I *hate* that.

I am angry that I am writing a book that might get banned in some places because we think it's important to acknowledge sex and intimacy as part of the ADHD experience. I hate that I get hate mail and threats calling me a slut and a whore and telling me I'm going to burn in hell because I educate about intimacy online. I hate that I, as a femme-presenting being, am simultaneously sexualized while also being constantly purity-tested. It's exhausting. People will pay to see my spicy photos, but if I talk about the importance of the clitoris in pleasure, I get told I'm being too clinical and gross.

My advice to you, dear reader, is simple. YOU DO NOT HAVE TO BE PART OF THE PROBLEM. Talk about sex. Discuss it. With your partner, with your family, with your friends. Talk about intimacy. Destigmatize it. Find a community that aligns with your beliefs. Get comfortable having fearlessly unapologetic conversations about your wants and needs.

I truly believe that taking ownership of your pleasure is one of the bravest and most vulnerable things you can do for yourself. It can be scary, especially in a relationship where you aren't treated well, or your partner rejects your needs in support of their own. But you have one glorious, exciting life to live, and you deserve to live without having to feel awkward about asking to be tied up or spanked, or just to be held, cherished, and loved.

You deserve so much more than so many of us were given, so I give you permission, dear reader, to claim that pleasure for yourself, and I hope this chapter helps, in some way, to at least get you started on that journey.

Wherever you are on that path, however you feel—right now, today—know that I am right here next to you, cheering you on, supporting you, and that you are never, ever alone.

16

THE
Chapter for Loved Ones

An exceedingly common phenomenon for loved ones of ADHDers is to feel a lot of guilt.

If only you'd noticed sooner, if only you'd been a little more patient, if only you would have known more about ADHD beforehand and could have supported them.

I want to validate those feelings. My own mom has struggled a lot with that. That's not to say she wasn't a good mom, but I know she has many regrets about things she said and did before she understood my neurodivergence and the way she expressed that frustration with me as a kid. (Yelling. There was a lot of yelling.)

I'm here to tell you that part of strengthening any relationship is forgiving yourself and giving yourself grace. It is admirable and kind to want to do better for the person with ADHD in your life, but I don't want you to forget that YOU also deserve kindness. You didn't know what you didn't know, you believed what you were taught to believe, and every day we are given an opportunity to grow and develop into a better version of ourselves.

Sometimes, being the best loved one you can be means needing to have honest, tough conversations about how to improve, or even repair, your relationship. It doesn't mean that anyone is at fault, it doesn't mean that anybody did anything wrong, it means that as we learn and grow and develop new systems and strategies, our needs and expectations may change. It's also valid to struggle with or need time to navigate those changes and the impact they may have on your own life.

Supporting an ADHD loved one doesn't mean allowing yourself to be steamrolled or accepting a parentified relationship in which you do all the work—it means working to find a balance and equity that supports you both. We hope this chapter can help.

—Cate

I think my PARTNER might have ADHD. How do I bring it up with them?

 Always try to come from a place of compassion. You're not accusing them of something. You're saying, "Hey, I think there might be something going on that's worth looking into." **You can also try to use "I" statements.** "*I've noticed it's been hard for you to keep the clutter from piling up.*" Sit down, maybe go out to dinner, or take a walk together.

And remind them that getting a diagnosis doesn't change anything. **You don't *get* ADHD when you receive a diagnosis.** You always had it, and now you know for sure. You're gaining information.

 There's also a phenomenon that can happen in relationships where you're upset about things like your partner being messy around the house, but there also needs to be some introspection: **Are you concerned that they have ADHD and you want to support them in finding the appropriate treatment? Or are you just annoyed at them 'cause they leave their shoes everywhere?**

Those can be two different discussions or part of the same discussion. It's two separate points: "Hey, maybe you have ADHD; we can talk about getting a diagnosis and getting treatment," and also "We need to talk about the immediate things that are affecting me and affecting our partnership and our life together, so we can address those separately." Addressing those issues is something that often needs to happen in a healthy partnership.

What are some ways that I can SUPPORT my ADHD PARTNER or FRIENDS?

Before we start spouting off a bunch of stuff, I think it's important to address a very important concept when it comes to supporting a neurodivergent person: *permission*.

A few years ago, Cate and I entered into a little agreement. See, in my natural state, I will forget my keys when leaving the house about half the time. So Cate and I discussed whether it would be okay if she occasionally asked me if I had my keys when I left the house. Although I knew it would occasionally annoy me, I said yes.

It often does annoy me when she asks, but in those moments I remember that I, of sound mind, gave her *explicit permission to do so*. And frankly, it stops me from forgetting my keys like half the time.

The reality is, a lot of the things that you can do to support someone with ADHD can be really embarrassing for them, which may cause them to resent and reject the help if it's offered unprompted.

Wow, am I really that much of a child that my partner/friend feels the need to step in and help me with basic things? Is it that obvious?

If you notice something your ADHD comrade frequently struggles with, and you have an idea for how you can help in the future, *ask for their permission*. This will likely be uncomfortable, they will likely be embarrassed, and they will likely be hesitant to accept help, viewing their need for it as some sort of failure. If you do get permission, they will at least let you help, if begrudgingly. Eventually, the benefit of the help will outweigh their embarrassment for needing it.

For people with ADHD, deliberately forming habits is extremely difficult. Everything we do is manual—nothing comes automatically. So a lot of times, the path of least resistance is the easiest, since you don't have to spend any brainpower.

For example, I put bins on the top of the shoe rack so I don't have to find individual spaces for each pair of shoes. Spending that brainpower is just awful for me. **One of the most powerful things you can do for your loved one is to have them talk themselves through their thought process.** Sometimes it's not about providing solutions or fixing anything. It's about giving your friends and family space to exist as they are, but with a better understanding of each other. In the case of my shoes, adding the bins is an attainable step for me, and I don't drive myself or anyone else bananas with the shoe mountain.

 This may go without saying, but never make fun of them for it. We may constantly feel shame and anger about these things—the clutter, the messiness, the lack of routine—and even hate ourselves for it. Don't make fun.

Clarifying your language is important, too—your definition of clean might be different from mine. Cate might say, "Hey, Erik, before I get home at seven, could you clean the guest room?" And I make the bed, tidy up, and pick up any trash. Then Cate gets home and goes, "Why didn't you vacuum or change the sheets?" Clarifying language with your loved one who has ADHD will go a long way. **The point is not to "win." The point is to arrive at a shared definition and to coexist peacefully.** That can take time.

 This is a note specifically for parents, rather than partners or friends. **It's common for parents to incentivize things like keeping a room clean, but what they're inadvertently doing is setting their ADHD kid up to fail.** When I was a kid, my mom said if I could keep my room clean for a month, I could have a dog. And I literally couldn't do it. To this day, I'm secretly worried that somebody's going to take my dog away because my room isn't clean in adulthood, either.

If your ADHD partner is changing something—rearranging furniture, switching up where the cups go in the kitchen, or moving the patio chairs—it's not really about the change being *better*, it's about the arrangement being *new*. That's the real reason they have the urge to do that. It's the novelty. So if you're okay with it, just let them do it. It helps.

It also helps to narrow down what's important to you and communicate that. In my house growing up, my parents said, "Your rooms are your rooms. We don't care how they look. But the rest of the house needs to be kept clean." So with an ADHD partner, you may want to say, "I need the kitchen to be clean. That's important to me." And let the rest just happen. **Because for your ADHD loved one, they have a really hard time prioritizing.** Your partner's office or workshop? If that's not important to you, let it go. Be clear about what matters to you.

 ## If you could tell your parents one thing about what it's like to live in your brain, you'd want them to know:

> If you heard how often I scream at myself and how much that voice sounds like yours, maybe you wouldn't have called me lazy for so long and might have actually gotten me help.

—Adrianna from London, Ontario

> It doesn't turn off. It's always chattering. It's why I wear headphones all the time. (My mom called them my "ears" when I was a kid.)

—Kim Greenawalt

CHAPTER 16:
The Chapter for Loved Ones

FORKING OFF

> **When your ADHD partner** is struggling with getting something done, it's likely due to some combination of consistently forgetting to do it and other executive dysfunction fuckery that causes them to drop the task and do something else ("forking off"). And repeat. The cycle looks something like this:

Forgetting > Remembering > Executive Dysfunction Fuckery > Forking Off

Forgetting > Remembering > Executive Dysfunction Fuckery > Forking Off

Forgetting > Remembering > Executive Dysfunction Fuckery > Forking Off

So, if you're aiming to help your partner, it's best to figure out where in this cycle they get most tripped up. When they remember the thing they have to do, is it always at an inopportune time where addressing it right then is impossible? (In the car? In the shower? At the supermarket?)

When they start to do the task, do they start emotionally dysregulating, priority-shuffling, or efficiency-obsessing to the point where they aren't actually doing the thing anymore?

You can also help your loved one by helping them assess their **task debt. If you have a string of tasks, each preventing you from doing the other, you're in task debt.**

For example: You ask your partner to do the dishes, only to come back to find them organizing the pantry. At first glance, this may seem like forking off, but nay, dear reader. They were chipping away at their task debt. Here's what happened:

They went to do the dishes (let's call this Task A), but the dishwasher was full. So they went to unload the dishwasher (Task B), but the cupboards were full of stuff that should be in the pantry. So they went to move the pantry stuff back to the pantry (Task C), but there was no room because the pantry was so disorganized. So then they had to organize the pantry (Task D) to clear room in the cupboard (Task C) so they could unload the dishwasher (Task B) so they could do the dishes (Task A).

Many people with ADHD are in serious task debt, and sometimes the chain of tasks gets so long that we decide it's virtually impossible to get all the way back to zero. So we mentally default on our debt and resign ourselves to living with all those tasks undone. I'll remind you that ADHD is often comorbid with depression.

As this person's loved one, try to follow the trail of task debt. Maybe your partner is mid-freakout about cleaning floor space, but what they really need is a different place to put the broken-down boxes since the trash cans are full. Help them with *that* task first and work backward. **Help them with the backlog. Help them with the debt.**

Another tip is to "be the compass." If your loved one gets new pots, for example, and needs to find homes for them in the kitchen, they may come up with fourteen different ways to rearrange things to put the pots away. People with ADHD are generally really good **prospectors**.

We're great at coming up with many, many different ways of doing something. We are terrible at choosing one of those ways and sticking to it. So another way to help your loved one is to help them choose *one* way of doing something, just *one* system, and sticking to it.

My PARTNER won't take their ADHD MEDICATION. What should I do?

 If they're forgetting, which is entirely possible—if not likely—remind them. That can be annoying to us, so tread carefully. Watch their routines, because it's harder to notice our own patterns than to notice those of others. **The best place to put your medication is a place that you go every day.** Maybe a good spot would be at the coffeemaker. Or their computer. Or something novel, like . . .

 . . . a gumball machine.

 A gumball machine! And at all costs, avoid losing the meds. Especially after traveling, because when you're away from home, your systems change.

 One of the more difficult parts about being in a relationship with somebody with ADHD is that it can be really easy to step into a parentification role. And you don't want that. **It's okay to support your partner, but it's not your responsibility to keep track of their meds.**

Out of compassion, you can say, "Hey, I can't help but notice that it's been a few days since you took your antidepressant." And they may realize that the meds are in their suitcase because they forgot they existed. That's okay. But it can be detrimental to a relationship (and lead to resentment) when you become your partner's personal assistant.

It might be a conversation that begins: "When you don't take your medication, it does affect me. It affects your ability to function and to wake up in the morning. It affects our relationship. So I need you to take ownership of this if we are going to continue to be in a relationship."

❓ My PARTNER has ADHD, and they use it as an excuse for BAD BEHAVIOR all the time. What should I do?

  Once again, no amount of mental illness is an excuse for bad behavior, dear reader.

PTOUGH LOVE PTERODACTYL

 One of the most difficult things about ADHD is that there are associated behaviors—like interrupting, being emotionally dysregulated, or speaking out of turn—that are generally considered rude. It's easy to be like, *Well, I'm gonna go find friends who don't care if I interrupt them! I'm going to find the people who understand!*

There's a difference between understanding and supporting those moments of making a mistake and the desire to find people who let you walk all over them with your bad behavior.

Real relationships come with a give-and-take, right? Erik and I interrupt each other all the time, but we don't get mad about it. We just say, "Oh, sorry, you go."

 One idea to keep in mind is not making any statements for someone else. **Don't say, "You're always so . . ." This never ends well. Make statements about yourself. Because those can't be refuted.** If you say, "When you do such and such, it makes me feel this way," the other person can't say, "No, it doesn't!"

  **There's a difference between a consistent pattern of bad behavior that harms you and harms the people around you and the occasional "Oh, I got excited and I interrupted."**

PTOUGH LOVE PTERODACTYL

CHAPTER 16: The Chapter for Loved Ones

As I've done before, I like to compare people blaming their ADHD for bad behavior to a made-up disorder that causes you to compulsively punch people in the face. It's really hard for you not to do it, and you have to work at it to keep it from happening. **Despite having this disorder, *you still shouldn't punch people in the face*. Nothing is gonna make that okay.** The people in your life are hopefully patient with you and understand that it takes a lot of effort for you to not punch people in the face.

In terms of actual steps for you to take, first communicate to your loved one: "Hey, that really affects me when you do that, so please make an effort not to do that. I'm willing to help and work on it together."

If that doesn't work, do the actual sit-down. And then you can say, "I've brought this up a couple of times." Be patient—you're still on their team. Having a sit-down is a pattern break for a person with ADHD, like, *Oh, something new is happening. We're sitting down and talking.* That can really help an ADHD person sort of go, *Oh, this is serious enough to break normal routines.*

 I like going for walks. That's something that helps a lot of people with ADHD, since there's stuff to do. There's stuff to look at. You don't have to make tense, awkward eye contact. Sometimes having an additional thing during conversation can be really helpful.

 If you've already tried communicating and having the sit-down but you still need more, consider an intermediary, like couples counseling.

? I don't like that my partner talks about me in **THERAPY**. What should I do?

PTOUGH LOVE PTERODACTYL

What your partner talks about in therapy is none of your business. Legally speaking, it just isn't. It is privileged information. Therapy is meant to heal; it's about your partner getting better. **They need to be able to give the complete picture of their life to their therapist.**

That being said, yeah, it's kind of uncomfortable sometimes to know that your partner might be talking about you in therapy. At some point, you have to trust your partner to know what they need to address in that setting. **A therapist is a professional, and they should be impartial. Think of a therapist like a brain mechanic.** So if your partner is in therapy to understand how their brain works, learning how to function in a relationship when you have ADHD is a natural part of the process.

There can be this idea that talking about someone is always negative—like criticism. But therapy is a place to process. Talking about someone in therapy does not necessarily mean that you're talking shit. Often it doesn't! Part of being in therapy is learning how to reframe and to break certain thought patterns. **So if your partner is talking about you in therapy, it's not necessarily a bad thing.** It may be that they are seeking resources or wanting to understand how their ADHD works within the context of their relationship.

To conclude this chapter,

we wanted you to hear from members of our community in their own words. We hope this helps you understand your own loved one with ADHD just a little bit better. And we thank you for reading.

 **If you were going to give someone a short and sweet summation of what it's like to navigate the world with ADHD, what would you say?**

> I would say that I can't control whether something catches and holds my attention, and ask that they please not take it personally.

—Shawna Jacques

> It's like trying to paddle a canoe with pool noodles for oars. It's a lot of work to make a little progress. Not impossible, but very hard to do without learning tools and getting support.

—mandolin913

> I am not sure myself. I have no sense of direction and get lost at every turn when I think I have a handle on my ADHD.

—Hayle Nicole from Hawaii

> My brain is like an Internet browser, and I always have about 180 tabs open at any given time. Some of them are sensory inputs from the real world. Some are stuff like work or art I'll get around to . . . eventually. There is a calendar open to remind me of stuff . . . Somewhere. There are several tabs with music and shows going off at the same time, and there's a tab that has my most embarrassing moments playing on loop that always pops off at the worst moments.

—@ZeinDarkuzss

> ❝ The speed on everything is off. It's either going too slow and you just want to get on with it because you see exactly where everything is going, or it's too fast and you can't keep up. All while the third verse of the "Macarena" is playing in the background on repeat.
>
> **—Marshall Stephens from Virginia**

> ❝ You will run way ahead on paths that interest you, and you will struggle and need help to navigate the ones that don't.
>
> **—Karen from New Jersey**

> ❝ It's like carrying eight squirming kittens in your arms with a small frog scream/singing in your ear while your parents look at you in disappointment.
>
> **—Ashtan (@cricketandlace)**

Afterword

Signing Off ... for Now

  Whelp. This is it—it's the end of the book, dear reader. Erik and I have put off writing this section until quite literally the very last minute because we are overwhelmed with what we could possibly say that'd leave you with everything we wish and hope and dream for you.

I've never been particularly good at goodbyes, so I suppose I will be direct. **If you take nothing else away from this book, remember that you are worthy of love and care, just as you are.**

In closing ...

While it's true that systems and structures to support your ADHD aren't going to build themselves, remember that you don't have to figure it all out at once.

Follow your passions. Whatever topic or interest or hobby brings you joy, follow it. Joy is rare and brief and beautiful. Cling to it. Revel in it. Take a moment every day to learn something new, or look at a leaf, or squish your dog and embrace that joy.

Speaking of: "Cringe" doesn't exist. If you live your life in such a way that you avoid "being cringe," you are going to miss out on a lot of joy.

Keep learning more about the world and about yourself. Keep striving to understand the "why" of things.

Remember that in learning, sometimes experiments must fail for data to be gathered. It doesn't mean you did anything wrong, and it doesn't mean it wasn't worth your time. Don't punish yourself.

Don't feed the trolls. Many people out there will hide behind their keyboard and say terrible, awful things about how ADHD doesn't exist and it's all a scam. Don't waste your time with those people. Your experience is valid. Your struggles are valid. It's not silly if it makes your life easier.

Lastly, be nice to yourself. If you're a person who rolls their eyes when you hear someone say that, maybe ask yourself why. Treat yourself like you'd treat your best friend. Give yourself grace, give yourself compassion, give yourself the benefit of the doubt.

Thank you for reading, and thank you for helping us get here.

Remember to eat a snack, remember to drink some water, remember to take your meds, remember to be kind to yourself, remember to be kind to others, and above all, remember that YOU ARE NOT A FUCKUP.

You can always find us on the Infinite Quest podcast, @catieosaurus and @erikgude on TikTok, and Catieosaurus on YouTube and Instagram.

Appendix

ADHD Evaluations

What is the SNAP survey? The SWAN survey? The Go/No-Go Test?

These are diagnostic tools that practitioners use in evaluating whether someone has ADHD. Years ago, it was the SNAP survey—a list of questions for a child and their parents to fill out about the child. It has since been updated and it's now called the SWAN survey. It's also one of several surveys used in diagnosis.

Here's a breakdown of some pretty commonly used tools in diagnosing ADHD.

The Strengths and Weaknesses of Attention-Deficit/Hyperactivity Symptoms and Normal Behaviors (SWAN) Rating Scale[1]

The SWAN rating scale is used in diagnosing ADHD in children. It is usually filled out by a child's guardian or teacher, or another adult familiar with the kid's behavior. If you're getting evaluated as an adult, it's unlikely that you will encounter it.

Adult ADHD Self-Report Scale (ASRS-v1.1) Symptom Checklist[2]

Sometime around 2005, we realized adults may need to be screened for ADHD sometimes, too, so researchers at the World Health Organization made the ASRS. If you're an adult going in for an evaluation, you will almost certainly see it.

I think some questions on common ADHD rating scales could be worded better. For example, question eighteen in the ASRS is "How often do you interrupt others when they

← GRIEVANCES GARGOYLE

are busy?" Your answer may be "Rarely," but only because you've learned over twenty years that you have an extreme tendency to interrupt people, so you spend half your energy trying to not interrupt people. A better wording might be "How often do you have trouble not interrupting others when they are busy?" That way the question is about your relationship to interrupting people, not just how frequently you do it.

Barkley Adult ADHD Rating Scale–IV (BAARS–IV)

In my opinion, this is the one you want. It is a set of several rating scales, some for you to fill out and some for a person/people close to you. Since ADHD is a neurodevelopmental disorder, it also asks about childhood to gain insight from your, well, developmental years. It combines the best bits of the rating scales that came before it.

The Go/No-Go Test

The Go/No-Go Test is essentially a video game diagnostic tool that is meant to be very easy and very boring. For example, you sit down in front of a computer and you click a button whenever a star with four points appears. The whole idea is that it's an incredibly easy task. Four points: click. Five points: no click.

The concept here is that a person without ADHD can deliberately decide to focus on that incredibly boring task. They know it's boring, but it's the task at hand. *Okay, I'll sit here and click on the thing.* A person with ADHD cannot do that. We cannot deliberately make ourselves pay attention to something that we find incredibly boring. And that shows up in the results.

> **RELATED NOTE:** The process of diagnosing ADHD is not standardized. It's all over the place. Ideally, there would be a really good standardized method, but because our methods aren't great yet—we're still not amazing at detecting ADHD in people—it's kind of a good thing that it's not standardized because that means practitioners are trying all sorts of things. Sometimes it will be a longer process to get diagnosed, and other times it's short and simple. It just depends on the individual.

Acknowledgments

 To Caroline Marsiglia and Rick Richter at Aevitas for seeing in us what we didn't see in ourselves. To Rennie Dyball for being the lighthouse in the storm of ADHD chaos that was this writing process. To Lauren Spiegel, Taylor Rondestvedt, and the whole team at Gallery: thank you for believing in our book.

To my oldest friends and the newest: to the Fellowship, to the Magi, to the Prisoners of Azkaban, thank you for being my friends and my companions. To Abby and to Emily. To Kelley for reminding me to put my feet up the wall. To Joe and Wolfgang and Alex, the big brothers I needed, not the ones I ever deserved. To Lillian, the surprise Sestra I never expected. To Jeff and Patrick Adamson for teaching me how to be funny on my own terms and to Adam Lewis for all the BS. To Nick and Mike and Pat and Shane for welcoming me to the table.

To Moon, Anne, Tsukino, Leah, Craig, Derpo, 2Lemons, 2Doodles, and the rest of Fruitsnack Nation who have been with us since the very beginning and never stopped rooting for us. To Max—did you eat today? To Dani and Dusty and Jess and KC, thank you for being such great role models turned friends. To my beleaguered and beloved assistant, Jenn, you will never know how much I appreciate you.

To the Prenzie Players, for my very first Titus and all that came after. To Aaron Sullivan, for Act 4, Scene 1. To Mrs. Ertel, Mrs. DeMeulenaere, and Mrs. Titus; to Dan LaCorte, Matt Davies, Doreen Bechtol, Paul Menzer, and Ralph Cohen; to Cory Johnson and Michael Kennedy and Dan Hale and Kris Eitrham; to Katie Williams and Kay O'Brien and Dianne Dye, thank you for being the teachers who saw me, who encouraged me, who put up with my bullshit and kept my love of learning alive.

To my newfound TTRPG family.

To my mom, who always did her best. I love you.

To Chris, for knowing me before, for seeing me through, for yes-anding the volcano and for always speaking BoxTroll.

To Erik. You know.

To my dad, who always said I'd be a writer. I wish you were here.

To Mom, for teaching me that learning to be kind to yourself is a lifelong process.

To Dad, for showing me that you can be a serious adult without being a *serious* adult.

To Cole, for being my friend.

To Abby, for teaching me how to play.

To Bailey, for reminding me I still can. To Grammy and Tzir, for always being curious.

To Bull Bear, for laughing with me. (You can go down with three!)

To Jordan Tripp aka C Dubs. Thanks for helping me out of the gutter.

To Will Parsons, for showing me who I am.

To the Hamik family, for keeping me out of the gutter.

To Chef Nick Robinson, for making the choice to be my teacher and showing me what joy can be found in skill and service.

To David Belkovski, Asa Bryce, and Donnie Spackman for challenging me.

To Mrs. Foreman and Mr. Gendreau for helping me survive eighth grade with my curiosity intact.

To Anne, Moon, Leah, Tsukino, and all my good beans for being there from the beginning.

To Enki. Thank you for making QuestCraft possible and for keeping it together when I left.

To Catherine Marie Osborn. I love you. I love you. I love you.

Notes

Chapter 1: The Technical Stuff

1. Oxford Languages, https://languages.oup.com/google-dictionary-en/.

2. "What Is Dyscalculia?" Cleveland Clinic, last reviewed 8/2/22, https://my.clevelandclinic.org/health/diseases/23949-dyscalculia#:~:text=What%20is%20dyscalculia%3F,of%20people%20without%20this%20disorder.

3. "Dysgraphia," National Institute of Neurological Disorders and Stroke, *Glossary of Neurological Terms*, https://www.ninds.nih.gov/health-information/disorders/dysgraphia#:~:text=What%20is%20dysgraphia%3F,are%20first%20introduced%20to%20writing.

4. Esther Sobanski, "Psychiatric Comorbidity in Adults with Attention-Deficit/Hyperactivity Disorder (ADHD)," *European Archives of Psychiatry and Clinical Neuroscience* 256 (Suppl 1) (2006): i26–i31, https://doi.org/10.1007/s00406-006-1004-4; and Joseph Biederman, Sarah W. Ball, et al., "New Insights into the Comorbidity Between ADHD and Major Depression in Adolescent and Young Adult Females," *Journal of the American Academy of Child & Adolescent Psychiatry* 47, no. 4 (2008): 426–34, https://doi.org/10.1097/chi.0b013e31816429d3.

5. Susan D. Mayes, Rosanna P. Breaux, et al., "High Prevalence of Dysgraphia in Elementary Through High School Students with ADHD and Autism," *Journal of Attention Disorders* 23, no. 8 (2019): 787–96, doi: 10.1177/1087054717720721.

6. Javant Mahadevan, Arun Kandasamy, and Vivek Benegal, "Situating adult attention-deficit/hyperactivity disorder in the externalizing spectrum: Etiological, diagnostic, and treatment considerations," *Indian Journal of Psychiatry* 61, no. 1 (2019): 3–12, https://pmc.ncbi.nlm.nih.gov/articles/PMC6341912/.

7. "Patricia Quinn, MD," *ADDitude*, https://www.additudemag.com/author/dr-patricia-quinn-m-d/.

8. Linda Karanzalis, "Executive Functioning," ADDvantages Learning Center with Linda K, https://addvantageslearningcenter.com/executive-functioning/.

9. Laurence Jerome, Alvin Segal, and Liat Habinski, "What We Know About ADHD and Driving Risk: A Literature Review, Meta-Analysis and Critique," *Journal of the Canadian Academy of Child and Adolescent Psychiatry* 15, no. 3 (2006): 105–125, https://pmc.ncbi.nlm.nih.gov/articles/PMC2277254/; Richard L. Merkel, J. Quyen Nichols, et al., "Comparison of On-Road Driving Between Young Adults With and Without ADHD," *Journal of Attention Disorders* 20, no. 3 (February 2013); https://doi.org/10.1177/1087054712473832; and Amanda Thompson, Brooke S.G. Molina, et al., "Risky Driving in Adolescents and Young Adults with Childhood ADHD," *Journal of Pediatric Psychology* 32, no. 7 (2007): 745–59, https://doi.org/10.1093/jpepsy/jsm002.

10. Anna Smith, Eric Taylor, et al., "Evidence for a pure time perception deficit in children with ADHD," *Journal of Child Psychology and Psychiatry* 43, no. 4 (2002): 529–42, https://doi.org/10.1111/1469-7610.00043; Julie B. Meoux and John J. Chelonis, "Time perception differences in children with and without ADHD," *Journal of Pediatric Health Care* 17, no. 2 (2003): 64–71, https://doi.org/10.1067/mph.2003.26; B. Yang, R. C. K. Chan, et al., "Time perception deficit in children with ADHD," *Brain Research* 1170, 90–96, https://psycnet.apa.org/doi/10.1016/j.brainres.2007.07.021; R. A. Barkley, K. R. Murphy, and T. Bush, "Time perception and reproduction in young adults with attention deficit hyperactivity disorder," *Neuropsychology* 15, no. 3 (2001): 351–360, https://psycnet.apa.org/doi/10.1037/0894-4105.15.3.351; Radek Ptacek, Simon Weissenberger, et al., "Clinical Implications of the Perception of Time in Attention Deficit Hyperactivity Disorder (ADHD): A Review," *Medical Science Monitor* 25 (2019): 3918–24; and Christian Mette, "Time Perception in Adult ADHD: Findings from a Decade—A Review," *International Journal of Environmental Research and Public Health* 20, no. 4 (2023): 3098, https://doi.org/10.3390/ijerph20043098.

11. Dienke J. Bos, Bob Oranje, et al., "Reduced Symptoms of Inattention after Omega-3 Fatty Acid Supplementation in Boys with and without Attention Deficit/Hyperactivity Disorder," *Neuropsychopharmacology* 40 (2015): 2298–2306, https://www.nature.com/articles/npp201573; Muhammad Abdullah, Benjamin Jowett, et al., "The effectiveness of omega-3 supplementation in reducing ADHD associated symptoms in children as measured by the Conners' rating scales: A systematic review of randomized controlled trials," *Journal of Psychiatric Research* 110 (2019): 64–73, https://doi.org/10.1016/j.jpsychires.2018.12.002; and Jonathan Armstrong, Allison Louis, et al., "Are omega-3 fatty acids effective in the treatment of children with ADHD?," *Evidence-Based Practice* 24, no. 8 (2021): 19–20, https://doi.org/10.1097/EBP.0000000000001089.

12. *Potential Neurobehavioral Effects of Synthetic Food Dyes in Children*, Office of Environmental Health Hazard Assessment, Children's Environmental Health Center, California Environmental Protection Agency: Health Effects Assessment (Report), April 2021, https://oehha.ca.gov/media/downloads/risk-assessment/report/healtheffectsassess041621.pdf.

Chapter 1B: A Bonus History of ADHD

1. Mahesh Shreshtha, Julianna Lautenschleger, Neelkamal Soares, "Non-pharmacologic management of attention-deficit/hyperactivity disorder in children and adolescents: a review," *Translational Pediatrics* 9, suppl 1 (2020): S114–S124, doi: 10.21037/tp.2019.10.01.

2. Klaus-Jürgen Neumärker, "The Kramer-Pollnow syndrome: a contribution on the life and work of Franz Kramer and Hans Pollnow," *History of Psychiatry* 16, no. 4 (2005): 435–51, https://doi.org/10.1177/0957154X05054708.

3. Klaus W. Lange, Susanne Reichl, et al., "The history of attention deficit hyperactivity disorder," *ADHD Attention Deficit and Hyperactivity Disorders* 2, no. 4 (2010): 241–55, https://doi.org/10.1007/s12402-010-0045-8.

Chapter 2: ADHD and . . . Comorbidities

1. Stephen V. Faraone, Tobias Banaschewski, et al., "The World Federation of ADHD International Consensus Statement: 208 Evidence-based conclusions about the disorder," *Neuroscience & Biobehavioral Reviews* 128 (September 2021): 789–818, https://doi.org/10.1016/j.neubiorev.2021.01.022.

2. Susan Young, Larry Klassen, et al., "Let's Talk About Sex . . . and ADHD: Findings from an Anonymous Online Survey," *International Journal of Environmental Research and Public Health* 20, no. 3 (2023): h2037, https://doi.org/10.3390/ijerph20032037; Samaneh Amani Jabalkandi, Firoozeh Raisi, et al., "A study on sexual functioning in adults with attention-deficit/hyperactivity disorder," *Perspectives in Psychiatric Care*, February 2020, https://doi.org/10.1111/ppc.12480; and Lorenzo Soldati, Francesco Bianchi-Demicheli, et al., "Sexual Function, Sexual Dysfunctions, and ADHD: A Systematic Literature Review," *Journal of Sexual Medicine* 17, no. 9 (2020): 1653–64, https://doi.org/10.1016/j.jsxm.2020.03.019.

3. Dara E. Babinski, Kristina A. Neely, et al., "Depression and Suicidal Behavior in Young Adult Men and Women with ADHD: Evidence from Claims Data," *Journal of Clinical Psychiatry* 81, no. 6 (2020): 19m13130, https://doi.org/10.4088/jcp.19m13130; Elizabeth B. Owens, Christine Zalecki, et al., "Girls with childhood ADHD as adults: Cross-domain outcomes by diagnostic persistence," *Journal of Consultation and Clinical Psychology* 85, no. 7 (2017): 723–36, https://doi.org/10.1037/ccp0000217; and William Dodson, "The ADHD-Depression Link: symptom Parallels and Distinctions," ADDitude, updated April 7, 2024, https://www.additudemag.com/adhd-depression-link-symptoms-diagnosis-treatments/#:~:text=Comorbidity%20studies%20vary%20widely%2C%20but,type%201%20depressive%20mood%20phases.

4. Esther Sobanski, "Psychiatric comorbidity in adults with attention-deficit/hyperactivity disorder (ADHD)," *European Archives of Psychiatry and Clinical Neuroscience* 256 (September 2006): i26–i31; Martin Katzman, Timothy S. Bilkey, et al., "Adult ADHD and comorbid disorders: clinical implications of a dimensional approach," *BMC Psychiatry* 17, 302 (August 2017), https://doi.org/10.1186/s12888-017-1463-3; and Stephen V. Faraone, Tobias Banaschewski, et al., "The World Federation of ADHD International Consensus Statement: 208 Evidence-based conclusions about the disorder," *Neuroscience & Biobehavioral Reviews* 128 (September 2021): 789–818, https://doi.org/10.1016/j.neubiorev.2021.01.022.

5. David Beck Schatz and Anthony L. Rostain, "ADHD with Comorbid Anxiety: A Review of the Current Literature," *Journal of Attention Disorders* 10, no. 2 (2006), https://doi.org/10.1177/1087054706286698; Elisa D'Agati, Paolo Curatolo, and Luigi Mazzone, "Comorbidity between ADHD and anxiety disorders across the lifespan," *International Journal of Psychiatry in Clinical Practice* 23, no. 4 (2019): 238–44, https://doi.org/10.1080/13651501.2019.1628277; Amitai Abramovich and Avraham Schweiger, "Unwanted intrusive and worrisome thoughts in adults with Attention Deficit/Hyperactivity Disorder," *Psychiatry Research* 168, no. 3 (August 2009): 230–33, https://doi.org/10.1016/j.psychres.2008.06.004; Sue Hyeon Paek, Ahmed M. Abdulla, and Bonnie Cramond, "A Meta-Analysis of the Relationship Between Three Common Psychopathologies—ADHD, Anxiety, and Depression—and Indicators of Little-c Creativity," *Gifted Child Quarterly* 60, no. 2 (2016) 117–33, https://doi.org/10.1177/0016986216630600; Frederick W. Reimherr, Barry K. Marchant et al., "ADHD and Anxiety: Clinical Significance and Treatment Implications," *Current Psychiatry Reports* 19, 109 (2017), https://doi.org/10.1007/s11920-017-0859-6; R. Tannock "ADHD with anxiety disorders," in *ADHD Comorbidities: Handbook for ADHD Complications in Children and Adults*, ed. T. E. Brown (American Psychiatric Publishing, 2009), 131–55; "Comorbid anxiety and depression in school-aged children with attention deficit hyperactivity disorder (ADHD) and self-reported symptoms of ADHD, anxiety, and depression among parents of school-aged children with and without ADHD," Weiping, Xia, Lixiao Shen, and Jinsong Zhang, *Shanghai Archives of Psychiatry* 27, no. 6 (2015): 356–67, https://pmc.ncbi.nlm.nih.gov/articles/PMC4858507/.

6. Nanda N. Rommelse, Barbara Franke, et al., "Shared heritability of attention-deficit/hyperactivity disorder and autism spectrum disorder," *European Child & Adolescent Psychiatry* 19, no. 3 (2010): 281–95, https://doi.org/10.1007/s00787-010-0092-x.

7. Suzan W. N. Vogel, Denise Bijlenga et al., "Attention deficit hyperactivity disorder symptom severity and sleep problems in adult participants of the Netherlands sleep registry," *Sleep Medicine* 40 (December 2017): 94–102, https://doi.org/10.1016/j.sleep.2017.09.027.

8. Amitai Abramovitch, Reuven Dar et al., "Don't judge a book by its cover: ADHD-like symptoms in obsessive compulsive disorder," *Journal of Obsessive-Compulsive and Related Disorders* 2, no. 1 (2013): 53–61, https://doi.org/10.1016/j.jocrd.2012.09.001; Azadeh Kushki, Eydokia Anagnostou et al., "Examining overlap and homogeneity in ASD, ADHD, and OCD: a data-driven, diagnosis-agnostic approach," *Translational Psychiatry* 9, 318 (2019), https://doi.org/10.1038/s41398-019-0631-2; Amitai Abramovitch, Reuven Dar et al., "Comorbidity Between Attention Deficit/Hyperactivity Disorder and Obsessive-Compulsive Disorder Across the Lifespan: A Systematic and Critical Review," *Harvard Review of Psychiatry* 23, no. 4 (July/August 2015): 245–62, https://doi.org/10.1097/HRP.0000000000000050; Valérie La Buissonnière-Ariza, Jeffrey Alvaro, et al., "Body-focused repetitive behaviors in youth with mental health conditions: A preliminary study on their prevalence and clinical correlates," *International Journal of Mental Health* 50, no. 1 (2020): 33–52, https://doi.org/10.1080/00207411.2020.1824111; S. Brem, E. Grünblatt et al., "The neurobiological link between OCD and ADHD," *ADHD Attention Deficit and Hyperactivity Disorders* 6 (2014): 175–202, https://doi.org/10.1007/s12402-014-0146-x; Brooke Sheppard, Denise Chavira, et al., "ADHD prevalence and association with hoarding behaviors in childhood-onset OCD," *Depression and Anxiety* (2010), https://doi.org/10.1002/da.20691.

9. Miquel A. Fullana, Gemma Vilagut et al., "Is ADHD in Childhood Associated with Lifetime Hoarding Symptoms? An Epidemiological Study," *Depression and Anxiety* (2013), https://doi.org/10.1002/da.22123; and Blaise Warden and David Talin, "A pilot exploration of ADHD symptoms in hoarding disorder: Co-occurring disorders or part of the hoarding syndrome?," *Journal of Affective Disorders Reports* 13 (2013), https://doi.org/10.1016/j.jadr.2023.100588.

10. Zahra Saif and Haitham Jahrami, "Eating Disorders in Children and Adolescents with Attention Deficit Hyperactivity Disorder," in *Eating Disorders*, eds. V. Patel and V. Preedy (Springer Publishing, 2022), https://doi.org/10.1007/978-3-030-67929-3_9-1; F. M. Villa, A. Crippa, et al., "ADHD and eating disorders in childhood and adolescence: An updated minireview," *Journal of Affective Disorders* 321 (2023): 265–71, https://doi.org/10.1016/j.jad.2022.10.016; Prithvi Rathi and Safeera Khan, "Attention Deficit Hyperactivity Disorder: Association with

Obesity and Eating Disorders," *Cureus* 12, no. 12 (December 2020): e12085, https://assets.cureus.com/uploads/review_article/pdf/45275/1612431666-1612431661-20210204-30437-5uoa6a.pdf; Jessica Baraskewich and Emma A. Climie, "The relation between symptoms of ADHD and symptoms of eating disorders in university students," *Journal of General Psychology* 149, no. 3 (2022): 405–19, https://doi.org/10.1080/00221309.2021.1874862.

11. F. M. Villa, A. Crippa, et al., "ADHD and eating disorders in childhood and adolescence: An updated minireview."

Chapter 3: How ADHD Affects Your Body and Brain

1. Jatta Berberat, Ruth Huggenberger, et al., "Brain activation patterns in medicated versus medication-naïve adults with attention-deficit hyperactivity disorder during fMRI tasks of motor inhibition and cognitive switching," *BMC Medical Imaging* 21, 53 (2021), https://doi.org/10.1186/s12880-021-00579-3; and Liv Larsen Stray, Øistein Kristensen, et al., "Motor regulation problems and pain in adults diagnosed with ADHD," *Behavior and Brain Functions* 9, 18 (2013), https://doi.org/10.1186/1744-9081-9-18.

2. Elisa D'Agati, Thomas Hoegl, et al., "Motor cortical inhibition in ADHD: modulation of the transcranial magnetic stimulation-evoked N100 in a response control task," *Journal of Neural Transmission* 121 (2014): 315–25, https://doi.org/10.1007/s00702-013-1097-7.

3. "What Is Misophonia?," WebMD, September 17, 2024, https://www.webmd.com/mental-health/what-is-misophonia#.

4. Ana Paula Francisco, Grace Lethbridge, et al., "Cannabis Use in Attention-Deficit/Hyperactivity Disorder (ADHD): A Scoping Review," *Journal of Psychiatric Research* 157 (January 2023): 239–56, https://www.sciencedirect.com/science/article/abs/pii/S0022395622006549; Amanda Stueber and Carrie Cuttler, "Self-Reported Effects of Cannabis on ADHD Symptoms, ADHD Medication Side Effects, and ADHD-Related Executive Dysfunction," *Journal of Attention Disorders* 26, no. 6 (2021): 942–55, https://doi.org/10.1177/10870547211050949.

5. "Neurodevelopmental Effects of Cannabis Use in Adolescents and Emerging Adults with ADHD: A Systematic Review," *Harvard Review of Psychiatry* 29, no. 4 (2021): 251–61, https://doi.org/10.1097/HRP.0000000000000303.

6. Daniel P. Notzon, Martina Pavlicova, et al., "ADHD Is Highly Prevalent in Patients Seeking Treatment for Cannabis Use Disorders," *Journal of Attention Disorders* 24, no. 11 (2020): 1487–92, https://doi.org/10.1177/1087054716640109. Leanne Tamm, Jeffrey N. Epstein, et al., "Impact of ADHD and cannabis use on executive functioning in young adults," *Drug and Alcohol Dependence* 133, no. 2 (2013): 607–14, https://doi.org/10.1016/j.drugalcdep.2013.08.001; David M. Fergusson and Joseph M. Baden, "Cannabis use and adult ADHD symptoms," *Drug and Alcohol Dependence* 95, no. 1-2 (2008): 90–96, https://doi.org/10.1016/j.drugalcdep.2007.12.012; and Ana Paula Francisco, Grace Lethbridge, et al., "Cannabis Use in Attention-Deficit/Hyperactivity Disorder (ADHD): A Scoping Review."

7. Rabia Khan, Sadiq Naveed, et al., "The therapeutic role of Cannabidiol in mental health: a systematic review," *Journal of Cannabis Research* 2, 2 (2020), https://doi.org/10.1186/s42238-019-0012-y; Hani F. Ayyash, Michael Ogundele, et al., "G632 Effectiveness of Cannabidiol oil in the management of ADHD and its comorbidities: Review of the evidence," *Archives of Disease in Childhood* 105, Suppl 1 (2020): A228, https://doi.org/10.1136/archdischild-2020-rcpch.546.

8. Robert N. Jamison, Tracy Sbrocco, et al., "The Influence of Problems with Concentration and Memory on Emotional Distress and Daily Activities in Chronic Pain Patients," *International Journal of Psychiatry in Medicine* 18, no. 2 (1989): 183–91, https://doi.org/10.2190/FTR1-F9VX-CB8T-WPMC.

9. Le Zhang, Ebba Du Rietz, et al., "Attention-deficit/hyperactivity disorder and Alzheimer's disease and any dementia: A multi-generation cohort study in Sweden," *Alzheimer's & Dementia* 18, no. 6 (2022): 1155–63, https://doi.org/10.1002/alz.12462; Douglas Leffa, João Pedro Ferrari-Souza, et al., "Genetic risk for attention-deficit/hyperactivity disorder predicts cognitive decline and development of Alzheimer's disease pathophysiology in cognitively unimpaired older adults," *Molecular Psychiatry* 28 (2023): 1248–55, https://doi.org/10.1038/s41380-022-01867-2; Marcos

Altable and Juan Moisés de la Serna, "ADHD in Elderly Age," ResearchGate (2020), https://doi.org/10.13140/RG.2.2.15353.49763.

10. Ronit Haimov-Kochman and Itai Berger, "Cognitive functions of regularly cycling women may differ throughout the month, depending on sex hormone status; a possible explanation to conflicting results of studies of ADHD in females," *Frontiers in Human Neuroscience* 8 (2014), https://doi.org/10.3389/fnhum.2014.00191.

11. Farangis Dorani, Denise Bijlenga, et al., "Prevalence of hormone-related mood disorder symptoms in women with ADHD," *Journal of Psychiatric Research* 133 (2021): 10-15, https://doi.org/10.1016/j.jpsychires.2020.12.005.

12. Sabri Hergüner, Hatice Harmancı, and Harun Toy, "Attention deficit-hyperactivity disorder symptoms in women with polycystic ovary syndrome," *International Journal of Psychiatry in Medicine* 50, no. 3 (2015): 317-25, https://doi.org/10.1177/0091217415610311.

13. "Premenstrual Dysphoric Disorder (PMDD)," *Health*, Johns Hopkins Medicine, https://www.hopkinsmedicine.org/health/conditions-and-diseases/premenstrual-dysphoric-disorder-pmdd.

14. Jeanette Wasserstein, Gerry A. Stefanatos, and Mary V. Solanto, "2 Perimenopause, Menopause and ADHD," *Journal of the International Neuropsychological Society* 29 (Suppl 1) (2023): 881, https://doi.org/10.1017/S1355617723010846.

15. Arnt F. A. Schellekens, Wim van den Brink et al., "Often Overlooked and Ignored, but Do Not Underestimate Its Relevance: ADHD in Addiction," *European Addiction Research* 26, no. 4-5 (2020): 169-72, https://doi.org/10.1159/000509267; and Paul Brunault, Julie Frammery et al., "Adult and childhood ADHD in patients consulting for obesity is associated with food addiction and binge eating, but not sleep apnea syndrome," *Appetite* 136 (2019): 25-32, https://doi.org/10.1016/j.appet.2019.01.013.

16. Zheng Chang, Paul Lichtenstein et al., "Stimulant ADHD medication and risk for substance abuse," *Journal of Child Psychology and Psychiatry* 55, no. 8 (2014): 878-85, https://doi.org/10.1111/jcpp.12164; Alice Charach, Emanuela Yeung, et al., "Childhood Attention-Deficit/Hyperactivity Disorder and Future Substance Use Disorders: Comparative Meta-Analyses," *Journal of the American Academy of Child & Adolescent Psychiatry* 50, no. 1 (2011): 9-21, https://doi.org/10.1016/j.jaac.2010.09.019; and Sean Esteban McCabe, Kara Dickinson, et al., "Age of Onset, Duration, and Type of Medication Therapy for Attention-Deficit/Hyperactivity Disorder (ADHD) and Substance Use During Adolescence: A Multi-Cohort National Study," *Journal of the American Academy of Child & Adolescent Psychiatry* 55, no. 6 (2016): 479-86, https://doi.org/10.1016/j.jaac.2016.03.011.

17. Gemma Mestre-Bach, Trevor Steward, et al., "The Role of ADHD Symptomatology and Emotion Dysregulation in Gambling Disorder," *Journal of Attention Disorders* 25, no. 9 (2019): 1230-39, https://doi.org/10.1177/1087054719894378.

18. Melissa Mulraney, Nardia Zendarski, and David Coghill, "Suicidality and self-harm in adolescents with attention-deficit/hyperactivity disorder and subsyndromal ADHD," *Journal of the American Academy of Child & Adolescent Psychiatry* 60, no. 9 (2021): 1049-51, http://dx.doi.org/10.1016/j.jaac.2021.03.004; Petter Olsson, Stefan Wiktorsson, et al., "Attention deficit hyperactivity disorder in adults who present with self-harm: a comparative 6-month follow-up study," *BMC Psychiatry* 22, 428 (2022), https://doi.org/10.1186/s12888-022-04057-0; John Headley Ward and Sarah Curran, "Self-harm as the first presentation of attention deficit hyperactivity disorder in adolescents," *Child and Adolescent Mental Health* 26, no. 4 (2021): 303-309, https://doi.org/10.1111/camh.12502; and Jocelyn Meza, Elizabeth Owens, and Stephen Hinshaw, "Childhood predictors and moderators of lifetime risk of self-harm in girls with and without attention-deficit/hyperactivity disorder," *Development and Psychopathology* 33, no. 4 (2021): 1351-67, https://doi.org/10.1017/S0954579420000553.

19. John Headley Ward and Sarah Curran, "Self-harm as the first presentation of attention deficit hyperactivity disorder in adolescents," *Child and Adolescent Mental Health*.

20. Esme Fuller-Thomson, Raphaël Nahar Rivière, et al., "The Dark Side of ADHD: Factors Associated With Suicide Attempts Among Those With ADHD in a National Representative Canadian Sample," *Archives of Suicide Research* 26, no. 3 (2022): 1122-40, https://doi.org

/10.1080/13811118.2020.1856258; Yanmei Shen, Bella Siu Man Chan, et. al., "Suicide behaviors and attention deficit hyperactivity disorders (ADHD): a cross-sectional study among Chinese medical college students," *BMC Psychiatry* 21, 258 (2021), https://doi.org/10.1186/s12888-021-03247-6; Jill Seladi-Schulman, "What to Know About the Link Between ADHD and Suicide," *Healthline*, June 29, 2022, https://www.healthline.com/health/adhd-suicide; Artemios Pehlivanidis, Katerina Papanikolaou, et al., "Trait-Based Dimensions Discriminating Adults with Attention Deficit Hyperactivity Disorder (ADHD), Autism Spectrum Disorder (ASD) and, Co-occurring ADHD/ASD," *Brain Sciences* 11, no. 1: 18 (2021), https://doi.org/10.3390/brainsci11010018; Judit Balazs and Agnes Kereszteny, "Attention-deficit/hyperactivity disorder and suicide: A systematic review," *World Journal of Psychiatry* 7, no. 1 (2017): 44–59, https://doi.org/10.5498/wjp.v7.i1.44; and Peter Garas and Judit Balasz, "Long-Term Suicide Risk of Children and Adolescents with Attention Deficit and Hyperactivity Disorder—A Systematic Review," *Frontiers in Psychiatry* 11:557909 (2020), https://doi.org/10.3389/fpsyt.2020.557909.

21. David M. Doyle, Tom O. G. Lewis, and Manuela Barreto, "A systematic review of psychosocial functioning changes after gender-affirming hormone therapy among transgender people," *Nature Human Behaviour* 7 (2023): 1320–1331, https://doi.org/10.1038/s41562-023-01605-w.

Chapter 4: Coping with ADHD: Stress, Boredom, and Other Experiences

1. Hung-Yu Lin, "The Effects of White Noise on Attentional Performance and On-Task Behaviors in Preschoolers with ADHD," *International Journal of Environmental Research and Public Health* 19, no. 22 (2022): 15391, https://doi.org/10.3390/ijerph192215391; and D. Daley and J. Birchwood, "ADHD and academic performance: why does ADHD impact on academic performance and what can be done to support ADHD children in the classroom?," *Child: Care, Health and Development* 36, no. 4 (2010): 455–64, https://doi.org/10.1111/j.1365-2214.2009.01046.x.

2. Peter Castagna and Susan Mayes, "Relationship between ADHD, Oppositional Defiant, Conduct, and Disruptive Mood Dysregulation Disorder Symptoms and Age in Children with ADHD and Autism," *International Journal of Clinical Psychiatry and Mental Health* 8, no. 1 (2020): 47–57, https://doi.org/10.12970/2310-8231.2020.08.08; and Russell Barkley, "ADHD and Truthfulness," *The ADHD Report* 27, no. 1 (2019): 7–8, https://doi.org/10.1521/adhd.2019.27.1.7.

3. Rebecca Bondü and Günter Esser, "Justice and rejection sensitivity in children and adolescents with ADHD symptoms," *European Child & Adolescent Psychiatry* 24 (2015): 185–98, https://doi.org/10.1007/s00787-014-0560-9; M. Scharf, A. Oshri, et al., "Adolescents' ADHD symptoms and adjustment: The role of attachment and rejection sensitivity," *American Journal of Orthopsychiatry* 84, no. 2 (2014): 209–17, https://psycnet.apa.org/doi/10.1037/h0099391; Will H. Canu and Caryn L. Carlson, "Rejection Sensitivity and Social Outcomes of Young Adult Men with ADHD," *Journal of Attention Disorders* 10, no. 3 (2007): 261–75, https://doi.org/10.1177/1087054706288106; and Dara Babinski, Autumn Kujawa, et al., "Sensitivity to Peer Feedback in Young Adolescents with Symptoms of ADHD: Examination of Neurophysiological and Self-Report Measures," *Journal of Abnormal Child Psychology* 47 (2019): 605–17, https://doi.org/10.1007/s10802-018-0470-2.

4. W. Dodson, "Emotional regulation and ADHD: A guide for understanding and managing emotional challenges," *Attention Magazine* (October 2016): 8–11, https://chadd.org/wp-content/uploads/2016/10/ATTN_10_16_EmotionalRegulation.pdf.

Chapter 5: ADHD and Identity

1. Martine Hoogman, Marije Stolte, et al., "Creativity and ADHD: A review of behavioral studies, the effect of psychostimulants and neural underpinnings," *Neuroscience & Biobehavioral Reviews* 119 (2020): 66–85, https://doi.org/10.1016/j.neubiorev.2020.09.029.

Chapter 7: Making It Official: ADHD and Diagnosis

1. V. Harpin, L. Mazzone, et al., "Long-Term Outcomes of ADHD: A Systematic Review of Self-Esteem and Social Function," *Journal of Attention Disorders* 20, no. 4 (2013): 295–305, https://doi.org/10.1177/1087054713486516.

2. Zheng Chang, Paul Lichtenstein, et al., "Stimulant ADHD medication and risk for substance abuse," *Journal of Child Psychology and Psychiatry* 55, no. 8 (2014): 878–85, https://doi.org/10.1111/jcpp.12164.

Chapter 8: Time and Task Management

1. Anna Smith, Eric Taylor, et al., "Evidence for a pure time perception deficit in children with ADHD," *Journal of Child Psychology and Psychiatry* 43, no. 4 (2002): 529–42, https://doi.org/10.1111/1469-7610.00043; and Julie B. Meoux and John J. Chelonis, "Time perception differences in children with and without ADHD," *Journal of Pediatric Health Care* 17, no. 2 (2003): 64–71, https://doi.org/10.1067/mph.2003.26.

Chapter 9B: Setting an Alarm to Pee and Other Personal Hygiene Systems

1. A. D. Craig, "How do you feel? Interoception: the sense of the physiological condition of the body," *Nature Reviews Neuroscience* 3 (2002): 655–66, https://doi.org/10.1038/nrn894.

2. M. Blomqvist, S. Ahadi, et al., "Dental caries in adolescents with attention deficit hyperactivity disorder: a population-based follow-up study," *European Journal of Oral Sciences* 119, no. 5 (2011): 381–85, https://doi.org/10.1111/j.1600-0722.2011.00844.x; Sandra Rosenberg, Sajeesh Kumar, and Nancy J. Williams, "Attention Deficit/Hyperactivity Disorder Medication and Dental Caries in Children," *Journal of Dental Hygiene* 88, no. 6 (2014): 342–47, https://jdh.adha.org/content/88/6/342.short; J. M. Broadbent, K. M. S. Ayers, and W. M. Thomson, "Is Attention-Deficit Hyperactivity Disorder a Risk Factor for Dental Caries?: A Case-Control Study," *Caries Research* 38, no. 1 (2004): 29–33, https://doi.org/10.1159/000073917; My Blomqvist, Kristen Holmberg, et al., "Dental caries and oral health behavior in children with attention deficit hyperactivity disorder," *European Journal of Oral Sciences* 115, no. 3 (2007): 186–91, https://doi.org/10.1111/j.1600-0722.2007.00451.x; and Maria Mielnik-Błaszczak, Monika Maslanko, et al., "Occurrence of dental caries in people with attention deficit hyperactivity disorder (ADHD)—literature review," *Journal of Stomatology* 70 (2017), https://doi.org/10.5604/01.3001.0010.7488.

Chapter 10: So, You Need to Eat and Sleep, Huh?

1. Stephen Becker, "ADHD and sleep: recent advances and future directions," *Current Opinion in Psychology* 34 (2020): 50–56, https://doi.org/10.1016/j.copsyc.2019.09.006; Scout McWilliams, Ted Zhou, et al., "Sleep as an outcome measure in ADHD randomized controlled trials: A scoping review," *Sleep Medicine Reviews* 63 (2022): 101613, https://doi.org/10.1016/j.smrv.2022.101613; Stephen Becker, Joshua Langberg, et al., "Sleep and daytime sleepiness in adolescents with and without ADHD: differences across ratings, daily diary, and actigraphy," *Journal of Child Psychology and Psychiatry* 60, no. 9 (2019): 1021–31, https://doi.org/10.1111/jcpp.13061; Jane Nikles, Geoffrey Keith Mitchell, et al., "A systematic review of the effectiveness of sleep hygiene in children with ADHD," *Psychology, Health & Medicine* 25, no. 4 (2020): 497–518, https://doi.org/10.1080/13548506.2020.1732431; Matilda Frick, Jenny Meyer, and Johan Isaksson, "The Role of Comorbid Symptoms in Perceived Stress and Sleep Problems in Adolescent ADHD," *Child Psychiatry & Human Development* 54 (2023): 1141–51, https://doi.org/10.1007/s10578-022-01320-z; Jessica Lunsford-Avery and Scott Kollins, "Delayed Circadian Rhythm Phase: A Cause of Late-Onset ADHD among Adolescents?" *Journal of Child Psychology and Psychiatry* 59, no. 12 (2018): 1248–51, https://doi.org/10.1111/jcpp.12956.

2. Lunsford-Avery and Kollins, "Delayed Circadian Rhythm Phase: A Cause of Late-Onset ADHD among Adolescents?"

3. "Food Loss and Waste," US Food & Drug Administration, last updated December 3, 2024, https://www.fda.gov/food/consumers/food-loss-and-waste.

Chapter 11: Why Folding Socks Is Overrated, aka the Household and Organization Chapter

1. Saya Des Marais, "How Can a Service Dog Help with ADHD?: Benefits, Breeds, and How to Apply," *PsychCentral*, updated on July 14, 2022, https://psychcentral.com/adhd/adhd-service-dog.

Chapter 13: Money: It's a Gas

1. Donald Wayne Black, Martha Shaw, et al., "Neuropsychological performance, impulsivity, ADHD symptoms, and novelty seeking in compulsive buying disorder," *Psychiatry Research* 200, no. 2-3 (2012): 581-87; https://doi.org/10.1016/j.psychres.2012.06.003; Dorian F. Bangma, Laura Tucha, et al., "Financial decision-making in a community sample of adults with and without current symptoms of ADHD," *PLoS ONE* 15, no 10 (2020): e0239343, https://doi.org/10.1371/journal.pone.0239343; D. Bijlenga, J. A. Vroege and A. J. M. Stammen, "Prevalence of sexual dysfunctions and other sexual disorders in adults with attention-deficit/hyperactivity disorder compared to the general population," *ADHD Attention Deficit and Hyperactivity Disorders*, 10, no. 2 (2018): 87-96, https://doi.org/10.1007/s12402-017-0237-6; and Dorien Bangma, Janneke Koerts, et al., "Financial decision-making in adults with ADHD," *Neuropsychology* 33, no. 8 (2019): 1065-77, https://psycnet.apa.org/doi/10.1037/neu0000571.

Chapter 14: All About Relationships

1. Nouchine Hadjikhani, Jakob Åsberg Johnels, et al., "Look me in the eyes: constraining gaze in the eye-region provokes abnormally high subcortical activation in autism," *Scientific Reports* 7, 3163 (2017), https://doi.org/10.1038/s41598-017-03378-5; Robert Joseph, Kelly Ehrman, et al., "Affective response to eye contact and face recognition ability in children with ASD," *Journal of the International Neuropsychological Society* 14, no. 6 (2008): 947-55, https://doi.org/10.1017/s1355617708081344; Kim Dalton, Brendon Nacewicz, et al., "Gaze fixation and the neural circuitry of face processing in autism," *Nature Neuroscience* 8, no. 4 (2005): 519-26, https://doi.org/10.1038/nn1421; Anneli Kylliäinen, Simon Wallace, et al., "Affective-motivational brain responses to direct gaze in children with autism spectrum disorder," *Journal of Child Psychology and Psychiatry* 53, no. 7 (2012): 790-97, https://doi.org/10.1111/j.1469-7610.2011.02522.x; and Dominic Trevisan, Nicole Roberts, et al., "How do adults and teens with self-declared Autism Spectrum Disorder experience eye contact? A qualitative analysis of first-hand accounts," *PLoS ONE* 12, no. 11 (2017): e0188446, https://doi.org/10.1371/journal.pone.0188446.

2. "The World Federation of ADHD International Consensus Statement," The World Federation of ADHD, 2021, https://www.adhd-federation.org/publications/international-consensus-statement.html.

3. Patrick Palines, Angela Rabbitt, et al., "Comparing mental health disorders among sex trafficked children and three groups of youth at high-risk for trafficking: A dual retrospective cohort and scoping review," *Child Abuse & Neglect* 100 (2020): 104196, https://doi.org/10.1016/j.chiabu.2019.104196; Dominique Roe-Sepowitz and Kara Jabola-Carolus, "Sex trafficking experiences of help-seeking individuals in Hawai'i," *Journal of Human Behavior in the Social Environment* 32, no. 1 (2021): 109-28, https://doi.org/10.1080/10911359.2021.1875097; and Allison Curry, Benjamin Yerys, et al., "Traffic Crashes, Violations, and Suspensions Among Young Drivers with ADHD," *Pediatrics* 143, no. 6 (2019): e20182305, https://doi.org/10.1542/peds.2018-2305.

Chapter 15: Let's Talk About Sex

1. D. Bijlenga, J. A. Vroege, et al., "Prevalence of sexual dysfunctions and other sexual disorders in adults with attention-deficit/hyperactivity disorder compared to the general population," *ADHD Attention Deficit and Hyperactivity Disorders* 10 (2018): 87-96, https://doi.org/10.1007/s12402-017-0237-6.

2. "What Does Queer Mean?" Planned Parenthood, https://www.plannedparenthood.org/learn/teens/sexual-orientation/what-does-queer-mean.

3. Mu-Hong Chen, Ju-Wei Hsu, et al., "Sexually Transmitted Infection Among Adolescents and Young Adults with Attention-Deficit/Hyperactivity Disorder: A Nationwide Longitudinal

Study," *Adolescent Psychiatry* 57, no. 1 (2018): 48–53, https://doi.org/10.1016/j.jaac.2017.09.438; Alyssa Francis, Danielle R. Oster, et al., "Factor Structure of the Sexual Risk Survey Among U.S. College Students with and without ADHD: Assessing Clinical Utility with a High-Risk Population," *Archives of Sexual Behavior* 51 (2022): 2931–42, https://doi.org/10.1007/s10508-021-02249-5; Kate Flory, William Pelham, et al., "Childhood ADHD Predicts Risky Sexual Behavior in Young Adulthood," *Journal of Clinical Child & Adolescent Psychology* 35, no. 4 (2006): 571–77, https://www.researchgate.net/profile/Bradley-Smith-17/publication/6786333_Childhood_ADHD_Predicts_Risky_Sexual_Behavior_in_Young_Adulthood/links/0fcfd511c12e625133000000/Childhood-ADHD-Predicts-Risky-Sexual-Behavior-in-Young-Adulthood.pdf; and G. M. Monawar Hosain, Abbey Berenson, et al., "Attention Deficit Hyperactivity Symptoms and Risky Sexual Behavior in Young Adult Women," *Journal of Women's Health* 21, no. 4 (2012), https://doi.org/10.1089/jwh.2011.2825.

4. R. George and M. A. Stokes, "Sexual Orientation in Autism Spectrum Disorder," *Autism Research* 11, no. 1 (2018): 133–41, https://doi.org/10.1002/aur.1892; Varun Warrier, David Greenberg, et al., "Elevated rates of autism, other neurodevelopmental and psychiatric diagnoses, and autistic traits in transgender and gender-diverse individuals," *Nature Communications* 11, 3959 (2020), https://doi.org/10.1038/s41467-020-17794-1; Anne Moyerbrailean, "Neurodivergence in the LGBTQ+ Community," Pride Center of VT, December 22, 2021, https://www.pridecentervt.org/2021/12/22/neurodivergence-in-the-lgbtq-community/; Devrupa Rakshit, "The Link Between Neurodivergence and Queerness, Explained," *The SWDL*, April 28, 2023, https://www.theswaddle.com/why-theres-more-gender-and-sexuality-diversity-in-the-neurodivergent-community; and Varun Warrier and Simon Baron-Cohen, "Transgender and gender diverse people up to six times more likely to be autistic—new study," *The Conversation*, August 7, 2020, https://theconversation.com/transgender-and-gender-diverse-people-up-to-six-times-more-likely-to-be-autistic-new-study-144085.

5. Hillary Bush, Lindsey Williams, and Eva Mendes, "Brief Report: Asexuality and Young Women on the Autism Spectrum," *Journal of Autism and Developmental Disorders* 51 (2020): 725–33, https://doi.org/10.1007/s10803-020-04565-6; Aimilia Kallitsounaki, David Williams, and Sophie Lind, "Links Between Autistic Traits, Feelings of Gender Dysphoria, and Mentalising Ability: Replication and Extension of Previous Findings from the General Population," *Journal of Autism and Developmental Disorders* 51 (2021): 1458–65, https://doi.org/10.1007/s10803-020-04626-w; and R. George and M. A. Stokes, "Sexual Orientation in Autism Spectrum Disorder," *Autism Research* 11, no. 1 (2018): 133–41, https://doi.org/10.1002/aur.1892.

Appendix: ADHD Evaluations

1. The SWAN* Rating Scale for ADHD, Amerihealth.com, Adapted from James M. Swanson, PhD, University of California, Irvine, https://www.amerihealth.com/pdfs/providers/resources/worksheets/prevhealth_swan.pdf.

2. Adult ADHD Self-Report Scale (ASRS-v1.1) Symptom Checklist, https://add.org/wp-content/uploads/2015/03/adhd-questionnaire-ASRS111.pdf.

Index

A

accommodations, 164, 176, 303-4, 305
ADD (attention deficit disorder), 33-34
addiction, 99, 174, 307-15. see also substance abuse
ADHD (attention deficit hyperactivity disorder). see also body and brain with ADHD; comorbid issues; coping with ADHD; diagnosis; eating; help with ADHD; household management; identity; loved ones; money; relationships; sex and intimacy; sleep issues; systems; time and task management; work
   cures, lack of, 17, 46-47, 48
   defined, 15, 26, 48
   as disability, 27-29, 129
   enjoyable aspects, 30, 134
   explanation, 23-48
   heredity, 19, 45, 48, 171
   history, 33, 49-55
   lifetime of, 19, 32, 43-44, 48, 97
   myths, 46-47, 48
   overview, 12-14, 48
   presentations, 34-35, 43-44, 48
   prevalence, 17-20
   as superpower, 129
   terminology, 33-34, 54
Alzheimer's, 89
anxiety, 36, 38, 57, 59, 66-71, 81, 113, 172-73, 308-9, 311
aphantasia, 83
attention deficit disorder, 33-34
attention deficit hyperactivity disorder. see ADHD
Autism, 33, 36, 57, 72-74, 84-85, 128, 168, 330

B

BIPOC (Black, Indigenous, and Persons of Color), 18, 134-43
body and brain with ADHD, 78-103. see also comorbid issues; executive functions; sensory issues
   addiction, 99
   aging, 88-89
   aphantasia, 83
   birth control, 102
   body temperature, 81, 231, 244
   cannabis and, 86-87
   clumsiness, 82
   cognitive distortions, 116-17, 120-21, 122
   disabilities, 27-29, 31, 60, 79-80, 88, 129
   hormones, 35, 48, 57, 90-98, 102, 144, 347-48
   interoception and, 81, 231
   neurodevelopmental disorder, 15, 26, 32, 48
   overview, 15-16, 79-80
   repetitive behaviors, 74, 75
   self-harm or suicide, 100-101
   time perception, 40-43, 182-83
   whole self approach, 102-3
body-doubling, 154, 158, 272
body-focused repetitive behaviors, 74, 75
boredom, 41, 42-43, 100-101, 245, 327, 347-49

Bradley, Charles, 51
budgets, 252, 309–11, 319–20

C

cannabis/cannabidiol, 86–87
car maintenance, 283
catastrophizing, 117, 120–21, 122
choice paralysis, 106, 195–96
cleaning, 273–75
clothes, 83, 219, 222, 223, 248, 267–68, 274, 277–79. see also laundry; shoes
clumsiness, 82
cognitive distortions, 116–17, 120–21, 122
communication, 142, 147, 329–34, 337, 349–50, 352, 359, 363, 373–74
comorbid issues, 56–77
 anxiety, 36, 38, 57, 59, 66–71
 Autism, 33, 36, 57, 72–74, 168
 common, 59–60
 defined, 28, 58
 depression, 36, 38, 57, 59, 61–66
 diagnosis, 33, 167–68, 170–71
 disabilities, 79–80, 88
 eating disorders, 57, 59, 76
 homotypic, 32
 OCD, 75
 overview, 28, 57–58, 77
 sensory issues, 73, 84–85
 sexual, 60–61, 347
 sleep issues, 57, 59, 240–43, 265
 substance abuse, 57, 59, 99
 whole self approach, 102–3
cooking, 254–56, 257–59
Cook, Lesley, 172
coping with ADHD, 104–22
 cognitive distortions, 116–17, 120–21, 122
 forgetfulness, 64, 66, 108–10
 lived experiences of, 105–6, 118–19, 220–21
 lying, 110–11
 rejection sensitivity, 112–15, 122
 skill development, 122
 stress, 107–8, 122
 train of thought, 108–10
creativity, 133, 174
Crichton, Sir Alexander, 52
culture, 18, 125, 137, 141–43. see also gender; race

D

debt, 307, 310, 323
delayed sleep phase syndrome, 239, 240, 241–42, 246
dental care, 222, 229–30, 233–34
depression, 36, 38, 57, 59, 61–66, 81, 101, 172–73, 311–12, 372
diagnosis, 161–79
 access, 170–71
 accommodations, 164, 176
 age, 19, 30–33, 171
 alternative, 170–71, 175
 authors', 24–25, 91–93, 163, 177–79
 comorbid, 33, 167–68, 170–71
 disclosure, 128–29, 130–31, 176–77
 effects, 127, 168–69, 179
 emotional response, 176–77
 evaluations, 166–68, 175, 380–81
 gender and, 18, 34–35, 147, 171
 hormones and, 91–93, 96–98
 lack of adequate, 17–19, 30, 98
 life changes and, 19, 32–33, 45
 limitations of, 165
 loved ones and, 164, 169, 366
 medication and, 165, 170, 172–74, 175
 purpose/value, 164–65, 171
 race and, 18
 self-assessment, 162–63
 self-diagnosis, 170, 175–76
 terminology, 33–34, 54, 147
Diagnostic and Statistical Manual of Mental Disorders, 18, 33–34, 54, 72, 147

disabilities, 27-29, 31, 60, 79-80, 88, 129
disorder, 29
dopamine, 37, 76, 97, 99, 172, 206, 245, 309-10, 312-13, 354
dyscalculia, 27, 311
dysgraphia, 28, 31
dyslexia, 27, 60
dyspraxia, 82

E

eating, 251-65
  bodily stimuli, 230-31
  convenience foods, 264
  cooking, 254-56, 257-59
  disposable dishes, 264
  food waste, 261
  kitchen organization, 253-54, 255
  lived experiences with, 256
  myths on, 46
  recipes, 262-63
  shopping, 251-52
  sleep and, 250-51
  stocking kitchen, 257-59
eating disorders, 57, 59, 76, 259
emotional control, 37, 76, 112-15, 122
erectile dysfunction, 60-61
executive dysfunction, 36
executive functions. *see also* emotional control; impulse control; organization; planning/prioritizing; task initiation
  ADHD effects, 15-16, 36-39, 48, 220
  aging effects, 88
  comorbidity effects, 36, 38, 57, 76, 77
  defined, 15, 36-39, 48
  household and, 268-69
  sex and, 347
  sleep and, 243

externalization, 108-9
externalizing spectrum, 32
eye contact, 330-31, 359

F

face blindness, 83
family. *see* loved ones
15-minute rule, 293
flexible thinking, 37
food. *see* eating
forgetfulness, 41, 64, 66, 88-89, 108-10, 232-35

G

gambling, 99
gender. *see also* women
  diagnosis and, 18, 34-35, 147, 171
  gender roles, 141
  hormones, 35, 48, 90-98, 102
  trans/nonbinary, 18, 102, 136-39, 144-48, 355
guilt, 65, 103, 365

H

handwriting, 31, 82
help with ADHD, 151-60
  acceptability of asking, 155-57
  advice as, 157
  buddy system, 159
  lived experiences of, 152-53, 156
  by loved ones, 155-58, 367-71
  methods of requesting, 158
  overview, 152
  payment, 154
  permission for, 367
  questions on, 160
  types, 154
heredity, 19, 45, 48, 171
heterotypic continuity, 19, 32, 43-44, 48, 97
history of ADHD, 33, 49-55
hoarding, 75, 311
Hoffman, Heinrich, 53
homotypic comorbidities, 32

hormones, 35, 48, 57, 90–98, 102, 144, 347–48
household management, 266–87. *see also* systems
  bathroom cleaning, 273–75
  car maintenance, 283
  clothes, 277–79
  floor cleaning, 273
  home organization, 268–72
  house maintenance, 283–84
  kitchen organization, 253–54, 255
  laundry, 80, 202, 206, 208–10, 212–13, 218, 223, 232–33, 260, 274, 275–76
  lived experiences with, 218, 260, 267–68, 272, 274, 281
  loved ones and, 271, 272, 368–69
  overview, 286–87
  pets, 285–86
  shoes, 202, 280–81, 287, 368
  tools, 282
  wallets, 284–85
hyperfixation, 41, 338
hyperfocus, 41, 42

I

identity, 123–49
  Autistic, 72
  BIPOC, 134–43
  correlated traits, 133
  diagnosis and, 127–29, 130–31, 147
  disclosure of ADHD, 128–29, 130–31
  disliking ADHD, 126
  good aspects of ADHD, 134
  lived experiences of, 124–25, 127, 130–31, 136–39
  overview, 125, 149
  personality, 126–27
  superpowers, 129
  trans/nonbinary, 136–39, 144–48
  wrong/right perceptions, 132

impulse control, 37, 76, 100–101, 110, 252, 308–15, 323
interoception, 81, 231
interrupting, 332–34, 337, 373

J

Johnson, Monica, 140

K

kitchen organization, 253–54, 255. *see also* eating
Kramer and Pollnow, 51

L

laundry, 80, 202, 206, 208–10, 212–13, 218, 223, 232–33, 260, 274, 275–76
laziness, 213
learning disabilities, 27–28, 31, 60
Leikam, Katie, 145
LGBTQIA+ people, 18, 102, 136–39, 144–48, 355
life changes, 19, 32–33, 45
lifetime of ADHD, 19, 32, 43–44, 48, 97
light, 73, 244, 350, 361
listening, 329, 359
Love, Amariah, 147
loved ones, 364–77. *see also* relationships; sex and intimacy
  behavior injuring, 373–74
  diagnosis and, 164, 169, 366
  help from, 155–58, 367–71
  heredity, 19, 45, 48, 171
  household management, 271, 272, 368–69
  hurtful comments by, 89, 177–78, 368
  lived experiences, 365, 369, 376–77
  medication management, 372
  systems support, 207, 371
  therapy on, 375

Index

M

medication
  access, 165, 170, 175
  ADHD, 68, 81, 99, 165, 170, 172–75, 243, 244, 372
  anxiety, 68, 81, 172–73
  cannabidiol, 87
  depression, 81, 172–73, 372
  FAQs, 172–74
  hormones, 97, 102, 144
  loved ones and, 372
  sleep and, 243, 244, 245, 250
  supplements vs., 175
menopause, 35, 97–98
menstruation, 35, 57, 90, 94–97, 236
misophonia, 84, 85
money, 306–23
  assistance, 311, 319, 323
  budgeting, 252, 309–11, 319–20
  decision chart, 314–15
  food, 251–52
  frugality, 321–22
  lived experiences with, 307–9
  questions on, 323
  rent payment, 40, 206, 316–18
  shopping and, 252, 307–15, 323
  socioeconomics, 141, 148
  structuring finances, 318
  time perception and, 40

N

neurodevelopmental disorder, 15, 26, 32, 48
neurodivergence, 18, 29, 55, 129, 227
  disclosing, 138–31,
  hormones and, 97
  masking, 168
nonbinary, 18, 102, 138–39, 144, 145–46
note-taking, 109, 198, 301–2, 350–51

O

object permanence, 254, 255
OCD (obsessive-compulsive disorder), 75
organization, 39, 253–54, 255, 268–72. see also household management; systems; time and task management

P

people-pleasing, 68, 113, 187
personal hygiene, 214–15, 222, 228–37. see also showering; dental care
personality, 126–27, 173
pets, 285–86
planning/prioritizing, 39, 40, 185, 189–92, 196–98, 302
PMDD (premenstrual dysphoric disorder), 57, 96–97
pregnancy, 35, 94, 97

R

rejection sensitive dysphoria, 112–15, 122, 333, 336, 345, 352
relationships, 325–42. see also loved ones; sex and intimacy
  abusive, 339–41, 342
  ADHD deniers in, 339–41
  annoying behavior, 337
  behavior management, 335–37, 342, 373–74
  commitment issues, 338
  diagnosis and, 129
  eye contact in, 330–31
  hurtful behavior, 326–27, 335–37, 339–41, 342, 373–74
  interrupting in, 332–34, 337, 373
  listening in, 329
  lived experiences with, 326–28, 331, 335
  maintaining, 328, 331, 335, 338
  overview, 342

Index

relationships (*cont.*)
    rejection sensitivity, 112–15, 333, 336
rent, 40, 206, 316–18
revenge bedtime procrastination, 246–47

S

self-harm, 100–101
self-monitoring, 38
sensory issues, 73, 81, 84–85, 214–15, 259, 302, 347, 350–52, 360–62
sex and intimacy, 343–63
    asexual spectrum, 356–58
    boredom/distraction, 347–49
    comorbid issues, 60–61, 347
    dangerous situations, 354
    defined, 345–46
    desire, 347–48, 351
    hyper-/hyposexual, 345, 353–54
    intimacy/connection building, 358–60
    kinkiness, 351–52, 354
    lived experiences with, 344
    masturbation, 60, 244, 356, 362
    note-taking, 350–51
    overview, 344–45, 362–63
    polyamorous, 355
    queer, 355
    rejection sensitivity, 345, 352
    sensory issues, 347, 350–52, 360–62
    talking and, 349–50, 352, 363
shame, 65, 109
shoes, 202, 280–81, 287, 368
shopping, 251–52, 307–15, 323
showering, 214–15, 218, 229–30, 232, 234–35
side effects, medication, 87, 172–74
sleep issues, 238–51
    common, 241–43
    comorbid, 57, 59, 240–43, 265
    coping with fatigue, 249–51
    lived experiences of, 239–41, 247–48
    medication and, 243, 244, 245, 250
    revenge bedtime procrastination and, 246–47
    tips to improve, 243–46, 247–48
socioeconomic status, 141, 148. *see also* money
spending, 35, 37, 309–10. *see also* money
stigmas, 18, 55, 128–29, 141, 168–69
Still, Sir George Frederic, 53
stims/stimming, 74
stress, 107–8, 122
substance abuse, 57, 59, 86, 99, 174
suicide, 101
systems, 200–237. *see also* household management; time and task management
    adapting, 202, 205–6, 209, 211–12
    brainstorming on, 209, 210
    building, 202–3, 208–12
    characteristics of good, 204–6
    defined, 203
    failed, 219
    lived experiences with, 201–2, 209–10, 218, 227–28
    loved ones and, 207, 371
    need for, 220–21
    personal hygiene, 214–15, 222, 228–37
    questions on, 203, 209, 210, 211
    seasonal, 219
    sensory issues, 214–15
    starting to use, 212–14
    suitable, 215–17
    testing, 211
    useful, 222–26
    workplace, 299–302, 305

T

task debt, 370–71
task initiation, 39, 62, 212–14

taxes, 311
time and task management, 181–99. *see also* coping with ADHD
   assistants, 194, 195–96
   car maintenance, 283
   choice paralysis, 195–96
   deadlines, 193–94, 299, 302
   lived experiences with, 179, 186
   loved ones and, 370–71
   methods, 189–92, 199
   overcommitment, 187–88
   pets, 285–86
   schedules/planners, 185, 193, 196–98, 299–300
   storage containers, 63
   structure, 184–85, 193–94
   systems, 213–14 (*see also* systems)
   time perceptions, 40–43, 182–83
   work-related, 245–46, 292–93, 294, 299–302, 305
time blindness, 40, 42, 76
tools, 282
toothbrushing. *see* dental care
trans/nonbinary people, 18, 102, 136–39, 144–48, 355

W

Weikard, Melchior, 51
Wilson, Karen I., 141
women
   diagnosis, 18, 34–35, 91–93, 96–98, 168, 171
   hormones/menstruation, 35, 48, 57, 90–98, 236
   identity, 136–37
   money management, 307, 310
work, 289–305
   accommodations, 164, 176, 303–4, 305
   ADHD deniers, 303, 304, 305
   arriving on time, 292–93

diagnosis disclosure, 128–29, 130–31
   hours/schedule, 245–46, 292, 294, 305
   job choice, 295–98, 304, 305
   lived experiences with, 290–91, 294
   sleep and, 239–41, 245–46
   systems, 299–302, 305
working memory, 38, 268–69

About the Authors

Cate Osborn is the host of *Sorry I Missed This* on Understood.org, which focuses on ADHD's impact on relationships, communication, and intimacy, and she is the cohost of the podcast *Catie and Erik's Infinite Quest: An ADHD Adventure*. A certified sex educator, she has had her work and commentary featured in *Cosmopolitan*, *The New York Times*, *GQ*, *Playboy*, *HuffPost*, and other outlets. Find out more at Catieosaurus.com.

Erik Gude, along with Cate Osborn, is an educator and advocate for people with ADHD. He cohosts *Catie and Erik's Infinite Quest: An ADHD Adventure* and, with Cate Osborn, frequently hosts panels at conventions about the intersection of ADHD and gaming, including Dragon Con, Emerald City Comic Con, Gen Con, MomoCon, and San Diego Comic-Con. Erik's ADHD Crafting Challenge was a huge success on TikTok with over twenty million views. A former cook, he is now a prop maker and fabricator at the legendary Fonco Studios. Follow him on TikTok and Instagram: @HeyGude.